Organizing from the Right Side of the Brain

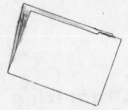

ALSO BY LEE SILBER

NONFICTION

Money Management for the Creative Person

Self-Promotion for the Creative Person

Career Management for the Creative Person

Time Management for the Creative Person

Aim First

Notes, Quotes and Advice

Successful San Diegans

Dating in San Diego

FICTION

Summer Stories

ORGANIZING
from the RIGHT SIDE
of the BRAIN

A Creative Approach to
Getting Organized

Lee Silber

Thomas Dunne Books
St. Martin's Griffin ☙ New York

THOMAS DUNNE BOOKS
An imprint of St. Martin's Press

www.stmartins.com

Library of Congress Cataloging-in-Publication Data

Silber, Lee T.
    Organizing from the right side of the brain : a creative approach to
getting organized / Lee Silber.
        p. cm.
    ISBN 0-312-31816-2
    EAN 978-0312-31816-1
        1. Paperwork (Office practice)—Management. 2. Storage in the
home. 3. Housekeeping.
    I. Title.

    HF5547.15.S56 2004
    648'.8—dc22   2004049745

10 9 8 7 6 5 4

To all the creative right-brain people who never seem to get organized in a way their neatnik left-brain counterparts can understand—it's your time to shine.

CONTENTS

ACKNOWLEDGMENTS

Many times it's easier to sort your stuff than it is your thoughts. Since I should lead by example, I organized my thank-you's in alphabetical order beginning with my wife, Andrea. Not only is she first on this list, she is the most important person in my life—even if this book did take up all of my time for months and months. Annette, my mom, who took me to the library as a kid and encouraged me to read—and write. Betty Edwards, for writing the first real right-brain book (*Drawing on the Right Side of the Brain*) that opened the door for people like me. Carolyn Chu, my editor. She is my "without whom this would not be possible" person. THANK YOU for everything! Harvey, my dad, who taught me how to be in my "right" mind and what it really means to be a pack rat. Jessica Matthes, for taking my sketches and bringing them to life. Scott Kramer, a friend (and magazine editor) who helped cut this book down to size. Toni Lopopolo, my literary agent for the past ten years. She does the deals and gets things done behind the scenes. Finally, I would like to thank you, the reader. If it weren't for right-brainers like you, this world would be a very dull place. Stay true to yourselves and remember: right-brainers rule!

When I asked others for organizing ideas I was overwhelmed by the response. I want to personally thank each and every person who contributed an idea or insight into organizing the right-brain way (whether they made it into the book or not). John Aliano, Tera Allison, Carla Bange, Dr. Robert Black, Sunshine Blake, Jill Baldwin Bodonsky, Felicia Borges, Andrew Chapman, Diana Costello, Sue Cotch, Sher Denton, Marion Dickes, Michelle Downey, Paulette Ensign, Edith Fine, Andrea Glass, Mark Golik, Evelyn Gray, Shannon Grissom, Kevin Hall, Becky

Hawley, Anna-Marie Hawthorne, Janis Isaman, Paula Jhong, Judith Josephson, Marie Kinnaman, Antoinette Kuritz, Peter Lloyd, Laura Love, Jacqueline Marcell, Seretta Martin, Jennifer Matlock, Mike Metz, Howard Meyer, Julie Morgenstern, Seth Odam, Kristine Porter, Nicole Pugh, Leslie Ray, Eileen Roth, Jennifer Shore, Kathy Stamps, Jennifer Stults, Kitty Torres, Eleanor Traubman, and Sue Viders.

INTRODUCTION

The goal of all inanimate objects is to resist
man and ultimately defeat him.

—Russell Baker

Are people critical of the piles of paper on your desk? Do they gibe you
with comments like, "A messy desk is the sign of a messy mind"? Does it
drive those around you nuts that you wait until the last minute to get
something done—and that goes for every one of the several projects you
are currently working on? Does your computer hard drive look like the
top of your desk—things all over the place with no rhyme or reason?

Let me guess. You've already read a book or two on being organized.
You found them boring, confusing, and frustrating—not to mention unrealistic. So you took a "Get Organized" seminar. They told you to put
everything away and to throw out anything you haven't used in a year.
Yeah, right. You even bought some cool containers and other organizing
products thinking that these tools would help you get organized once
and for all. Now they just clutter up your space and serve as a painful reminder of yet another attempt to get organized gone awry.

Literally hundreds of thousands of people out there are dealing with
these and similar problems. Good people—creative, innovative, imaginative people who simply find it hard to get organized. People like
you—and me. Sadly, there are no little elves who will magically clean up
and organize the clutter in your life. That doesn't mean you can't be organized. With a right-brain approach, it will feel right and fit your style.
You'll wake up each morning excited by how your environment reflects

who you are and how it is organized in a creative way that works the way you do. This is what you have been waiting for—to finally organize everything in your life. I'm here to tell you, it's possible!

I'm on your side. I'm not going to make you clean off your desk or tell you that you can't continue to pile your papers. If you want to write notes to yourself on paper scraps, that's okay, too. I'm serious. Want proof? I wrote this book's opening sentences on a napkin while performing on stage with my band (between songs) and then later piled them with my other notes. I sat behind my drums wondering if having our gear neater and more organized would make us play any better. The answer was—No! (Nothing would, ha, ha, ha.) However, I also knew that without some organization, we wouldn't have landed the gig in the first place, let alone had a set list or the equipment connected correctly. There has to be a balance between being overly organized and being able to find what you need when you need it—despite what it may look like to others. Sometimes what we do and create is more important than the environment we live and work in. Some overly organized people insist that organizing is everything. They'll spend a sunny Saturday color-coding their sock drawer while the rest of us are out living life. Some sense of organization is healthy and helpful, but it should not rule your life. This book balances the need to get organized with your desire for freedom.

If you expect to hear the same old virtues of filing every piece of paper, forget it. Piling isn't a problem when it works. I'll show you how to do it effectively. Irritating people who are forced to find things in your mess, getting a poor work review for failing to follow through, or losing your good credit because you don't pay bills—those are problems. Working on several projects at once is not a problem—and often leads to inspiration for right-brainers. Taking on too much and failing to meet your deadlines can be a problem. So we'll find ways you can juggle without dropping the ball. You can hang onto your clutter if you have the room. I would never make you part with your prized possessions. The problem is when everything is out and in the way. There are several solutions for making the most of your space and safely storing (and finding again) the things that don't deserve prime positions in your home and office. Hooray! In this book you will find that you don't have to fight your natural tendencies. Instead, we will work with them to get organized in a way that makes sense and sticks.

You don't have to change who you are to become an organized person, and I'll prove it. We (right-brainers) can be just as organized as our left-brain counterparts (maybe more so), but we prefer to do it in our own unique way—with a little savoir faire. We're knocked for being disorganized, undisciplined, and messy; yet we get things done and have fun doing it. Organizing actually comes naturally to us, but not organizing that anybody else might recognize as such. Admittedly, we can be distracted, impatient, sloppy, and offbeat. We loathe routine, abhor structure and rules, rarely write things down, take a wait-and-see approach more often than not, like everything out where we can see it, and have difficulty making and sticking to decisions. We're also oblivious to time, don't mind being surrounded by clutter, and tend to lose things more often than others. It's easy to understand why getting organized (in the classic sense) is such a tough sell for real right-brainers.

Most books on getting organized are incredibly big and boring. This book is different. It's creative, solution oriented, relevant, and fun to read—anything but boring. It's easygoing, anecdotal, and sprinkled with inspirational and interesting "sound bites"—quotes, factoids, and examples. Each chapter includes specific-action items that can be put into use right away. We needed one of our own to write a book about how to become more organized without transforming us into a linear, left-brain person! That's why I personally took a test-drive with all of the tips in this book to make sure they didn't pull us too much to the left.

This book takes a fresh and unconventional look at all aspects of organizing. I touch on the basics and the "rules" but quickly veer into new territory that will click for you. This is a hands-on, how-to book that will produce lasting change. It goes farther and offers more than any other organizing book. It's more innovative and incorporates some of the classic ideas from organization experts, but it adds a creative twist. You can't force a square peg into a round hole, so why try? Let's find the right fit for your temperament, style, and environment. Using this book can help you get it together and make lasting changes that will not only help you get organized but improve all aspects of your life. These are such simple techniques that are easily implemented so that it's almost easier to do them than not. It will take some thought and effort on your part, but it won't require changing who you are and how you see the world around you. It will have a profound effect on the quality of your work and relationships—and your sanity. You'll see immediate, positive, tangible changes (and so will those around you). Some of the suggestions will fit into your style; others will inspire you to find variations. The beauty is, you will understand the basics of organizing and then you can apply these principles to anything and everything.

Watch any of the TV makeover shows and you'll notice two things. The designers try to capture the essence of the people they're redesigning rooms for and include as much of their personality into it as possible. They try their best to make the rooms functional and funky. Those two actions are also keys to organizing. You'll notice that once a room is redesigned, former "messies" are both amazed and excited about the possibilities. They are more confident, enjoy the new space, and want to show it off. Most importantly, they are so stoked with the makeover, they vow to maintain it. My solutions and suggestions also help "disorganized" people become organized on their own terms so that they will be proud to show off their newfound skills.

One of the first things you notice when you walk into my office or studio is how organized it is. I have developed right-brain ways to find a place for everything and put everything in its place without compromising my creativity. This system is colorful, visual, and VERY unusual. And it works! Everything looks nice and neat—and it is—but it is also set up to work in concert with my style, not in conflict with it—switching off from task to task, project to project. It allows for things to be out without being a distraction. I discovered that I was able to find creative ways to take control of the information, papers, and projects that flow in and out of my life. This wasn't always the case. I have come a long way and learned a lot about being organized despite my natural, right-brain tendency to want to hang onto everything I have ever owned (or borrowed) and keep it out where I can see it.

Just as I wouldn't want to read a book full of the same old (irrelevant) stuff about organizing, I wouldn't expect you to either. That's why these are NOT recycled organizing tips. They're a collectively creative approach for creative people. It's new, different, and better. It takes existing organizing advice and molds it to our unorthodox lifestyle. Ask any right-brainer about getting organized and we typically laugh—out loud. This is usually NOT our greatest strength. That's why this book will be a big boost to helping you get it together. Getting organized may be one of the most difficult things for you to do, but—it's also crucial to your health, happiness, and success. The ideas in this book work wonders. Here's to the new, organized you. The first step is to turn the page and begin reading about how right-brainers like yourself can be more organized without making major changes to their lives. Hey, if I can do it, anyone can.

Note: You will notice that some of the same organizing tips and techniques are included in more than one place. There is a good reason for this. This is a book written by and for right-brainers. I don't expect you to read this book in any particular order. I also know you will likely jump to the first chapter that catches your eye. That's why I felt it was imperative that some of the most important organizing ideas and insights be repeated. So whether you read this book chronologically or haphazardly, you will not miss the most important points.

Also, if you are interested in seeing examples of many of the tips and techniques included in this book, go to www.creativelee.com and click on "Organizing Photos."

HOW TO GET YOUR FREE BONUS CHAPTER

To make this book more manageable, I had to cut one of my favorite chapters. If you would like to read "Thinking Inside the Box: Tools That Make Organizing Easier" simply send me a self-addressed, stamped envelope (with $1.00 in postage) to the address below. (Or, go to www.creativelee.com to find out how to have a portable document format (PDF) version e-mailed to you.)

Lee Silber
www.creativelee.com
c/o CreativeLee Speaking
822 Redondo Court
San Diego, CA 92109

For photos of the tips and techniques presented in this book, please visit www.creativelee.com and click on "Organizing Photos."

Part One

WHERE ARE YOU NOW?

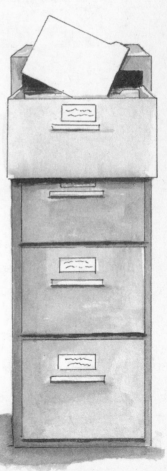

one

ORGANIZING THE RIGHT-BRAIN WAY

How Right-Brainers Can Be Organized in a Left-Brain World

Scientists say a woman listens with her whole brain, while a man only listens with half his brain. The other half is trying to picture her naked.

—Jay Leno

"Clean up that mess!" "Get those piles of papers off your desk and into a file." "Why can't you be more neat and organized like everyone else?" As a right-brainer, certainly you have heard statements like these at one time or another. The reason behind comments like these is that society is made up mostly of left-brainers, who, being the majority, feel their way of doing almost everything is the best, or only, way—especially when it comes to organizing. To them, organizing is easy. To us, it's a constant struggle against all that makes us who we are. So we try to come up with all kinds of creative and crazy ways to deal with clutter, which only another right-brainer would appreciate. This doesn't always work out so well though.

If you have ever wondered whether you were predisposed to being disorganized, you may have been onto something. Being a right-brainer does make it less likely you were born with a natural ability or the tools to organize things in a traditional way—and that's okay, up to a point. We can take your unique, unorthodox approach and be better organized in a comfortable, natural way—your way. Maybe you believe that organizing is a neat and tidy perfect little home. This is both impossible and improbable for the right-brainer. It's okay to be a bit messy. The main thing is, does it work or doesn't it? Is it comfortable to you and those you live or work with? (I know, who cares what *they* think. Well, we want some harmony in the house, right?) What we are looking for is a tiny bit of tweaking to get you to the point where you are organized (in a right-brain way) and stay that way. In most cases you will be able to continue to do things the way you do and stay in your comfort zone. What we are searching for are solutions for the areas that are NOT working. The goal isn't to turn you into some kind of obsessive, organizing freak. No, the goal is to organize things so that you are still able to let your style and personality shine through but create a system that is designed to work the way you do.

"Research has shown that men usually sleep on the right side of the bed. Even in their sleep they have to be right," jokes comedienne Rita Rudner. Very funny. Well, in defense of both men and right-brainers, we can't help it. What you do and say is a direct result of your brain style and dominance. When you are in your "right" mind, it's hard to see things any other way. We are the few, the proud, the right-brain thinkers. By using the right side of our brains, we may have some decidedly different ideas about what being organized is all about and how to do it, but that doesn't mean our approach is all wrong.

Step one is to better understand yourself and why you put things where you do and to come up with an organizing style and system that suits your personal style and preferences. As Emo Phillips said, "I used to think the brain was the most fascinating part of the body. Then I realized, well, look what's telling me that." Maybe we should listen a little bit more to what our brain is telling us. Let's face it, these are lifelong preferences that take time to change—assuming they need to be changed at all.

The solution is to make the most of your right brain while awakening your left brain to come up with a whole-brain approach to getting organized. We want to organize *our* way as much as our left-brain counterparts would like to see us adopt *their* style and adapt to *their* systems. It could be a messy battle (pun intended) if we aren't willing to at least look at how the left-brainers organize and see if we can borrow the best of their ideas and throw away the rest. This way we will have a better idea as to which organizing tips and techniques will work best for us (and what we'll stick with).

Nobody only uses his right brain. (I'm serious.) We all switch off between the two hemispheres of our brain depending on the task; but at the end of the day, one side of the brain dominates what we do. A whole-brain approach to almost anything is preferable. So some of the suggestions in this book will seem a little left-brain, but I encourage you to try them out. A slight shift to the left is helpful with many of the tasks that need to be mastered when it comes to organizing. We will also discuss why being almost exclusively in our "right" minds is crazy. It's not cute or creative to be double booked, running late, flailing around, and failing to get the right things done. It's also embarrassing (and dangerous) when people come over to visit and have to avoid being buried under falling piles of paper or tripping over lots of loose items, or fear that clutter could come pouring out of the coat closet. It's a potentially stressful way to live for you and those around you. It's also not good for your health, finances, friendships, or your career aspirations.

Your brain is as strong as its weakest link or your best asset when it comes to getting and staying organized. We can bemoan our weaknesses or strengthen our strengths and *work around* our weaknesses. My advice is to do things that bring out your best side and hide the handicaps. Someone once said, "You can't change the way your brain works. You can only change the way you use it." Amen, brother. The best organizing system is one that supports us and our goals. It takes advantage of our right-brain way of doing things. It feels so natural that we don't even have to work at it. (It's a "no-brainer.") It's you at your best. Instead of beating yourself up for being who you are, celebrate your right-brain strengths. You can get mad at your disorganization, but not at yourself.

This is not an excuse, and I am certainly not saying that because we are right-brainers we are therefore disorganized. I also want to dispel the myth that being organized will kill the creative, fun-loving, quirky people we are. We organize so that we can be spontaneous. We organize so that we aren't all stressed out looking for lost and misplaced things. We organize so that we can come up with innovative ideas and create great works of art and do something positive with them or, at the very least, save them in a safe place. I have found that true creativity is a disciplined process for the most part, and when we can harness the enormous power of focus and concentration and keep the light shining on the task at hand, we can achieve a high-quality result in half the time. This is good, no?

While I was researching this book, I would go into people's homes and offices and see several organizing books sitting on the shelf. Judging by the complete chaos of their situation, my guess is they either never read them or they read them but couldn't use them because these books didn't take into account their uniqueness. Most organizing books take a one-size-fits-all approach. I believe that you begin by accepting your style and work with that. No style of organizing is wrong—whoever you are, wherever you are, work with it. There is only wrong for you.

I have also come to discover that you can be organized without becoming a left-brainer. Don't let left-brainers make you feel inferior just because you don't do things their way. You have some very special gifts that they don't. Celebrate your uniqueness. Organizing is simply a way to make the most of what you have to give the world. A way to allow you to be all you can be. It's more than tips and tricks. It's a way of life that keeps disorganization from pulling you under and drowning your dreams. It's very important to create systems that keep key things flowing in and out of your life and to put items away in places that allow you to find and retrieve them quickly and easily. Organizing is like hide-and-seek, except you know where everything is hiding and you are playing with your eyes open (and it's not considered cheating). This is such a powerful (and peaceful) feeling.

Here's some more good news. Everyone is able to do something well; it's just that society puts a premium on left-brain skills. That's changing with the times. There is now an appreciation for creativity and innovative thinking. Employers are starting to overlook any shortcomings that accompany these valued traits—like being disorganized. Whew, that's a relief. What works is translating our strange behavior into a system we will understand and embrace to stay organized. Remember, though, we live in a left-brain world where structure, time lines, attention to detail, focus, priorities, and paperwork are rewarded. Our unusual and unorthodox way of organizing isn't a problem unless we let important things get completely out of control. We may hate structure, but we also know we need it. The thing I noticed about myself is that I don't mind structure as long as I create it. What I don't do well with is when other people put restrictions and requirements on me or my time. I am miserable when my calendar is full of appointments and things to do that I didn't put on there myself. It's the same with organizing. We like to come up with creative solutions for storing stuff and clever uses for old and odd items.

Because organizing and fun reside in opposite sides of the brain, they make for some interesting battles between good and evil. Some people allow their right brain (spontaneous, fun, imaginative, creative, distracted) to rule. Others are able to make peace with their left brain (focused, disciplined, linear, logical, and rational) and have a balance between both sides of the brain so that they are able to have fun and get things done. Like anything else, balance and compromise are needed to be organized enough to get others off our case. (Sure, we could just push over a pile of papers and bury them so they are never found. But like a lot of things that get lost in our clutter, what if we need to find them again?) We have to get a handle on, and reel in, our right brain when it wants to overdo too much of a good thing. (For example, we may tend to overorganize or come up with too many different systems that don't support one another.) That certainly doesn't mean we have to stop the party; it just means we need a bouncer and curfew. We aren't imbeciles or incapable of organizing, it just isn't what we do best. Most likely because we were never taught how. We are trained in other areas. We say we aren't good at organizing, but that isn't always true. With some knowledge and experience, we can do it. We need to know what to do, how to do it, and have the discipline to follow through. It comes with practice and patience. (Uh-oh.)

You have a right-brain dominance that is natural, but you can train your brain to do just about anything, including organizing. Neither side is better or worse, right or wrong (although being a right-brainer has its advantages). We need interaction from both sides as we shift back and forth all day long, depending on the activity. It's just that we feel more comfortable using one side or the other and use it predominantly. The better we are able to tap into our less dominant side, the better we become. To use both halves of our brain to full capacity is the goal. A healthy balance between the two halves leads to more creativity and productivity, and you get the best of both worlds and the maximum power. When the two halves work in harmony (rather than bicker back and forth) you also have inner peace.

In this chapter we will examine some of your personal preferences and suggest some organizing ideas that can be adapted to your own unique situation. This means looking at your habits and patterns, likes and dislikes, skills and strengths, past and present successes, and your overall organizing style. It may be painful to look back at your life and all your failed attempts at becoming more organized for clues about what won't work. But it's worth it. "The heroes of mythology are not perfect people but people with very obvious strengths and very obvious weaknesses. What we see as heroism is a negotiation between strengths and weaknesses," says Ken Burns. He's right. It's a process and since we like to make changes to our lives and environment as often as the moon is full, we need an approach to organizing that we can keep up—one that is flexible and adaptable. This is done by education, experience, and self-exploration. So here we go.

DO YOU HAVE THE "RIGHT" STUFF?

I never set out to be weird. It was always other people who called me weird.

—Frank Zappa

When you read the descriptions and suggestions in this chapter put yourself in the picture and ask, "How does this apply to me?" Look for connections to your situation. Try to picture the points visually. We may not be as neat and tidy as our left-brain counterparts, but some of our strengths, different as they are, can be beneficial in the organizing process. We (right-brainers) can be superheroes under the right circumstances. Our kryptonite, however, is dealing with details, planning, practicality, prioritizing, structure, time lines, tidiness, logic, limits, order, routine, rules, and the mundane. Did I miss anything? Take the following quiz to find out which traits you share with others of our kind. For the characteristics you checked off, I made it easy to find out more about each one with a quick scan index. It's interesting to learn why you do the things you do and then learn organizing solutions that will work with each tendency. I'd recommend reading each one or you can just jump around and read whatever strikes your fancy. The key thing to realize is that there is an antidote for whatever ails you in your attempt to become organized.

Check off those right-brain traits that apply to you and then look them up later in this chapter to learn more. Ready? Okay, here we go. Are you . . .

___Absentminded	See page 10
___Addictive	See page 11
___Adrenaline Junkie	See page 12
___All or Nothing	See page 13
___Altruistic	See page 13
___Amazing	See page 14
___Big-Picture Thinker	See page 16
___Busy, Busy, Busy	See page 17
___Clutterer	See page 18
___Cool with Chaos	See page 19
___Creative	See page 20
___Curious	See page 21
___Defensive/Sensitive	See page 23
___Disinterested in Organizing	See page 24
___Disorganized	See page 27
___Divergent Thinker/ Easily Distracted	See page 28
___Dramatic/Eccentric	See page 30
___Emotional	See page 31
___Fun/Playful	See page 32
___Generous	See page 34
___Impatient	See page 34
___Impulsive	See page 36
___Inconsistent	See page 36
___Indecisive	See page 37
___Independent	See page 38
___Inventive	See page 40

continued on next page

Absentminded

During high school one of my summer jobs was as a janitor at a think tank. Since these brilliant minds didn't adhere to regular hours, I would see some of them when I arrived for work in the early evening. It was an almost daily occurrence for me when I walked in the door for someone to ask me to find something they had misplaced or lost. Since they were so preoccupied with solving some sort of top-secret scenario (I didn't ask or have the clearance), they didn't pay much attention to where they put their keys, glasses, and, in a few instances, important papers (not good). One of the things I learned that summer was how we right-brainers recall where we put things differently than most people. We have a nonverbal, symbolic, or holistic method of memory (we can recall faces, but not names) with a random-access retrieval system for information. To master this trait or tendency is the secret to solving the most frustrating affliction known to modern man—where are my missing keys?

TRY THIS. To become better organized, we should put our stuff in a place where it makes sense to *us*. Put "key" items in our path or leave them out, so it is almost impossible to not see them. This works well for the right-brainer, but we can't leave everything out all the time or we would be buried and *nothing* would stand out. (That's where clear containers work really well.) When it comes to putting things away and remembering where we put them, we need to associate ideas with items and make personal connections in order to remember and retrieve stuff stored out of sight. To do this, keep like items together. On Tuesday nights I play in a softball league so I put my glove, bat, cleats (and sunflower seeds) together in a gear bag so I can just grab 'em and go. You can do this for just about anything by creating zones based on what you do in a certain area and store the stuff you use there. You can do this when you are about to go on a trip, too. Leave your luggage out and throw things in as you remember them. Just seeing the suitcase and a few items in it will trigger your memory. Because we can get great ideas at any time, carry a personal digital assistant (PDA), microrecorder, or an idea journal with you and store these in a safe place. (Later, group these together for easy retrieval by category, project, or date.) We can borrow a page from the left-brain approach to organizing by having a place for everything and putting it all back in that place, or (and you'll like this) put things in piles but do it with a purpose. A pile by the phone means these papers are waiting for a call. A pile by the door means these go with you when you leave, and so on. Finally (and there are a LOT more suggestions included later in this book), make the most of the traits you possess. If you are like me, pictures really are worth a thousand words so instead of using words to label boxes use a picture, drawing, or a symbol.

Addictive

It's in our nature to take things to the extreme. Instead of saving some of the things we find interesting, useful, or sentimental, we save everything. For instance, when my buddy first got interested in collecting baseball cards he did it as a "hobby." At some point the line between hobby and habit got blurred, and he had spent tens of thousands of dollars on cards and collectibles. As his collection grew in size, so did the space it took up. He eventually dedicated an entire room to his sports memorabilia. The problem was (other than the money and time he spent on his obsession) his lack of organization. He had so much stuff he couldn't remember what he had or find what he wanted when he wanted it. Whenever I'd ask to see something in his collection, he would say, "I know it's here somewhere." Sometimes he'd find the card in question (by chance). Most times it was "like" it was LOST.

TRY THIS. The solution was so simple. I helped him install shelves and we made cool display cases for his best stuff and put it on display. Now it was out where he (and others) could see it. I helped him sort the cards by year, and he put them in protective plastic sleeves in different-colored binders with the spines clearly labeled with what was inside. These were all kept on a shelf in the closet. He also had boxed sets of cards and we organized them by year and marked the outside. We made a bat rack and other storage units to safely display his sports stuff. Now he knew what he had and was able to show it off a lot better. To keep it organized and under control he set limits. Once he filled the space he had to use, he had to apply the "one-in-one-out rule" and sell off something if he wanted to add something. He was pleased with this setup but more importantly, his wife was ecstatic. (My work there was done.)

Adrenaline Junkies

Do you find it a rush to wait until the very last minute to do something? Well, you are not alone. Many of us find some stress stimulating and may even create scenarios where scurrying around in a state of panic is part of the plan. When it comes to organizing, this could mean that straightening up amounts to shoving things in the closet or under the bed minutes before your guests are to arrive. Waiting to get gas until you are running on fumes. Rushing to the post office to get your tax return in the mail the day before it's due. Don't be a victim because you are disorganized.

TRY THIS. Without deadlines, nothing gets done. Set up incremental deadlines instead of one GIANT one. Give yourself a drop-dead deadline. One friend of mine had put off unpacking (after moving) for months. To finally get organized she sent out invitations to her housewarming party set for two weeks later. Needless to say, she finally unpacked and put everything away before the big date. Do it NOW if it's easy and takes a few minutes. As for the thrill-seeking, find other outlets.

All or Nothing

When it comes to organizing projects, we don't like to take sips, we want to swig the whole thing in one big gulp. "Why just clean out the closet?" we'll say. "Let's organize the whole house!" Yikes! It's that kind of thinking, along with no real sense of time, that gets us in trouble. After that big burst of energy and enthusiasm wears off, we realize we have bitten off more then we can chew and give up. (Talk about a hangover.) Now, not only is everything from the closet on the floor, we have also emptied out the cabinets and other containers and it's a bigger mess than before. It's that extreme mind-set of wanting to do something grand that gets us in trouble. When reality sets in, we lose interest, intensity, and eventually run out of steam—especially when we get to the boring part of the project. With organizing projects, we make more of a mess when we don't complete them and never gain any momentum or get the satisfaction of seeing something to completion.

TRY THIS. When I start writing a new book, the euphoria of being signed to a book deal begins to wear off and the reality of having to research and write the thing sets in. If I didn't break the project down into bite-size morsels, I would, by nature, try to shove the whole thing down my throat and choke on it—or I wouldn't even nibble on it out of fear. (I'd be overwhelmed, not know where to begin, and wonder if I could pull it off.) The same thing is true with organizing. Take that energy and enthusiasm you have when you first decide to do something and focus it on an organizing project that you have the time to tackle in one sitting. Instead of trying to rearrange the whole closet, take on one shelf or one bar at a time. I realize this goes against our right-brain nature, but it allows us to work in short bursts, which is us at our best.

Altruistic

How can we waste time worrying whether or not our kitchen is clean when our beaches and bays are littered with trash? Why worry about all the paper clogging our lives when the world's rain forests are being logged into oblivion? I want to save the world, too, I just decided to begin in my own backyard. When we're faced with projects that touch our souls, make a difference in the world, challenge us, and provide some recognition for our talents, we can be dynamos. We don't need external motivation when we are doing things that have meaning. But it's the other stuff (like organizing) that sometimes slips through the cracks. Maybe you even have a bit of bohemian in your makeup and couldn't care less about style, order, and what Martha Stewart thinks organizing is. I agree. You should develop your own style of putting things away (or leaving them out). I also realize that even if you live in a van and travel around selling tie-dyed T-shirts at craft shows, being a bit more organized can help you have more freedom and free up time to make a difference in the world—while making sure you balance the books and properly promote your van-based business.

TRY THIS. Being the environmentalist and activist that I am, I came across a powerful book called *Selling the Dream* by Guy Kawasaki. A former Apple executive, Kawasaki explains the concept of evangelizing. In a nutshell, *evangelizing* means you get others so excited and motivated about your cause that it then becomes *their* mission and they help you do something you couldn't have done alone. What I have observed when it comes to making a difference and bringing about positive change in my community is that organizing helps, does not hurt, the cause. When championing any issue, it almost always requires letter writing and follow-up, building a following and a mailing list, making notes and keeping your records straight, planning and persistence, and maybe most of all rallying others to either take action or do something to influence decision makers. This is hard enough when you are organized. It's impossible when you are disorganized. Find the deeper meaning for getting your act together, whether it is to set a good example for your children to follow or to quit wasting time looking for lost and misplaced things and spend it on more meaningful pursuits. Or do it because it will make *you* feel good.

Amazing!

We can do as much as our left-brain counterpart (maybe more), but prefer to do it in our own unique way. Despite the negative bias against right-brainers as unproductive, undisciplined dreamers, we get things done. Be proud of who you are but excited about who you can be. Great minds have always faced strong opposition from lesser minds. The same traits that are a disadvantage when it comes to being organized prove to be an advantage in other areas of our lives. For example, some of the most accomplished people had many of the same characteristics you do. Many actors, artists, musicians, designers, and inventors favor the right side of their brain.

TRY THIS. "Professional organizers and planners are actually in a conspiracy to waste your time, not save it. Does any family truly need color-coded socks? Or alphabetized canned goods?" asks Lorraine Bodger. Use the tips and techniques from this book that make the most sense to you. Not everything will. You are unique (and special) and so are your circumstances. Pick and choose the ideas that you know will work with, not against, your natural tendencies. How will you know? When you read the right answer, you'll get a pit-of-the-stomach excitement or catch yourself smacking your forehead saying, "Aha! That would work!" Look around you and pay attention to what's working when it comes to organizing. Ask yourself why it's working. Look for clues. What's the common thread that makes you organized in some areas of your life and not in others? How can you learn from and build on these things? While you are at it, give yourself some credit and celebrate your successes.

RECYCLE

Odd objects that were once collecting dust can double as bookends. Neglected glass jars now hold soaps in the bathroom or odds and ends in your garage. An old tackle or toolbox becomes an art supply holder or makeup kit. Abandoned shoe boxes can hold all the supplies needed for bill paying or coupon clipping. Extra vases can be used to organize paintbrushes, fertilizer, or take-out menus. Ashtrays are perfect for corralling frequently lost or loose items like change, keys, and cuff links. Seldom-used Tupperware is very handy for organizing game pieces, strange screws, and office supplies. I'm sure you can come up with more ideas on how to recycle your under-utilized clutter.

Big-Picture Thinker

We are more interested in the bird's-eye view than the worm's-eye view. Combine that with a difficulty for dealing with details, an inability to prioritize or correctly estimate how long tasks take, not wanting to take the time to break down an idea into incremental steps, and you get either procrastination or incompletion. When I was organizing my garage, I didn't want to waste time measuring what would fit where. Instead, I went out and bought a bunch of shelving, hooks, containers, and boxes. I was more interested in the overall concept I had for organizing the garage than I was in the minutiae of things like planning. I got lucky and everything fit—which is rare. Organizing is about dividing up areas into zones based on how the space is used. It's about deciding which items are more important than others and putting them in prime places or out of the way. Organizing is also easier when taking it a little at a time and breaking down the daunting tasks into smaller, more manageable steps. Hmmm, sounds a little left-brain, doesn't it? It is and it isn't. Getting organized is a whole-brain affair. We can flex our right brains and also give our flabby, seldom-used left brains a workout, too.

TRY THIS. To use a whole-brain approach to organizing, visualize the outcome you seek and then look for connections on how to complete it with a mind map, sketch, or a rough plan. (This is for your right brain.) Then do a more detailed drawing with measurements and the steps you need to take in the order they need to be taken. (A little left brain is needed here.) For example, when it came time to organize my office, I took a different approach. I imagined it the way I wanted it to look and feel. Then I asked myself what activities I did where and created zones based on these activities. There were a copy cove, filing center, computer station, and so on. I then drew my office space (somewhat to scale) and cut out construction paper to represent my big pieces of equipment and furniture. I started experimenting by moving them around. (This was much easier on my back than actually moving my filing cabinets around.) Once I could see what fit where, I went to work. This is what I mean by taking a whole-brain approach to the problem.

Busy, Busy, Busy

We (right-brainers) usually like to have a lot going on in our lives or we are bored. We prefer to remain in perpetual motion. Am I right or am I right? We are always on the go and rarely slow down long enough to take care of trivial tasks, such as straightening up or organizing. Being right-brainers, we can juggle more than most, so multitasking is taken to Olympic proportions. Meg Ryan says, "Women have this ability to multitask, and I think because we are capable of it, we abuse ourselves with it. I think men are much more myopic and much more directional." Since we have our hands in so many things, we also wear many hats— freelancer, employee, artist, hobbyist, parent, spouse, friend, activist, housekeeper, gardener, cook, and the list goes on and on. The problem is, we don't feel organizing is worthy of our time, so it's last on the list to get done. (As if there were a list.) The problem with being busy may mean we never slow down long enough to get in touch with who we really ARE. We simply live from task to task. Being busy but never getting anything important done aren't good for long-term success. Organizing may not be among your top-ten favorite things to do, but I bet being more organized would help you have the time for the things that did make your top-ten list. Grammy-winning guitarist Norman Brown says, "Up until recently, being hyper and always on the go was part of my lifestyle, that was just me. Maybe it's getting older, but I realize that I can't be that way all the time anymore. I have to pace my energy output."

TRY THIS. Organizing helps us to determine what's important in our lives and makes us slow down just a little so we can enjoy that which means the most to us. When you are in the process of organizing, you tend to slow down and are able to take stock and realize what your priorities are. Think about it. When you sift through old photos, mementos, or love letters, how can you not help but notice what emotions this conjures up? Organizing also helps us get more done in less time. Wouldn't it take less time to dust and clean if clutter was in containers or out of the way? I rest my case. That means the maintenance tasks that take up so much time—and life is made up of mostly maintenance tasks with some joy thrown in to keep us from going completely crazy—can be done much faster and easier. Sure, we can then stuff even more things into our schedule—just make them more meaningful or enjoyable. Maybe you believe that downtime is wasted time. When you put your brain on autopilot and do something repetitive (like organizing), it may help you work your way through a creative block. Ever notice how you get those strokes of genius when you are doing the most mundane things? There is a reason for that. Your left brain—the critical side—is tuning out so that the right side—the creative side—can get a word in edgewise while the other side is busy.

Clutterers

The term "pack rat" is thrown around a lot when describing us. I am not so sure being described as a hairy rodent making a nest out of all sorts of stuff is the kind of terminology that will build up our self-esteem. There is nothing wrong with having and holding onto a lot of useful, interesting, or sentimental things as long as you have the room to hold them. If you have them organized in some fashion that isn't a health or fire hazard, what's the harm? If you can find what you need when you want it, it isn't a burden to you or those around you, and your hoarding doesn't hold you back from reaching your goals, what's the big deal? I understand that many right-brainers feel uncomfortable with empty space and clear counters. We would *prefer* to be surrounded by our stuff. It acts almost like a security blanket. There are a lot of things that really do come in handy someday. We would like to think we have almost everything for every imaginable situation. (It's impossible.) Then there's the stuff we save for the memories. Finally, some items may even be valuable. It's okay to keep all of these things. Just put them in places where you can get to them when you need them.

TRY THIS. Before buying out the Bed Bath & Beyond store, see if you can reorganize what you have. Look up, look down, look all around for spaces that may have escaped your eye—the attic or crawl space under the bed, the back of doors, in rafters, under stairs, between the washer and dryer, or inside empty luggage and coolers. Maybe you can skirt some of your furniture for additional storage space. Just don't store stuff you use regularly so out of the way you have to be Spiderman to get to it. You want to be able to get to it when you need it and more importantly, be able to put it away without a big hassle. Just remember, put things where you use them or based on how often you'll need to get to them. Long-term and out-of-the-way storage is for seasoned stuff.

Cool with Chaos

Some right-brainers prefer turmoil and think they thrive on constant chaos. Chaos isn't all bad, in regulated doses. It can be stimulating and even invigorating. Some tension is motivating, but the stress of having everything undone or in disarray can be taxing on you and those around you. Some people prefer to live on the edge by choice and find it more comfortable to be in a crisis mode. These "drama queens" seem to relish the problems being disorganized can cause. They will even put themselves in precarious positions (again and again) because they are bored when things are going well. So they create a crisis scenario through a lack of organization where one need not exist. (This includes not backing up our hard drive, not paying bills or even balancing our checkbooks, leaving valuables on the floor, not shredding personal documents, and loaning out items without writing down a reminder.) It seems strange that someone would actually want to live like this, but it happens. My guess is that we thrive on risk and like challenges so much we need to make sure we have enough of both to keep us stimulated and interested. Maybe we feel indestructible, omnipotent, powerful—or we simply don't fathom failing. Legendary drummer Buddy Rich played like he lived—fast and furious. He was always in motion, racing around town in fast cars. Many people like to live life in the fast lane. For them organizing isn't sexy, thrilling, or risky. It's boring. Instead, disorganization and all the risks that come with it are more interesting and stimulating. "The triumph over anything is a matter of organization," says Kurt Vonnegut. I tend to agree. Organizing brings some stability to your life, and that makes it worth the time it takes.

TRY THIS. Who says that organizing doesn't come with some risk? You could suffer a paper cut while filing. If you need more risk, try putting your keys in a fishbowl filled with live piranhas or sort through your piles of papers in the nude—with the window open. How about inviting a friend over to tackle a tough area to organize? Dig through your old stuff with a few friends and share some of the drama that went with each purchase—then get rid of or stash anything that causes a painful memory and organize the rest.

Creative

We fear that too much organizing will kill our creativity. If you think that, you're wrong. To prove it, organize a little area and see what happens. Look at it as an experiment. I bet you will see that it actually helps, does not hurt, your creative abilities. Art Fry, the inventor of the Post-it note, says, "Some people are going to be creative if you put them in a packing crate. Others need the stimulation that a good environment produces." I will say, creativity comes from confidence. Having things around that remind you of how wonderful you are can only help your creative side to flourish. Beyonce of Destiny's Child has a reflection room where she keeps plaques on the walls. Howie Dorough of Backstreet Boys also has his awards up where he can see them. Leave items out and put up things that build your self-esteem and make you feel good. I save all my fan mail and press clippings in a binder. Put your love letters in a shoe box. Keep mementos from your childhood in a treasure chest under your desk. Surround yourself with things that make you feel alive, creative, soothed, calm, content, happy, free. Get rid of anything that drags you down—items that produce bad memories, stuff that's broken, things that no longer serve you or your life.

TRY THIS. Where do you get your best ideas? What would an idea space be like? Light or dark? Quiet or noisy? What sort of tools or materials would you like to have around you? What type of work surface? Clean or cluttered? What would the walls have on them? Do you work during the day or at night? The answers are different for everyone, but the one thing we all have in common is that there is no one place where inspiration hits. It can come at any time. However, we tend to spend a great deal of our creative time in one place—our office or studio—and we need to make it a space that encourages creative thought. How you do this is your personal preference. One writer I know lined the walls of her writing room with cork so that she could pin up anything that inspired her—quotes, clippings, and all kinds of crazy things. An artist I admire who works with wood likes to leave the shavings on the floor of his studio. When he walks around barefoot the sensation is stimulating. A musician leaves all of his gear set up so that all he has to do is flip a few switches and he can play and record whenever inspiration hits. Maybe you do your creative thinking in an office. Most companies that foster creativity encourage their people to play. (Hooray!) These places allow their people to paint their walls, make piles, and have toys in their office. I have seen everything from Slinkys, Nerf balls, Godzilla inflatables, squirt guns, *Star Wars* and *Star Trek* gear, PEZ dispensers, and more. These things make people smile as they stay in touch with their inner child. This, in turn, inspires innovative thought. Add some stuff to your desk that increases your creativity. Maybe you can't change everything about your environment at work, but you can add a few fun things. Keep a few toys around to play with when you are stuck. This allows your right brain to get a word in while your left brain is busy playing with Silly Putty.

VISUAL VARIETY

The right brain works best when it is able to look around and make connections with odd items. Your creative side also needs visual variety. Shake things up from time to time. Turn pictures on your desk upside down. Reposition other things on your desktop just because you feel like it. See, your left brain will label things, and you don't really notice them. Your right brain kicks in when things are a little off and tries to put the puzzle together.

Curious

We are lifelong learners and an inquisitive bunch. Most people ask, "Why?" We ask, "Why not?" We will gather obscure facts, figures, and other "intellectual" finds and want to save them—all. Before we know it we are buried under a pile of books, magazines, and printouts. When surfing the Web, we are like kids in a candy store. We are interested in everything, and that means our hard drives are littered with all kinds of interesting (and probably unrelated) bits of information. When it comes to hobbies we prefer to get all the gear and *then* decide if we are truly interested. The problem is we can't get rid of anything we deem useful—and everything seems useful. That makes organizing very difficult. Another reason right-brainers tend to save stuff is that we want to find a solution to a problem nobody else seems to be able to solve. To do that we like to have a lot of seemingly useless information and items at our disposal. (Things others would have disposed of a long time ago.) We see illogical patterns that others miss. What others see as a mess, we see as solutions sitting in a pile of papers. What can we say? We are able to do a lot of different things and do them well. Don't apologize. The only drawback is we end up having to organize a variety of items that go with each of our interests and pursuits. The other problem is that a lot of random stuff lying around makes it hard to categorize and thus difficult to group together and put away.

TRY THIS. Einstein came up with the theory of relativity, but much of our stuff isn't relative and we have no theories about where it goes. So we just shrug and say, "Einstein had a messy desk, so I am a genius, too." Well, we are no Einsteins. That doesn't mean we can't be curious. Actor Matt Keeslar says, "When I get depressed and haven't been working, I start hanging around Barnes & Noble for hours, reading a book from every department." Good. You don't have to own every book in the store. Use the library and Internet instead. For the information you do want to keep, use binders, boxes, bins, and baskets to sort and store it. Look for broad categories and just throw the stuff into the right container. It's easy and it's better than a lot of loose paper strewn randomly all over the room. Create categories and files on your hard drive and treat them the same way—drop related information in the right folder for safekeeping and easy retrieval. When you have a wild idea about the new hobby you want to try, see if you can rent the gear until you are sure it's worth the expense and space to buy. (Sell some under-used items to make room and help pay for the new ones.) Here's a thought: use your natural curiosity and desire to try and tackle your organizing challenges. Set up "zones" for each activity and keep like items together. Because we work in processes, we should store and organize our paper, files, and supplies as works in progress. Pile by project or let them float around you in your space.

CURIOSITY PAYS OFF

To save space William Calderwood of Arizona patented lighter-than-air furniture. It levitates to the ceiling (using helium) when not in use. You pull it down when you want to sit on it. Clever.

Defensive/Sensitive

Deep down we want people to appreciate us for who we are, not who they think we should be. It hurts to hear all the negative comments about our unorthodox ways of doing things. Because we organize by gathering, associating, clustering, piling, and don't tend to alphabetize, prioritize, or categorize things "properly" by some predetermined acceptable system, we are ridiculed and reprimanded. Left-brainers see us as coming from "the wrong side of the tracks." They look at us with disdain. We are messy, disorganized, and couldn't care less about some of the same things they hold so near and dear, like routine, rules, and order. We flaunt our creativity in the way we think, act, and dress. It bothers them that we can't be more like they are—uptight, disciplined, and above all else, organized. Believe it or not, many of us do wear our disorganization as a badge of honor. We can be heard bragging, "I haven't seen the top of my desk in ten years." We can't be like them (nor do we want to) so we flaunt our mess as a means of deflecting their disdain. The truth is, they should lighten up a little and maybe we can control *some* of the clutter.

TRY THIS. Don't do things and live your life to try and please others. Do it for yourself and your sanity. It's okay to admire people who have have their act together. Maybe it's a sick fascination—like viewing an automobile accident—we want to get organized but we also realize we aren't interested in their kind of regimented, structured, right-angle style of organizing. There is no wrong way to organize as long as it's working. Famous *Chicago Tribune* columnist Mike Royko had piles and piles of paper all around him and was still able to get the job done. The "right" way to organize may be to just do more of what works and eliminate the things that don't. Or, and this is a biggie, we could look to the left for tips on how to organize and then tweak them with our creative brain to make them match our own unique circumstances. This "meeting of the minds" just may do the trick.

Disinterested in Organizing

"The great myth (and barrier) for the creative person is the belief that their creativity precludes them from being organized. The reality is that their disorganization can get in the way of their creativity," says professional organizer Odette Pollar. I agree. The answer is to use creative ways to get organized. Since organizing isn't a priority, we are perpetually disinterested and disorganized. It's maddening, but we plow through piles of papers and misplaced messes. We aren't organized people and don't want to be, so we never worry about the mess in our wake. We want to do it our way, even if it's not working. We can be supertalented, smart, clever, wonderful people, but when it comes to organizing, we get sort of stupid. It is our beliefs about organizing that do us in.

TRY THIS. I find organizing fascinating for a number of reasons. It involves a lot of skills a right-brainer is good at, including problem solving, innovative thinking, and design. Look at it as a challenge and a chance to flex your creative muscles. We are nonconformists and rebel against traditional techniques. That's good, because most organizing tools are made for left-brainers. I say create your own. I know a woman who mounted a strip of wood around her room and attached doorknobs every foot or so. It was meant to be a design element (don't ask), but it turned out to be quite functional for hanging clothes and clutter. How about turning the front of cabinets or closet doors into corkboards for displaying your kid's art? I didn't like any of the planners on the market so I invented my own whole-brain planner with lists on the left and doodle space on the right. If we just saw organizing as more than drudgery, it would be easier to get excited about it. Even if you don't like it, you still have to do it. Why? Organizing is the key that unlocks your true potential. If I was disorganized, I would never be able to juggle all the things I have going, and I wouldn't have achieved as much as I have. Find the links between organizing and the rest of your life. I bet there are some connections you may have missed. You'll feel better about yourself and your life when organized. Think about it—you'll save time, reduce stress, and feel empowered. Think about all the positive feedback you'll get when you do it. There will be an increase in your happiness and you'll enjoy your space a LOT more. It is worth the time and effort it takes. Look at it as a big adventure, a chance to do some soul-searching and gain a lot of insight and inspiration. Have a scavenger hunt. When you begin the process of organizing you will discover a lot about *YOU.* Your choices, good and bad. What's important to you. It's all there right in front of you in a pile.

SOME REASONS YOU SHOULD WANT TO BE ORGANIZED

My guess is that you are intimidated by others who are naturally organized. They will make comments that make you feel inferior. You have to defend yourself against these left-brainers with a superiority complex. Don't let their condescending attitude get you down. Instead, take action and prove them wrong. Come up with a better, more creative (and effective) approach. One you can proudly point to as your own. Then you can yell, "Take that, you anal-retentive, compulsive freak!" These people may never understand us, but if we have an organizing system that works, they can respect us.

1. **Do it for yourself.** Organizing can be the difference between being a doer and a dabbler. Do you want to be more than another frustrated person who didn't live up to his full potential because of disorganization?
2. **Do it for your career.** Once you are known for being reliable, as well as creative, people will want to work with you. It's a rare combination.
3. **Fewer people are pissed at you.** Generally others don't appreciate it when you forget their birthday, miss an anniversary, fail to return items you borrowed, don't return calls or respond to e-mails for months. You won't win friends or influence people when you show up late (or not at all) because you never write anything down or were looking for your lost keys. Do it for yourself, but a big benefit is that the people around you will be happy, too.
4. **Cleaning without clutter is easier.** Cleaning around clutter takes a ton of time. This is time that could be spent on better or more productive things.
5. **Control the chaos.** Happy people feel in control of their lives. Statistically, the most predictable *unhappy* people are those who lack control. To beat the blues, organizing is one of the best things you can do.
6. **It teaches discipline.** We are all about fun and games and that's good—up to a point. Some things in life are serious and need to get done. We waste a

continued on next page

lot of time and energy worrying about what we should have done, and *that* takes away from the fun.

7. **Your love life may improve.** One woman wouldn't date at all for fear that someone might see her place and her messy ways. Her kitchen and bathroom are clean, but her, uh, unmentionables are everywhere. I admit, women's underwear looks a lot better than a guy's hanging from the doorknob, but let's face it, nobody wants to see your "Granny panties" on a first date.

8. **Avoid embarrassment.** Are you afraid to give anyone a ride in your car because of the clutter? If you do give someone a ride and she comments on the smell or the mess and asks if you have a dog, you should always say yes, whether you do or don't.

9. **Entertain more often.** When you are organized, there's no mad dash to stash all of your stuff before answering the door. It's nice to welcome people into your home and not have to say, "Excuse the mess. The cleaning lady didn't come this week." Trust me, they aren't buying it.

10. **Find things.** I saw a commercial where a guy wins the lottery but can't find the ticket. In the ad, he blows it off and has a beer in a bar; but let me tell you something, that would suck. We waste a lot of our lives looking for lost and misplaced things because of disorganization, and it's very stressful.

11. **Focus.** If a home, office, studio, or workshop is overrun with clutter, it's harder to focus with constant reminders of what needs to be done all around you.

12. **Free up your brain for better things to think about.** When everything in your life is organized you can use your brain for more important things than looking for lost items and constantly cleaning up.

13. **Life is too complicated not to be orderly.** Right-brainers like to have a lot going on in their lives. How can you handle all the information and items that come into your life on a weekly basis if you don't have some way to make it work?

14. **There's no place like home.** An organized house is a more pleasant, peaceful, and relaxing place to come home to.

15. **R-E-S-P-E-C-T.** People treat you differently when you have your act together—they treat you with respect. You'll respect yourself, too. When you look good, you feel good.

16. **Romance.** Some people like it dirty, but most people prefer it clean. What am I talking about? Romance and relationships are improved by being organized.

17. **Saves time.** Life is short. It's shorter when you waste time. Being more organized can free up some time for fun things.

18. **More room.** Clutter makes a room look a lot smaller. (Imagine what it does to a car or a closet.) We need some open space to breathe, to think, and for visual relief.

AN IMPORTANT LESSON

Billionaire Richard Branson started his first business, a magazine, when he was just a teenager. He says he was more interested in the business side of running a magazine than the editorial stuff. "I realized that the strength of the magazine—the chaotic devil-may-care gaggle of creative types who camped out in our office—was also its weakness. The erratic artsiness was fine, but I, and I alone, was left to worry about the bills."

Disorganized

Are you forgetful, frequently late (poor judge of time), and known as "difficult" to work with? Are you caught up in your own world and do you have a lack of respect for others' time and agendas? Do you frustrate others when you have trouble finding important papers amid the mess? It's hard to admit this may be true of you, but if it is, needless to say, this style has a tremendous downside. It could be that your right brain sabotages your success. Not that this is an excuse, but your right brain may not know any better. Giving a right-brainer space is like giving a dog a computer. Chances are she will not use it wisely. Studies prove we have difficulty with where to put things because we have trouble with spacial tasks. (Aha! I knew it. It's in our DNA.) The other thing is, we like living this way—up to a point. Others may say, "What a mess. When are you going to get organized?" We reply, "What mess?" or "This mess? It's a work in progress," or, "It's organized chaos." I bet at some point you have picked up a design magazine, visited an organized home, or watched a makeover show on TV and felt a twinge of envy. Maybe you have tried to get organized before, but fell back into your old ways. Bought the books, took the seminar, and gave it a go with the best intentions; but it never sticks. Organizing seems to come easily for left-brainers. They put everything in its proper place and are naturally neat and tidy. They can also be compulsive, stressed, and uptight.

TRY THIS. Do you constantly say, "Excuse the mess," when someone comes into your home or office? Is that the first impression you want to make when people meet you? As you know, you never get a second chance to make a good first impression. People make opinions about YOU based on what they see, usually within the first few seconds. Make the entryway a highlight of your house. Create clutter-free zones by using clear containers to group and store your stuff. Organize your planner, portfolio, or purse if this is what others often see. To do this, get the right tools for the job. Good organizing products make your life easier and free you up to be more creative and spontaneous. Yes, you read that right, spontaneous. Anything that seems like too much trouble to implement, too structured, or boring should be left out. The key is deciding what is the most important thing you want (and must) get done and using these tools to help you do it. Whatever you do, find ways to get it together a little bit at a time. Organizing is becoming more and more important, even to the right-brainer who managed to get by on a wing and a prayer until now. With corporate downsizing and a tight economy, people are expected to do the work of two or three people. We need ways to stay on top of things or we will get buried. Organizing is the answer. With this book it's not only possible, it's probable!

ACTION ITEM

Visualize what it would be like to have everything organized. What would it look like? Feel like? What would others say? How would your life be better?

Divergent Thinkers/Easily Distracted

Mike Meyers described his brain as an airport without air-traffic controllers. He says he has about twelve ideas circling the airport and never knows which one will land. It's hard to be organized when you can't focus. We are divergent thinkers (a nice way of saying our minds are likely to jump around). Actor Mark Ruffalo said, "I always have eighteen things going on—I kinda have attention deficit disorder (ADD) that way." Uh, yeah. For us, new is definitely more exciting than status quo. There are problems with always seeking something new. For one, many times we aren't paid until we COMPLETE a project, and leaving a trail of unfinished projects just isn't profitable. Allowing (unpaid) distractions to get in the way of the paying work we should be doing can also be dangerous. An inability to focus can be a form of self-sabotage. We want it all (now), and when we try to do it all we spread ourselves too thin. Also, the ability to create endless possibilities isn't such a great trait when it comes to filing. A neighbor of mine was asked if he was tested for attention deficit disorder by his employer, and his "honest to God" reply was, "If they did, I don't remember it." Author Robert Shiller says, "The ability to focus attention on important things is a defining characteristic of intelligence." We won't succeed until we can focus. It's hard to stay organized when you are all over the place. So much switching off usually leaves a trail of half-finished tasks and related clutter. Mail is left all over the house. Laundry sits half-folded. Books are left unread all over the house. This compounds the problem because too many things left lying around are even more distracting. We are always looking for the next big thing to do. We are always trying to find fresh, fun, and interesting things to do. To us, new stuff is always better than old, but we can't possibly part with what we have. We like to jump around and do things out of order. We start one filing system and then start a new one. We're most comfortable when several things are going on simultaneously because we like to switch back and forth between projects and we welcome interruptions with glee. We are always changing and trying new things, zigzagging through life, which makes it tough to get and stay organized.

TRY THIS. Finish one thing, then start another is the advice often heard from well-meaning parents. Boooooooring. Instead, set limits and goals. I will focus for forty-five minutes, then I can goof off or go do something else. I will eliminate one piece of clutter per day. I will not let anything new into my home for one week. Goals and discipline go hand in hand. Give yourself a target and a way to measure how you're doing. Set challenges like, "I will clean up my home by 4:30 p.m. I will file loose papers by the end of the day. I will make a to-do list every day." Self-discipline is simply paying attention and altering your behavior. Become a little more practical and grounded in reality; be less controlled by impulse and emotion. Wow, did I just write that? Yes, I did. I wouldn't be where I am without some control over my tendency to go off in ten different directions at once and have my head in the clouds. Stuart Woods once wrote two books at one time. What he did was work on one in the morning and the other in the afternoon. Use your natural tendencies, like divergent thinking, to your advantage by multitasking. Maybe you can watch TV, answer e-mail, return calls, and eat dinner all at the same time. Get into the zone. We can be like ten year olds engrossed in a video game when we are interested. We can focus when we find something fascinating. Find ways to focus by making organizing fun, interesting, and challenging. Know your tendencies and make tasks last less long. Work in minicycles. (Break big organizing projects down into smaller tasks that take ten to twenty minutes.) Have places to put away unfinished projects. Write down what you were going to do next on a pad kept with what you were working on. You need constant stimulation. You can make this tendency work for you. Fisher-Price encourages its toy designers to get out and regularly visit such places as toy stores, day-care centers, trade shows, parks, and playgrounds. The change of scenery helps to produce original ideas. Rotate responsibility. "Boredom is a great motivator," boasts Uma Thurman. Plastic baskets are perfect for works in progress, things in various stages of disrepair, or just stuff you want to store. How about this for the person with a lot going on all at once? Use a briefcase for each project you are working on. When you are bored close up the case and everything is stored safely away. Everything stays together and travels well. Just grab and go.

Dramatic/Eccentric

Many of us enjoy shocking and surprising others. We wear our originality and eccentricity like a badge of honor. That's partly why we want them to say "wow" when they walk into a room and see a massive mess. Maybe we try to get a reaction with a strange collection of stuff. For example, a guy I met collects old and outdated Apple computers. It's cool but the clutter this collection creates is mind-boggling. It could be that you "recycled" an odd object to use as it was never intended to be. Just keep in mind that when you prefer stylish and cool over practical and functional, this can cause organizing problems. This is only a problem when you want to impress people with your disdain for order or an amazing amount of strange stuff or the tremendous (and tenuous) height of your piles. When organizing you want your personality to shine through—up to a point. (Some of us have personalities that are larger than life.) Einstein's office was so messy they always kept the door shut. (He also believed that his theological cat, Weltanschauung, was in cahoots with his academic rival. Go figure.) There is a fine line between genius and weirdo. You can be your "normal" nonconforming self and still be organized. I think some eccentricity is needed to personalize your space. If you prefer to paint a wall with chalkboard paint and provide colored chalk and encourage friends and family to make their mark in your home, I'm all for it. If you want to work by the light of a lava lamp, go for it. If you keep a collection of old fur balls from your cat in a jar on the shelf, who am I to judge?

TRY THIS. "You've got to be original, because if you're like someone else, what do they need you for?" says Bernadette Peters. What if you painted flowers all over your filing cabinets? How about coming up with a calendar that matches your moods rather than the months? An empty coffin could become a handy storage unit. A laundry line stretched across a room could be used to hang art, messages, or as a time line for bills. (Paint the cord in colors to reflect urgency or use stickers to indicate due dates.) Cut a surfboard in half and mount it on the wall for shelves. Use a truck bed coming out of the wall to store stuff. Thrift store suitcases stacked on top of one another serve as storage and end tables. Use meat-packing paper on a roll (attached to the wall) to write messages to yourself, doodle, or make a daily things-to-do list. How about a mannequin to hang the next day's outfit on so it's ready to go in the morning? See, you can be your old, odd, off-the-wall self and still be organized.

Emotional

I was watching TV late at night and bought a collection of hits from the seventies because they reminded me of when I was a kid. This emotion triggered a want to spend some money. (It doesn't take much.) Now, these are songs I hear on the radio all the time but I still *had* to have them. We tend to get emotionally attached to things because right-brainers feel things more deeply than others and make connections others ignore. We keep a lot of stuff around not because it's useful but because it's *meaningful* to us. It's fun to search through old things and relive the memories. We tend to make decisions with our hearts and not our heads. This leads to some very interesting choices about what we have to organize in our homes and offices. We may also suffer from MS (otherwise known as mood swings). Like a pendulum, we will swing from one mood to another with highs and lows like a roller-coaster. When we are up, we tend to go crazy and spend, spend, spend, which leads us to be bummed; and then we spend to try to make ourselves feel better. We may rally for a while, but eventually, when we get the bill, we are even more depressed than before. Then the pain passes (and we forget the, "I'll never do it again," admonishment we made to ourselves) and we go on another bender. And so it goes. The aftermath is a lot of stuff to store that doesn't fit in our space or our lives.

TRY THIS. My advice: Don't love anything that can't love you back. That said, there are some things that we just absolutely *love* having around. What if we set some limits? Limit your collection to one shelf or one room. Buy a treasure chest and throw things into it. When it's full, sift through and save only the things that produce a positive emotion. (Some writers save their rejection letters as a motivational tool. In this case a negative emotion produces a positive one.) How about a hot one hundred? This is the best of the best. These are your one hundred favorite photos, CDs, books, DVDs, or magazines. You can rotate them with stuff in storage if your mood shifts, but there are some parameters about just how much will fit. Maybe you can take the best stuff and make a collage, video, or compilation CD so that it takes up less space. Try keeping a piece of a keepsake, not the whole thing. I would recommend NOT making a big decision when you are at one or the other extreme. When your emotions are in a down cycle, you can sometimes blow things way out of proportion and everything feels hopeless. Not good. In general, when we are emotional (and when are we not?) we can make some whopping errors in judgment.

Fun/Playful

The song says, "Girls just wanna have some fun." So do right-brainers. We are the life of the party. We throw our hands in the air like we just don't care. We like to let the good times roll. Chances are we don't take things like organizing seriously, and my guess is we wouldn't say organizing is fun—so it doesn't get done. "You've got to keep the child alive; you can't create without it," says Joni Mitchell. Oh, and we do. You can protect your right to play and create a space that is stimulating but not distracting, cluttered but comfortable, playful but professional, and above all, organized but not overly orderly.

TRY THIS. At Nike, they get it. The culture at the corporate headquarters is one of continuous invention and innovation. They encourage the designers to draw inspiration from sources other than shoes. That means there is a lot of stuff lying around to get the creative juices flowing—odd artifacts, samples of origami, model cars. People make piles on their desks, and nobody cares. Most of the work is done outside of their "isolation" cubicles anyway. The creative director at Nike actually wants all hell to break loose and likes the loud music, late nights, and pizza parties that inspire creativity. (They understand that the process of creating can get messy.) They call the Design Department the "Innovation Kitchen," and it is not organized in a classic sense; but they want and like it that way. At the headquarters of Nickelodeon, a TV network that caters to kids, they also get it. Workers describe it as a place where they come to play. It's an attitude that's designed for maximum fun. The walls are made of chalkboard and cork and metal so that employees can post their art, jokes, ideas, thoughts, and wild ideas. Messy desks and crazy clutter are part of the culture. At Wham-O headquarters, where they make the Hula Hoop and the Frisbee, the company acknowledges that to develop fun products they have to have fun and that is the secret to their success. At Southwest Airlines headquarters the walls look like a family scrapbook and are covered with the photographs of workers. Aha! Organizing can be fun. It's all in how you look at it. Decide to become the Picasso of paper management, the Michelangelo of time management, and the da Vinci of details. What if you put all your organizing tasks on little slips of paper along with some fun things to do, dropped them in a jar, shook it up, and randomly chose one every hour? Add some fun and games to organizing by buying things that are functional but fun. How about adding a tape dispenser that is shaped like a shark? Pens with bobble heads on top? Custom file folders made out of rubber, plastic, or whatever? Cut out your own message slips in odd shapes and create your own unique pad. Make an in-box out of an old mailbox and mount it on the wall. Use a wood tiki as a business card holder. Make an OUT OF OFFICE sign using an old Halloween mask. It's still a functional office and it's neatly arranged so nobody complains.

Generous

Being people pleasers, we would give you the shirt off our backs. (And why not? We have a hundred more where that came from.) When you give away your time because you want to be liked and would feel guilty if you don't, you are giving away more than an hour here or an hour there—you are parting with a piece of your life. It also means that all those things you want to do are on the back burner because you put others' priorities ahead of your own. If you really want to get organized and stay that way but claim you don't have the time, could it be that you HAD the time but chose to give it away and to spend it elsewhere? I say, put people first, but charity begins at home. If you are helping others clean up their places but your own is a mess, shame on you. Learn how to say, "No!" or you will never get your own needs met or your own work done. If someone asks if she can store her stuff in your already cramped quarters, what do you say? "NO!" What are you, a martyr? Mother Teresa?

TRY THIS. It's good to give things away—almost as good as getting. Give away some of your clutter and free up some room. Donate your unused, unwanted, and just plain ugly stuff to a charity, museum, or your kids. I asked my parents for my inheritance early. Instead of money, they gave me bags and boxes full of a bunch of their excess clutter. Not what I had in mind. In all seriousness, the biggest burden all that disorganization creates is on those around you. You'd love to do more for people, but how can you when all your time and money are tied up in things? How much time do you waste fighting about and fighting through your clutter? I truly believe you have to make space in your life (and your house) so that better things can come in. It's true of all clutter—even people who are dragging you down. When you let go of a friend who takes advantage of you and treats you poorly, I guarantee you that eventually someone better will come along to take his or her place. It's the same with the things in your closet, garage, and files. Let go so you can let in something newer and better.

Impatient

We want quick and easy solutions. If organizing doesn't take right away, we aren't interested. "I Want It Now!" is our motto. Unfortunately, it takes time and discipline to get organized. Sorry. We can't give up at the boring part or we will never get it together. I think it's great to be in the moment. As right-brainers, this is one of our greatest strengths. There is magic in the moment, but after it passes we must face the future. By focusing on the future while paying attention to the present, we are able to enjoy the here and now and organize for what is coming next.

TRY THIS. Would you like to be able to wave a wand at your mess and have it all magically organize itself and returned to where it belongs? Go ahead, wave your magic wand (otherwise known as your credit card) at the problem. Huh? Hire some help in the form of a professional organizer to give you the initial boost you need. Let her deal with the most difficult organizing challenges you face. Then all you have to do is finish it off and maintain it. If you can't afford to hire some help, ask your family and friends to come over (bribe them with pizza and promise they get dibs on the stuff you no longer need) and have an organizing party. If you have to go it alone, here are some tips to make organizing fast and easy. Start with something simple so you can see some progress right away. Take it one pile at a time so you don't get discouraged when you barely make a dent in the overall problem. Work in short, concentrated bursts of thirty to forty minutes. If you feel like doing more, go with it. Because when you are in the mood to organize and your energy level is high, you have to ride it for all it's worth.

PICTURE THIS

Taping a Polaroid picture of what's in a box to its outside makes identifying what's inside quick and easy. (This is good for the visual person.) Another quick way to identify what's in a box or bin is to color code it. Use different-colored bins to match the color of the LEGO pieces to make it a no-brainer for kids to put their blocks away at the end of the day. For deep storage, put holiday decorations or seasonal clothes in boxes that make sense to you. Christmas decorations are in a red box and summer clothes are in a yellow bin.

Impulsive

Right-brainers are known to fall in love fast, buy things they really don't need, and make decisions without much thought. When it comes to organizing, impulsiveness can get in the way of getting it together. For example, we see a rave review for a new contact manager software program so we buy and begin to use it. That would be fine, except that we have various parts of our mailing list spread out over three *other* similar programs we bought on a whim. The other way impulsiveness plays out is when you start to organize without much thought about what should go where. (A little planning goes a long way when it comes to organizing.) When you give an impulsive person a credit card and send him to the store, watch out. He may buy tons of stuff he doesn't need now—or ever. Then these extra items have to be stored somewhere, making staying organized a real challenge.

TRY THIS. If someone wants to purchase a handgun, he is forced to wait at least a week. This kind of "cooling off" period should be instituted for all big purchases. Then you could step back and decide if you really need it (or just want it) and if you have the room to store it. When it comes to overbuying, freeze your credit card in a block of ice, and then when you want to make a purchase, you have to wait while it thaws and you may change you mind. You may also want to ask yourself when making a decision, does this help or hurt me when it comes to my goals? If your goal is to get organized, then limiting what's coming into your life makes sense. Subscribing to ten new magazines, volunteering to be the bookkeeper for a club or association you belong to, or ordering the *Encyclopædia Brittanica* (in book form) is counterproductive to your goals.

Inconsistent

If your space were a place it would probably look like New York City at rush hour—and everyone would be blindfolded. Things are all over the place, mixing and mingling without much thought as to where they are going or where they should end up. Not good. Hey, variety IS the spice of life, but when it comes to organizing, consistency is the key. Since we don't like to do the same thing the same way twice and prefer to jump around, over time our filing system can become a convoluted mess. There are ten different folders (filed in ten different places) for the same thing. Some receipts are in a shoe box for tax reasons, a few are stapled to manuals, and still others are crammed in your wallet. If you can decide on one place that makes the most sense, you will lose a lot less stuff and organizing will get easier. When you keep appointments in ten different places—your PDA, planner, pocket calendar, wall calendar, Post-it notes, and maybe worst of all, in your head—is it any wonder that it's hit or miss whether you make it there or not? Simplify!

TRY THIS. "Be regular and orderly in your life so that you may be violent and original in your work," said Gustave Flaubert. To make decisions about where to put things, limit the choices by creating slots, spaces, and dividers. Have homes or designated spots in which to put stuff. Instead of leaving your keys on the counter one day and in the bathroom the next, pick a place to leave them and make it a habit to always use the same place. Hang them on a hook by the door or put them in your purse (which hangs on a hook by the door). When things are working, leave them alone. If the temptation is to do something different—don't. If you can stick with ONE system long enough, it will become second nature and organizing will get a LOT easier.

Indecisive

Do you tend to take a wait-and-see approach with things? Do you flip-flop on decisions and are you known as being wishy-washy? If you put everything off until . . . (fill in the blank), nothing ever gets done. Stuff stays where you put it for the most part and attracts other things to keep it company. You're in the situation you are in because of the choices (or lack of choices) you've made. When it comes to organizing, this includes how much stuff you have decided to let into your life and where you put it. YOU have the power of choice. The better you choose, the better the result. What's worse are patterns of bad decisions that pile up. Indecision is a choice. You chose to do nothing. Choose to become more organized. That's the first step.

TRY THIS. Read the "Rules" chapter in this book and set up some boundaries to follow. For example, to simplify decision making simply put things where they are used. Have a box for the "I don't know what this is or where it should go." Make a "not sure" box or drawer for things that don't have a home. When it's full, make some decisions about what stays, where it goes, and what gets tossed. Patterns may form or after a while you may realize you don't need it and the decision of what to do is made for you. It's your life. Choose wisely. What exactly do you want your environment to look like, feel like, work like? Make decisions based on that vision and get in touch with why you want it. Make small choices that support the bigger picture—and the organized you. Choose not to put something down, but instead put it away. When you do this on a regular basis you end up more organized. Focus on what's in front of you and make good decisions about where to put this *one* thing. Just move it closer to where it goes. Make the best choice. It doesn't have to be perfect. Pick the path that has the least resistance. Maybe the decision is made for you. Notice where you drop things. To straighten up, put a "catcher" there. When it comes to deciding what stays and what goes, ask yourself, "Does this make me smile? Make a difference? Make me a better person/parent/professional?" Many things may catch your eye, but keep the things that touch your heart. Make decisions based on feelings first. We may be seen as wishy-washy because after the initial intuitive response we start to think rather than feel, and this causes indecision. The next time you ask yourself, "Where should I put this?", put it in the first place you would go to look for it.

Independent

Cats: They do what they want, when they want. They rarely listen to anyone. They are totally unpredictable. They whine when they are unhappy. When you want to play with them, they prefer to be left alone. They leave their hair everywhere. They expect you to cater to their every whim. They are moody. They drive you nuts. Conclusion: Cats are little, tiny women in fur coats—or right-brainers. I thought about using reverse psychology in this book so that the headstrong, rebellious, independent thinkers would believe they were bucking the system, when in reality they were doing exactly what I hoped they would when it came to organizing. The problem is, right-brainers are too sharp and would have seen right through that strategy. It's true that we have a very strong independent streak and will rebel any chance we get with dramatic effect. Did you know that Paul Gauguin was a banker before he became the talented Postimpressionist painter who left his restrictive job and moved to Tahiti to paint? That's my dream, too. But I have to live in the real world with deadlines, bills, paperwork—and organizing. Freedom is my highest value. How about you? Don't like to be boxed in or pinned down? Prefer to keep your options open and don't make a things-to-do list? Hate routine or committment and don't write anything down? Prefer variety and don't do anything the same way twice? I'm with you, man. We would prefer to do things our way, in our own sweet time with no outside interference. We also don't adhere to rules or regulations. One of our favorite things is to find new and neat ways to do things. Well, when it comes to organizing, some consistency and routine are a real help. Hey, I'd like to pay my bills once a year and file my taxes in October, but I don't think creditors or the Internal Revenue Service are going to go for it.

TRY THIS. "To enjoy freedom we have to control ourselves," said Virginia Woolf. I agree. To be truly creative you have to have some sense of order in your life. Some structure is needed because we have so many things going on we would never be able to keep it all straight. Working without a plan seems like a pleasure, but it can pose some problems. Too much free-form living will leave everything in your life constantly out of control. Important priorities will get shoved to the back burner, tasks will fall through the cracks, and our stuff will tend to pile up. We want to work on things when we want to work on them. I say, do whatever you FEEL like doing as long as it is something that needs to get done. Use your internal clock to guide you as to when to do what. We can't just go hog-wild and give in completely to our natural right-brain tendencies. A little left-brain activity is also helpful. When you are bored—and when are we not?—switching to a left-brain task can be a relief and a release. Put a basket by the computer with your mailing list updates and do them a little at a time. Things that need to be repaired can be kept in containers on a shelf in the garage so that you can easily get to them (but they are out of the way), and you can work on them whenever you feel like it. Write appointments and dates to remember in pencil or put them on sticky notes in your calendar so you can easily change them. Put chores on individual index cards and shuffle them and pick the one that matches your mood. Make a master list of organizing tasks and put it up where you will see it. Make it a work of art by doing it in calligraphy or with symbols for each item. We want a one-of-a-kind space that reflects our unique nature. We need space that is an expression of our personality. We want to organize in a way that opens our minds, engages us, and makes our spirits soar. No problem.

THIS IS IN-TENTS

Make tents (card stock folded in half so it's freestanding) with your desktop publishing software and an ink jet or laser printer so key information sits atop your piles. Make it a guide to what's in that pile. You can make your to-do list into a tent, too. This works well for important computer shortcuts. Make a mantra, goals, or reminders stand up and stand out.

Inventive

Right-brainers love to challenge themselves by solving problems with innovative thinking—which is exactly what organizing is. We are able to work around our disorganization with quick thinking and cleverness. Throughout this book I poke fun at my father for all the clutter he keeps around. Upon closer inspection, I realized there is a method to his madness. Over the years he has given new life to many old and abandoned items. If we look around the yard, for example, there are some really interesting and inventive uses for just about everything. I want to share some of these with you to prove that one person's clutter is, well, another's solution, with a little ingenuity. An old tire becomes a planter. A hose with a hole in it is made into a drip irrigation system when punctured with even more holes. Rubber bands are balled up and made into a chew toy for the dog. Egg cartons are now planters for seedlings. Used popsicle sticks stuck in the ground become markers for plant types. An old Halloween mask and ratty clothes mounted on an old broom handle become a scarecrow. An oar is attached to the fence and screws are added to form hooks to hang gardening tools. A water feature is created out of an old wheelbarrow and various other odds and ends. A wind chime is created from lengths of pipe and fishing line. My father says, "Clutter is stuff that wastes space because it doesn't earn its keep by being useful, enjoyable, or valuable." Once again, Father knows best.

TRY THIS. Did you know that the paper bag, the TV dinner, and the disposable diaper were all invented by women? I'll bet that's where the expression "mother of invention" comes from. We need to look at our disorganization as a problem to be solved, not a hopeless situation that is out of our control. We like putting puzzles together. We are good at seeing the big picture and patterns that others (left-brainers) miss. We are creative. This is the making of an organized person. Start by asking yourself, "What isn't working and why when it comes to organization?" Then come up with as many solutions as possible. The more creative, the better. Rise to the challenge. We love to look for creative solutions to everyday problems.

CREATIVE CLUTTER

Turn clutter into something useful using your creativity. Put a drawing board, blackboard, bulletin board on the wall. Cutlery trays meant for the kitchen become dividers for brushes and other craft tools. An old frame can be filled with cork to create a corkboard. A muffin pan can be (cleaned and) painted to hold small office supplies. A photo album with acetate sheets serves as the perfect place to keep song ideas scribbled on scraps of paper. Buckets are good to group cleaning supplies. A cleaned-up bicycle chain can become a bracelet. A coffee cup you can't part with becomes a pen holder. A ceramic figurine that's collecting dust can be a business card holder. An extra ice tray serves as an earring holder. Old coffee cans are perfect for all types of loose little items. A terra-cotta pot for plants can hold all kinds of things. Almost anything heavy can be a bookend. That old ashtray becomes a clutter buster. An empty fishbowl is a clear and clever place to put keys, jewelry, change, wallet, and any other pocket stuff, as well as coupons, take-out menus, or just about anything.

Live in the Moment

We like to live in the moment with an almost total disregard for the future. We won't think fifteen minutes ahead, let alone fifteen years. Go through my files and purge old papers? Nah. I'm too busy. I'll just get another filing cabinet. Inventory all the items in my home for insurance purposes? I'm invincible. Nothing will happen to me. Make a will and keep a copy in a safe place? Why bother. I could die tomorrow. Exactly. Maybe you feel as though everything will just magically work out somehow. Maybe you envision your White Knight coming to the rescue. Don't wait until it's too late or say, "I'll deal with it when the time comes."

TRY THIS. Find a balance between living for today and planning for tomorrow. List ten things that bug you about your home or office as it relates to being less than organized. Make room in your schedule to tackle them one at a time.

Messy

Kurt Cobain and Courtney Love lived like such pigs they had rotten food scattered all over their Seattle home. They tried to hire a maid, but when she walked in and saw the horror, she ran out of the house screaming, "Satan lives here!" I'm not that messy, but I will ask my wife, "Why should I clean up when I am just going to use it again tomorrow?" Sometimes when I am in the middle of a creative project it doesn't make sense to clean up until it's done. If you multiply that by ten ongoing projects you have quite a mess. My wife truly believes I was born with some sort of cleaning disability. I admit that it's hard to get organized in a "classic" sense; but as long as you can function and those around you don't want to kill you, what's the problem? A "messy desk" to the untrained eye might look like a disaster area, but there is a reason for leaving things out. Tom Peters said, "I get a little queasy over a clean desk." We don't do well with a neat, sterile environment, and there is (usually) a method to our messiness. The problem is that your appearance is 75 percent of the impression you make on others and a basis for their attitude toward you. It's also no fun when it's always "hunting" season, and you are looking for lost stuff due to the mess. I do a spring cleaning in my office once a month—regardless of the season.

TRY THIS. Washington sculptor Margaret Ford creates masterpieces from maple branches and twigs by adding heads, hands, and feet of clay to them. She lets some pieces of wood sit for years until she figures out how to use them. They are organized by size, type, and style in buckets, which are pushed to the corners of her studio. There is no excuse to be messy. You can say it's due to your creativity, but as the previous example illustrates, organization can actually enhance your artistic endeavors. If you claim you are too busy, what you are really saying is you don't consider organizing a priority. Look, you don't have to be neat, but being organized is worth the time it takes. When you can put your hands on anything in under ten minutes, it's a great feeling. You can still leave things out if you want. If a pile is by the phone, that means those papers are waiting for a reply. Things right in front of you are works in progress. Reading materials by your favorite chair (or in the bathroom) are waiting to be read. This way things are easy to find, and when you are bored with one thing, it's easy to move on to another. Having things out is actually a procrastination beater and an efficient and effective organizing system. Not everyone is so enlightened. So straighten up your piles, move loose items into clear containers, and keep clutter contained in designated areas.

"Mind-Full"/Rarely write things down

In the movie *National Lampoon's Van Wilder,* whenever Van says something profound ("Don't be a fool, stay in school"), he will turn to the person he is talking to and say, "Write that down." Good advice. You can call us a "head case" if you like because we like to keep things in our head rather than write anything down. Hey, less paper is good, but you can't trust your memory. The problems that result include forgetfulness, brain clutter, and no paper trail for others to follow. There is one benefit from putting things on paper that I bet you never considered. Writing things down gets you out of your right brain, which can be easily frightened. Making lists and organizing can calm it down. Even right-brainers like some sense of order and a little organization in their mind. It's too bad there isn't a scratch pad in the front of the brain and a filing cabinet in the back.

TRY THIS. "I write everything down I want to remember. That way instead of spending a lot of time trying to remember what it is I wrote down, I spend the time looking for the paper I wrote it down on," jokes Beryl Pfizer. To organize your ideas (and store them safely) write these strokes of genius down in an idea journal. To get in the habit of writing down reminders, put pads of paper and pens all over the house. For other reminders, put things in your path so you almost trip over them on your way out the door. If you prefer to write things on little random pieces of paper, simply staple these scraps to a larger piece of paper and voilà, you have a master list of things to do. Make a master list of quickie tasks you want to get done when you have a spare minute or two. When it comes to boxes, don't make it a guessing game. Mark the outside with images or a key word to give you a clue as to what's inside.

Moody

Studies prove that right-brainers experience mood disorders more often than other people in the general population. (This is news?) Carrie Fisher is best known for playing Princess Lea in *Stars Wars,* but since then she has written several screenplays and script-doctored countless others despite being diagnosed as manic-depressive. She is able to be productive by working in spurts that coordinate with her manic highs. That's not to say it's always been easy. Before being diagnosed, she had some obsessive tendencies. She says she has two moods: Roy, the manic extrovert, and Pam, the quiet introvert. "Roy decorated my house, and Pam has to live in it," she "jokes." Many creative people also suffer from some sort of moodiness. We do great work, but at what cost? Vincent van Gogh, Charles Mingus, Georgia O'Keeffe, and Ernest Hemingway all suffered from various mood disorders.

TRY THIS. When it comes to getting organized, we can use some of that manic energy to organize the whole house. When you are "on" and in the mood to get organized, go with it. However, when your mood shifts, organizing is probably the last thing you'll want to do. So keep your organizing systems simple so that it's almost easier to put something away than it is to leave it out—whatever mood you are in.

Oblivious (to Messes)

One teacher assigned her class a project to write a paper to convince us that a chair didn't exist. "What chair?" one student replied. (Give her an A+!) We couldn't care less what other people think of our disorganization. If it works for us, then it's fine. Peter Lloyd says, "Organized? I pride myself on staying utterly, randomly, and proudly disorganized. Yet order creeps in all over. While I close my eyes, you could go to my desk, dig around, and find a note, read it to me, and I could tell you where you found it! I feel that disorder more truly reflects the chaos at the core of existence. I choose to resonate with that chaos." This is what I mean. Yet you've bought this book so . . .

TRY THIS. Anyone can be organized—if she *wants* to. In the film *The End-less Summer II,* Pat O'Connell and his buddy Wingnut were packing for an around-the-world surf trip. Wingnut packed all of his clothes in nice, neat, orderly piles and then carefully put them in his suitcase. O'Connell just threw everything in a duffle bag and was done in a matter of minutes. In a later article about Pat O'Connell in *Surfer,* they did a photo shoot at his home. It's stylish and warm. Oh, and it's organized, too. He organized small, specific areas into zones all over the home and yard. "We're redoing the backyard at the moment, and I'm so stoked. It's like I've got all these little zones out there. I'm going to put in a few tables and it's going to be the hang zone." If this guy can do it, anyone can.

Optimistic

Maybe overly so. We think we can get it all done, but despite our positive outlook, things seems to pile up. Then we have piles on top of piles. That's when we realize we'll never get it all done. We are not good at estimating time. (Timekeeping is a function of the left brain.) We are also not great at keeping track of time, estimating time, or being on time. (These things are all related.) Tasks generally take longer than we think they will, and when they do, we get discouraged because it's taking too long. There is also a sort of *White-Knight,* or *The Big Fix* mentality with a lot of creative people. It's almost a total disregard for organizing because the thinking is that something or someone will come along and rescue us from ruin. Sometimes things do just work out somehow. A friend comes over and is so disgusted that she decides to help. Maybe a move makes us sort through our clutter. Other times, well, time runs out and disaster strikes. It is far better to be independent than dependent on others for that one clutter-clearing solution to save the day.

TRY THIS. Take charge of your environment (and your life), and if help does magically come to you (you hire a maid), great. If it doesn't, that's okay, too. Expect a miracle but plan for the realities of a messy life. You can be a dreamer, but think and act rationally when it comes to what is possible. We would much rather come up with the idea than carry it out. (You may have to hire help with organizing.) Don't romanticize about uncluttering in one afternoon. The reality is that it takes time. If you filter what you want through that mechanism called "fantasy land," where anything is possible, it is sooooo easy to rationalize just about anything. Put up more clocks to get a better sense of time. When planning, double your estimates. Things usually take twice as long as you think they will.

PAIN IN THE NECK

Making even small changes to your work environment can help you avoid a pain in the neck (literally and figuratively). Make things easier to reach. You don't want to be bending or twisting every time you get a printout. You spend a lot of time working, and you should make it comfortable.

Perfectionist

I had trouble setting up a filing system. I would get to a difficult decision about what to title a file or what paper went where and be paralyzed because I wanted to make the perfect choice—which is impossible. Decision making is difficult enough without the pressure of perfectionism. Being a perfectionist can be tiresome. Nothing ever feels like it's finished; and even when it is, you feel like a failure. I often wonder if the words of my father ringing in my head have something to do with my desire to do things to the best of my ability. He would often say, "Do it right, or don't do it at all." Some things related to organizing just need to be done right now—whether they are done right isn't really relevant. Who cares if you scribble a note to yourself on the back of an empty envelope? If you taped this note to your keys and thus remembered to get flowers for your anniversary on the way home, you succeeded. Thank God. Still, many of us want to do things right—or not at all. This explains why there are lots of unfinished projects left lying around. (Perfectionism and procrastination are first cousins.) Also, we like the excitement of doing things but fear finishing—and the judgment that comes with completion. If we finish something, then it means it's over and we will have to decide what to do next; and we worry that we won't know what this is. One more thing. Organizing is easier when you have help. The perfectionist prefers to do everything herself because nobody else would get it right. (Translation: Nobody would do it her way.) Having high standards is one thing; having unrealistic expectations is another. Allowing your kids to pitch in and help organize not only teaches them important skills, but it allows you to work on something else. Just remember, they are kids and not "Mini Me's." There comes a point when delegating some portion of organizing or "letting it go" is the best way.

TRY THIS. Organizing isn't brain surgery, and it's certainly not life or death. Doing something (even if it's not perfect) to be more organized is better than doing nothing. It's easier if others help with organizing, but we want to do it all ourselves. This is an imperfect world. For right-brainers, things are usually in a constant state of change. So when it comes to organizing, do your best and then move on and fix things as you go (and grow). If you have tried and failed at organizing in the past, stick with it. Consider designer James Dyson, who found 5,126 ways how NOT to reinvent the vacuum cleaner. Everything in the house bothered him, but he decided to do something about it. He took on the challenge to improve upon an appliance that everyone hated. He says, "There is a tendency in life to do things as they should be done. I like to try to think how they shouldn't be done and find a better way." Eventually he became a millionaire after inventing a bagless vacuum.

FOR FUN

Your right brain's connected to your . . . While sitting in a chair, make clockwise circles with your right foot. While doing this, draw the number "6" in the air with your right hand. What direction is your foot going in now?

Procrastinator

We waste time doing what doesn't need to be done or is easy to do, when the important stuff sits because we don't want to do it, don't know where to start, or don't have all the information. We will open the mail and fill in some dumb questionnaire but not pay or file the bills. We'll push papers into a drawer and feel like we don't have to deal with them. We're so distracted by outside stimuli, we don't focus long enough to start or finish a task. Or we wait for inspiration. We approach tasks in a disorganized fashion, which makes it difficult to know where to begin. Do you really want to be more organized? Then put this book down and do something, anything, right now to become more organized.

TRY THIS. Do a little at a time and work in short bursts. Every hour spend five minutes tackling a problem area. Do things when they are due. A mañana mind-set doesn't work for everything. (It's never better to wait when you can get it done now.) Identify something you have been procrastinating over and take a small step. Not everything needs to be done the minute it arrives. It is more important to do the key things while less important tasks sit in the in-box until you have time to tackle them. Do the easiest thing first to build some momentum. Make a list of things you want to organize and put a date to do them. Block out time on your calendar to tackle this area of your life. Get help if you have to. Focus on the feeling of being finished.

ASK A PRO: JULIE MORGENSTERN, BESTSELLING AUTHOR

"Use color coding and very cool, fun containers to design a system that reflects the person's individuality, creativity, and unique sense of style. Coming up with creative titles for files and drawers also works. For example, a storyteller I worked with hated marketing so we renamed her marketing drawer 'Sharing It with the World.' This changed her entire relationship to the folders inside."

Rebellious

Do you feel like left-brainers are always flaunting their organizing skills? Judging you? Talking down to you? Making you feel inferior? You say, "I did it *my* way." They say, "You did it the *wrong* way." If society tells us we should be organized, then guess what? We won't do it, at least not the way others want us to. We hate rules and structure and will rebel any chance we have. Let me ask you something. Who really wins when you rebel by being disorganized?

TRY THIS. Some left-brain organizing skills can help you reach your goals. Sadly, without these skills you will have a hard time being all you can be. It will hold you back. People think of Jimmy Buffett as a carefree beach bum. Not so. If he were, he would have been just another one-hit wonder ("Margaritaville" is his only real hit song and that was in the seventies), but instead he is a highly successful businessman with a solid career. To protect his party image, Jimmy would hide in his hotel room organizing receipts and invoices. If he didn't stay on top of these tasks, he would not be where he is today—sold-out concerts, his own line of clothes and tequila, his own record label and gold records, restaurants, shops, millions through mail order and bestselling books. You can't do this without being organized. This is the key to left-brainers' success. Being somewhat organized does make dreams come true. Being the dreamers we are is great. That's the big picture. What we need help with are the small steps to develop those dreams into reality. Clutter takes over your life and clogs up everything. It puts up roadblocks that keep you from getting where you want to go. Whether you want to write a novel, build a business, or travel around the world, being more organized will help you make it happen.

Self-Destructive

I believe low self-esteem is the root of all problems—disorganization being no exception. "I've tried and failed" is no excuse. (You haven't had this book to help you.) Why else would some people not pay their bills, miss appointments, forget to follow up, and risk their reputation? I'll tell you why. They feel unworthy and believe they don't deserve to have good things happen to them; and when they do, they do something seemingly stupid to sabotage their success so they can return to their comfort zone. Left-brainers can be very intimidating. When they are around, don't you feel like they are judging you? They are. When others see that you don't take care of yourself, your home, your stuff, they think less of you. If you want respect, show them you deserve it. When you look like a bag lady, they treat you like one. Your external world (disorganization) is a reflection of your inner self. Turmoil, indecision, laziness, a lack of discipline, low self-esteem, self-centeredness, and little respect for yourself—that's what disorganization says to the world, and people treat you accordingly.

TRY THIS. What's really bothering you? Think about how being a little more organized can help. Left-brainers believe they can organize anything because they have before. We need a success or two under our belts to believe we can do it. Wouldn't it be nice to stop worrying about what others think and say about your mess? To end the guilt? To stop feeling like a failure? Don't compare yourself to left-brainers. Focus on the positives. It's time to stop the endless searches for lost and misplaced things for our own sake. If you really feel that enough is enough, then do something about it. Get organized despite whatever you feel is holding you back. People with a lot less talent, skills, and creativity have gotten organized and so can you. Value yourself, your career, and your work. You deserve better. When you come home to a clean and organized abode it feels good; you feel good and better about everything. Just do it your way. It's not our ability that shows us who we are; it's our choices. Choose to be organized.

Sensitive to Your Surroundings

When my friend Christie was hired to head an in-house creative department she began by painting the walls yellow. It was bright, sunny, and said "hello" every time she walked into the room. She bought mixed-matched thrift shop furniture, and hers was the only department to use Macs. The lesson here is to create an environment that is in tune with you and the way you work and live. You shouldn't have to fight the environment you work and live in. Redesigning the space around us helps us recover the joy of living and be more creative. Use scents to help concentration, colors for creativity, textures, music— anything that makes you feel good about where you work and live. Right-brainers appreciate style and asthetics. Design does matter—to us. This is why getting a cool-looking organizing product may make it more likely you'll use it.

TRY THIS. Feng shui is all about less clutter. Feng shui wants an orderly, clean, and happy environment that is a joy to be in. Feng shui thinks about where you live and work and finds solutions, changes, likes and dislikes, to make you feel at ease. Clutter with a purpose can work. With feng shui you learn how to place things so that the energy flows despite the amount of stuff you have. Chi is the universal energy that feng shui is all about. It thrives on harmony, beauty, order, spaciousness, and gentle curves. It dislikes disorder, straight lines, and neglected areas. It gets results with less effort by placing things in their proper place to create a positive energy, a flow and harmony with surroundings. (This is one time when out-of-sight, out-of-mind is a good thing.) That's how I define feng shui. Apply this at home and at work. (I realize most cubicles make your bedroom closet look large. Most cubicles are too tight to be cozy. It's hard to use feng shui without the room needed. But it's possible.)

Spontaneous

No planning for us. We want to take action now. We like to wing it. Plans? No. Caution? Nope. Measure first? Nah. We are predictably unpredictable. Wild! You never know what to expect next from us. We do what we feel (but we need to *feel what we do* more). We never stop long enough to figure out what we really want out of life; instead, we just take it as it comes. It's exciting to live this way, but the downside is we could be going nowhere fast, leaving a big mess in our wake.

TRY THIS. A few forward-thinking companies are now using modular workstations that can be quickly rearranged based on the project and the people working on it. This is perfect. As people move from one project team to another, so does their office. It's both flexible and mobile. This approach can work for organizing a lot of things in our lives.

Stubborn

"Gina" is the most right-brain person I know. She shared this story with me that exemplified why she needed my help. One night she wanted to go to sleep but had a nagging feeling that she was forgetting something. She got out of bed and shuffled through the mess in her house for a clue. Nothing. So she thought she would see if the answer was in her car. Since it was late and dark, she snuck outside in her panties and a half shirt. She would have made it, too—if not for the motion-sensor light that illuminated her for all to see at the party going on in the house across the way. It was humiliating. In fact, forgetting things and looking for lost items were everyday occurrences for Gina. Her organizing was affecting all areas of her life. She admits that she is totally unorganized and totally reactive. In the past she has tried to get it together and organize, but it never seems to stick. Her life pulls her this way and that. One crisis after another undermines each attempt. When it comes to her disorganization she freely admits that she keeps doing the same things over and over and it's getting old. "You will do foolish things, but do them with enthusiasm," said Colette. And we tend to live by that credo. Why do we repeat past patterns even though they're not working? When you try to show a right-brainer a new or better way, he resists. We want to be right.

TRY THIS. With Gina we began by talking about what her goals were, and I explained that being a little more organized could help make her dreams become a reality. Otherwise her life would continue to be a nightmare. We came up with a vision of what being organized would mean to her. What it would look like. Feel like. How it would work. We discussed basic organizing principles and rules, and we made notes on what would work for her. We discussed why she was where she was. She agreed that she had made some bad choices and agreed to try a new way of organizing. She would start small and pick the area that bugged her the most.

Undisciplined

The instructions on the treadmill at my gym read: STAY CENTERED. AVOID STRAYING TO THE LEFT OR THE RIGHT. ALWAYS LOOK STRAIGHT AHEAD. Hmmm. Good advice. We admire self-discipline even though we rarely possess it. We generally don't do well with budgets, diets, or exercise programs. Serious creativity requires a balance between a childlike playfulness and serious adult skills, like discipline and punctuality. There are the wanna-be creatives, and then there are the truly creatives. The wanna-be's are people who have very low attention spans and are all over the place. They can come up with all kinds of truly wonderful ideas but rarely follow through on them. The second type of people are also extremely creative, but as it happens they are also extremely disciplined as well. It's a most remarkable combination.

TRY THIS. Realize that some rules and structure are helpful. A little planning is a good thing. Logic and rational thinking are okay. Most of all, the great geniuses of history have been extremely well disciplined. They developed the capacity to concentrate single-mindedly, to be totally focused on a single problem or question for a long period of time (almost to a fault). Sidetracking is the greatest single challenge for the creative person because when you're all over the place, you don't get anything done. Organizing is a whole lot easier with a little discipline and structure.

Unorthodox

"It's better to stand on the wrong side of the ball and hit it right than to stand on the right side and hit it wrong." That's the official motto of the National Association of Left-Handed Golfers (NALG). We will not follow the tried-and-true approach to being organized. We organize by clustering, using odd connections. We will zig when the books say zag. Visualize a perfectly organized environment. What is standing in the way? Where are the problem areas? People will simply not get it or you and your unusual approach to organizing. That's their problem, not yours. A lot of left-brain people are threatened when you don't fit into one of their little cubbyholes. We don't mind a good scavenger hunt filled with surprises and discoveries. "Huh, I didn't know I still had this old (fill in the blank)."

TRY THIS. "You learn your own rules, what's right for you," says Lauren Hutton. Maybe the best way to get people to think out of the box is not to create the box in the first place. Beach Boys singer Brian Wilson built a giant sandbox around his piano so that he could feel it under his feet as he wrote music. That sounds strange but when you really think about it, it makes perfect sense. Innovative drummer Terry Bozzio is always trying new things. There are some limitations about what drums go where (structure), but he has added layers of drums in places I have never seen before. It's organized to match the unusual styles of music he is playing. I couldn't play his set, but it works for him. On the organizing show *Clean Sweep,* the professional organizer made a client throw her shoes and "make a basket" to win the right to keep them. Although this book is LOADED with all kinds of creative ideas about how to get organized, I encourage you to mix and match and use your creativity to customize the tips until your organizing scheme makes sense to you.

Visual

We prefer to pile rather than file and use a "Pile" cabinet system (pile things on top of a cabinet rather then inside) for fear that what's out of sight is out of mind. This is despite being told that every piece of paper not in use at this moment should be in a file because otherwise it will get lost. Hmmmm. The fact is that anytime you file something, there IS a good chance it will get lost. The truth is, of what we file nearly 80 percent is never seen again. That's why we would rather leave things where we can see them. Not only are they within reach, they are out where they trip up our mind so we don't forget them. We see and we understand. We know where everything is amid the piles of papers. This "system" only works up to a point. If everything is out, it defeats the purpose and we'll *still* struggle to see and find things.

TRY THIS. Leave important things out as reminders. "People want to know why I do this, why I write such gross stuff. I like to tell them that I have the heart of a small boy—and I keep it in a jar on my desk," jokes Stephen King. (At least I think he's joking.) There is nothing wrong with leaving papers out where you can see them. Chances are you know where everything is. This book is loaded with suggestions on how to file or pile effectively. If you like to leave file folders out where you can see them, bend the bottom so it looks like a spine and write in large letters what's inside. For binders, buy tabs that stick out so you can see what's inside without even picking them up. When you do make piles, do it by design. Break files down by category and put them in the space that makes the most sense. Wrap a ribbon around a pile or use a rubber band to keep it together. We can also come up with our own visually based filing/piling system so everything isn't out in the open. Instead of putting a boring label (CRAP MY MOTHER-IN-LAW GAVE US) on a box, use your computer and create something that shows you what's inside instead of just saying it with words.

Wonderful the Way You Are

We come into this world as princes, and society tries to turn us into toads. When others tell you that you are stupid, lazy, crazy, and weird remember, they are just jealous. You have so many wonderful and positive traits going for you, how can you not be happy to be who you are? The best part is that you can be organized if you want to. You have it in you to do it. I believe in you.

ONE OF US: DR. ROBERT ALAN BLACK

"There are right-brain traits that actually can help us be more organized. These include the ability to see connections which helps us find things easier. The tendency to place strong emotional ties to items helps us find things and provides multiple variables to be used for cross-referencing later, especially since we prefer to work on multiple things simultaneously. What hurts or disrupts us when organizing is a tendency to keep multiple copies of things because we see multiple needs and connections. This, in turn, increases the size and number of our piles, boxes, and files. The complexity of our minds tends to create complexity in our organizing system (or collections of systems)."

two

GET OUT OF
YOUR OWN WAY

Overcoming the Obstacles Stopping
You from Being More Organized

I've always been big on deciding what I want
to happen and then making it happen.

—Catherine Bell

Ever have a funny feeling that you don't quite fit in? Well, you
don't. Thank God. We are unconventional people with unconventional ideas. Others don't know what to make of us—or how
we organize things—so they react out of fear of the unknown and try
to change us at every step. The truth is you can be your wonderful self
and still get organized—many right-brainers do. There are reasons
why you are the way you are. Maybe you've been called "scatterbrained" because you tend to flit from one thing to another, leaving a
trail of clutter in your wake. "Scatterbrained" is not only negative, it's
inaccurate. You're actually a "divergent thinker." That's not just a
pretty phrase. It's a scientific concept backed up by some significant
research. Because of this and other traits that make you special, generally accepted organizing techniques just don't work for you. There's
also a good explanation for those piles of stuff on your desk. People
who primarily operate in the right hemisphere of the brain tend to be
nonlinear and visual. Which means you need to see all those files and
papers you're working on. Don't be too hard on yourself if you went
back to your old habits a few hours or days after you read the latest
bestseller on organizing, took the seminar, or bought the brand-new
filing cabinet. The problem does not entirely lie with you. Conven-

tional organizing approaches don't take your natural tendencies into account.

THE REASONS WHY WE ARE DISORGANIZED

I arise each morning torn between a desire to save the world, and a desire to savor the world. That makes it hard to plan the day.

—E. B. White

ARTISTIC TEMPERAMENT

It was G. K. Chesterton who said, "The artistic temperament is a disease that affects amateurs." Get over yourself. Just because someone is disorganized, messy, or a pack rat does *not* make her an artist. In my years of interviewing people who work in the arts, I have found some of the most creative people prefer clutter around them. That's fine, but *the* most successful have a system to organize it all. Maybe you want to be seen as special—you don't have to be disorganized to do it. We are different and couldn't be more proud of that fact. If everyone else is organized, then we want to be disorganized. We march to the beat of own drummer and we can get away with it if we are creative types. But in the business world it can be a big burden to be branded as disorganized. You can express yourself and stand out and still be organized. Be one of the few artists who has an organizing system to keep track of your inspirational stuff and previous works. Heck, if you really want to stand out in the art world, be professional. Create a "Creativity Center" in your home or office where all your tools and inspiration are in one place. Your creative zone can be a mess if you want but keep other areas, like the kitchen, your business center, and the bathroom, organized and clean. You can have tons of cool stuff around, just get it up and out of the way. One department manager at Lucas Digital has what he calls his "Wall of Inspiration," which includes old comic strips, photos from *Aviation Week & Space Technology* magazine covers of music magazines, and illustrations of robots and 1950s-style spaceships.

BLAME GAME

You want to get and stay organized but OTHERS are in the way—the boss, roommate, kids, spouse, lover, or just life and the hectic pace of it. Even if they are sabotaging your organizing success, the blame game is not the best way to begin solving the situation. This is a victim mentality and defeatist mind-set. Control what you can and set some limits. One woman allows her husband one room in the house to do whatever he wants with, but his clutter and disorganization are NOT allowed to spill over into the rest of the house. She simply shuts the door to keep it out of sight and out of mind. I can't tell you how many people want to write a book but haven't because they want to wait until their kids are off to college, their husband cleans out the spare room, or they get that new laptop for their birthday. With that attitude, it's not gonna happen. Do what you can with what you have. It's the same with getting organized. Either lead by example, follow the trail of clutter, and come up with creative solutions, or get out of the way. Blaming others for your problems is NOT a solution.

B-O-R-I-N-G

Organizing and all that goes with it can seem tedious and time-consuming and, most of all, boring. In my opinion it all depends on how you look at it. If you make it personal, creative, and fun it isn't so bad—or boring. For some, cool containers will do it. For others, it could be a new PDA to plan the day or creative labels using desktop design software and a color ink jet printer to make labeling less boring. Maybe what it will take is inviting some of your closest friends over to clean out a clothes closet and share some of the stories behind your purchases. Have you ever tried combining organizing tasks with something you actually enjoy—filing and talking on the phone or dancing while doing the dishes?

CAN'T KEEP IT UP

Are you so busy you barely have time to breathe? Are there more things on your daily to-do list than any one normal person could handle in a week? Do you find that day by day, little by little you are falling further behind and getting and staying organized are at the bottom of the barrel? Life moves faster than ever, and technology is actually making matters worse. This is not good for left-brainers or right-brainers. Left-brainers are easily overwhelmed, but they also have the capacity to plan, break things down into smaller parts, and prioritize and focus. Right-brainers see this cool new stuff and want to sample it all; and without any natural skills in prioritizing, planning, or putting things away, you've got potential problems. There are people with more on their plate than you, and they are able to find the time to catch up and put things away after completing a project. We are master multitaskers and love a good challenge. We can get a handle on organizing if we make it a priority.

CH-CH-CHANGES

Things tend to get out of control during a transitional period. Maybe you moved into a smaller place, added a roommate, remodeled, started a new business, went back to school, divorced, married, or had a child. (Hopefully not all in the same month.) All of these things have an effect on how organized or disorganized you have become. What works for your life now? A good organizing system works with you and expands and contracts according to what's going on in your life. This book is all about teaching you the basics so that no matter what happens, you can stay on top of things.

CHAOS CREATORS

As I mentioned in the previous chapter, we like to live on the edge, and if life isn't stressful enough, we'll create a crisis to make it even more challenging. Safe and secure is boring and so is knowing where everything is. A last-minute search for something is stimulating but also stressful. We need some structure in our lives. A few routines allow us to flourish. We need goals, guidelines, and deadlines or nothing gets done. Yes, we like to let loose, do things when we feel like it, but bills need to be paid, taxes filed, and projects completed. Otherwise it's impossible to keep track of what's going on and follow up and stay on top of everything. Structure allows you to get more done, get the right things done, and not get overwhelmed.

CAN'T CONTAIN THE CLUTTER

We like to be surrounded with stuff, but it's extremely hard to be organized when there is clutter everywhere. Now, this isn't a problem if you are able to find what you need and you are getting everything done that you need to get done. I know this for a fact. My parents are pack rats. When I was growing up, every drawer in our house was a junk drawer. To this day, before I go to the hardware store I first call my father to see if he has what I need. This is an important main point. He has a LOT of stuff, but he can find almost anything in under a minute. The problem is (if there is one) that they are running out of room to store all his stuff. So he rearranges from time to time to make the most of his storage space. To others, their home looks a little like an old general store, but it's really a lot like a library—things are put in places where they can be found. Without some basic organizing skills, it would be overwhelming. Not all clutter bugs are this organized.

CLEAN, BUT NOT NEAT

My wife will often tell me I am *neat,* but not *clean.* Harsh, I know. Others are clean, but not neat. (Anyone who is both has a lot of free time on his hands.) The truth is, one isn't better or worse than the other. I understand the thinking here. If something is clean, it's okay to leave it out. That would explain the pile of laundry on the floor. It's clean, but it's out. I do like to make piles with my papers, but they are neat piles. When I do put things away, I throw them in a container and slap a lid on. It's simple and it's neat. I call it my "scoop and store" system—and it works really well for me. The goal isn't a perfectly clean, neat, or sterile environment. Instead, your home and office should be comfortable, workable, and functional. Leave things out where you can get to them if you frequently use them. Put them in clear containers if you want them away but like to see what's inside.

CONFUSING AND TOO COMPLEX

If your system of putting things away (or leaving them out) is actually a series of convoluted, incomplete failed attempts to organize, that can be the problem right there. How will you know where to put something away and find it again if you have ten different half-finished organizing systems all going at once? Maybe your first attempt at organizing didn't work so you tried again. Then, after years of inventing and reinventing yourself and your surroundings, you have what amounts to a mess. Since we have short attention spans and like new challenges, we can come up with ten different places to put something that make sense (to us), and we quickly lose sight of what should go where. Come up with some system that makes sense to you and stick with it. One of the most basic rules of organizing (all the rules are covered in a later chapter) is this: the easier you make something to do, the more likely you will do it. Let me give you a good example. My wife and I live by the beach and everything has to be covered to keep it from rusting—bikes, the barbecue, and anything else made of metal. So I bought covers (and locks) for everything and anything. After a short while I came to the conclusion that I would rather let everything rust than have to handle another wet, dirty, and difficult cover. My advice is this: SIMPLIFY. Make organizing easier by eliminating any extra steps or impediments to staying organized.

EVERYTHING AND THE KITCHEN SINK

Andy Warhol saved everything—from interesting to mundane—and tossed it in a box by his desk. When a box was full, it was packed up and stored. The result was six hundred boxes of treasures and trash. It took Sotheby's twelve days to auction off his estate.

CONSUMERISM

Who hasn't wanted to own the latest and greatest gadget or gear? It's human nature to want more, better, newer. Who can blame us? It's easy to believe that the items being hawked will save us time and make our lives easier. It's a never-ending barrage of messages that say you are only as good as the gear you've got and that you need more and better stuff. If you can afford to continually upgrade and update everything, what's to stop you? Price and space. Most of us can't possibly afford to buy and store all the things advertised on TV. I won't lecture you about overspending or debt (at least not in this book), but I will tell you, there is a cost to keeping clutter around. If an item you bought isn't consumable, then it takes up space. As they say, nothing is free. You pay per square foot to store that thing. If it's valuable, useful, and saves you time, then great. If not, then you have traded a piece of your life for this thing, and it's still costing you to store it. What am I talking about? For argument's sake, let's say you make ten dollars an hour (come on, work with me) and the item you bought cost you one hundred dollars. You had to work ten hours to pay for it. That's ten hours of your life that you will never get back. If you own or rent your place then you have to work to pay to live there. If an item takes up square footage, then you are paying a monthly fee to store it. (If you divide your rent by the square footage and how much space an item takes up, you can figure out what something costs to keep.) You either have to be selective or (and this is what I do) buy *and* SELL stuff. When I "need" new drum equipment, I will sell off something I no longer use. When I "need" new computer equipment, I donate my old stuff to a charity. Things flow in and out of my life, and it's a LOT easier to stay organized.

CREATIVE, IN A LEFT-BRAIN WAY

Is it possible to be too creative for our own good? Yes. Not everything needs to be a creative, right-brain affair. What's so wrong with an old-fashioned, functional file cabinet for sorting and storing papers? Why reinvent the wheel when we don't have to? I do think that coming up with clever and creative solutions to storing stuff is the answer for some special situations, but a little left-brain (did I just say that?) organizing is fine in most cases. Sure, we can easily conjure up a creative and elaborate system for organizing almost anything. But then we will lose interest in our grandiose idea, and what we are left with is a big mess. Maybe, just maybe, we could learn a little bit from our left-brain counterparts when it comes to organizing and save our right brains for bigger and better challenges. That's why I included some of the basic organizing principles later in this book. This way, at least, you know what the "rule" is so that when you break it, it's more fun.

CYNICAL

Do you tend to look at the dark side of things? Are you a "worst case scenario" person, who has already "what-iffed" every possible situation and bought all the gear to be ready in case of a catastrophe? We know that a depression-era mentality is the cause of a lot of clutter. Many of us are ready when the worst hits because we have backups and backups of our backups of everything. We certainly can't trust financial institutions, so we keep every ATM slip, old checkbook, and credit card bill from as far back as the Bush presidency—the OTHER President Bush. Being prepared is not only the Boy Scout's motto, it's also a way of life for a lot of us. However, we waste a lot of our lives worrying about things that will NEVER happen and storing stuff that we don't need to. The first step is to realize that the sky isn't falling. Things are going to be fine. You will be fine. How do I know this? Well, let's see. I have been through three IRS audits (won them all without having to even show 1 percent of the papers I had saved). I have kept and maintained an emergency kit for years and never had to use it—not once. I've been robbed, lost my wallet, and had my luggage lost more times than you can say DELTA (Don't Expect Luggage to Arrive). What's my secret? I expect the best *but* plan for the worst. I photocopied every card in my wallet. I took a video of all of my possessions. I own a fireproof safe for my valuables. I save the papers that need to be saved but they are stored out of the way. Organizing helps you deal with disaster, but don't let the fear of ending up a bag lady make you live like one now.

DIFFICULTY WITH MAKING DECISIONS

Sandra Bullock says, "I always leave the house questioning every single move I make, down to the shoes, the choice of cab, the timing of it. It's such a sick, sick cycle." (She should have "decided" to pass on *Speed II*, but that's another story.) All that angst isn't good. I know I covered indecision in the previous chapter, but deciding what goes where is at the heart of organizing and worth going over again. (What? You mean you didn't read the last chapter yet? You're skipping around and reading this book out of order? I knew it! It's okay.) If you are unsure where to put things, then they are more likely to stay put—which is usually in the way and taking up valuable space. Indecision is a big part of disorganization. We would put things away if we could just decide where and overcome the fear of making a mistake and putting them in the wrong place. Instead of making a decision, we push it aside or put it down wherever there is empty space and it begins to pile up. "He who considers too much will perform little" is an old (and accurate) German proverb. The main concept of organizing is to group like things together, put them where you use them, and keep the most often used items within reach and the rest out of the way. With parameters like these, deciding what to do with something shouldn't require a rocket scientist. Even if you put something in the wrong place, it's not the end of the world. Work around it or make it right. If things are piling up in one place, maybe that's where you want them to go. Put a bin, box, hook, or hang a shelf there. Don't fight it. The decision was made for you.

DISORGANIZED GENE

Many of you may feel you have been born without the organizing gene that allows the rest of the world to somehow magically get it all together with relative ease. You assume that hyperorganized people were born that way. I've never seen a baby born with a planner or file folders, have you? It's learned. Anyone can learn how to get organized. Anyone. It's just that you chose *not* to learn how to organize because you had better things to do. (Who can blame you?) No matter how much your parents probably punished you for not picking up after yourself, you just weren't interested. I am not saying you will ever be superorganized (unless you want to be), but you can certainly be more organized than you are now if you choose to. If all you can think about is how disorganized you have been, it can drag you into depression and affect all areas of your life. Let's put things into perspective. *Organizing is only one area of your life.* You are not a failure. You may have failed at being organized (in the past), but that doesn't mean you need to beat yourself up. Today is a new day, and what has happened in the past does not determine your future. (Events in your rearview mirror are worse than they appear.) Keep your eyes on the road and the task at hand. Let go of the outcome and focus on the process or, in other words, remain in the moment and usually the pressure and fear will disappear. Besides, when you remove the fear, everything is more fun; and when you are having fun, you tend to have more success.

DON'T KNOW HOW

If your parents were disorganized, raise your hand. (Mine is up.) If your parents were highly organized, raise your hand. What am I getting at? They say you either become your parents or rebel against them. So there you go. However, if your parents never sat you down for "the talk" (how to be organized), how were you to learn? How and where to put things away is not something you are likely to discuss with your friends. (When I tried my buddies threw popcorn and chips at me and told me to shut up and watch the game.) Organizing is not taught in school—although it should be! Without the proper training, it's hard to know how to get organized and stay that way. Aha! That's where this book comes into play. "Experience is a hard teacher because she gives the test first, the lessons afterwards," said Vernon Law. I am sharing all of my experiences and those of others in this book so that you don't have to learn how to organize the hard way.

DON'T LIKE WHERE YOU LIVE OR WORK

Have you ever considered that the reason you choose not to organize is that you hate your home, can't stand your office, or find your computer frustrating? The solution could be to beautify your home or jazz up your office. Pride of ownership is a powerful motivator when it comes to getting organized. Usually the first step is to declutter and clean. The second step is to redecorate, rethink, and then rearrange stuff. Voilà, you love your space, and you're organized. Okay, maybe it's not *that* simple, but it's possible.

DON'T WANT TO DEAL WITH OTHER ISSUES

Being organized doesn't equal happiness. Happiness is NOT a by-product of being organized. Happiness is in your head. If you feel like you are organized, then you probably are to a certain extent. There are people who have everything put away perfectly yet still don't feel like they are organized enough. Sad. They will say that as soon as they have everything they own perfectly put away, then they can enjoy their life. Even if you are struggling to stay organized, you can't stop at the first setback. Keep trying and ENJOY the process without the pressure of trying to make everything perfect. Stop every once in a while when you are struggling and take a look around and enjoy life, no matter how screwed up your filing system is. Don't dwell on the negatives. Focus on the positives and look for ways to improve. What can you do right now to fix your situation? There is a woman called the Fly Lady (flylady.com) who suggests you start to turn your life around by taking charge of one small area. Her advice is to start with keeping your sink neat and clean. Good advice, I'd say.

DON'T WANT TO DO IT

In many cases it isn't that we can't get organized, it's that we *choose* not to. I have witnessed many right-brainers who appeared to be totally incapable of keeping their homes in order but are highly organized at work. Why is that? I believe it's because being disorganized at work would mean losing a job or clients. So when faced with what is worse—being organized or suffering a career setback—they choose to be organized because they have to. That means that they can get organized if they need to. "Not tonight, honey, I have a headache," is a classic excuse for . . . not wanting to tackle tough organizing projects. To stay organized, a little action every day goes a long way. I was teaching a class on time management and organizing and one of the attendees would cut in on almost anything I suggested, would roll her eyes, scowl, and say, "I tried that and it didn't work." Secretly, or not so secretly, she really doesn't *want* to get organized. But she tries so that she can say to others (picture her with her hands on her hips, speaking matter-of-factly), "See, I tried organizing, but it doesn't work." I did my best to ignore her and help those who really wanted to have a home they could relax in, an office or studio that was professional and that they were proud to show off, and systems in which less was lost and the important items were easy to get to and put away. This naysayer won't become more organized until *she* decides she really wants to make it work. Her loss.

DON'T WANT TO SWEAT THE SMALL STUFF

We are big-picture people and that can mean more than just being visionaries. In our home smaller items (keys, pens, coins) start to collect in a corner or on a counter, and before we know it little things begin to pile up. Small clutter accumulates like litter. There is a youth hostel by the beach where I live where young people like to hang out and throw their trash on the sand and sidewalk. Then other tourists feel that it's okay to toss an empty soda can or fast-food wrapper on the sand, since there is already litter there. Before you can say "sunset," this small stretch of sand is covered with all kinds of clutter. It's like there is a magnet that pulls all this litter together. It's the same way with other stuff. This is one area where buying (or creating/converting) something to catch the clutter makes sense. For example, I began to notice that my countertop was covered with all kinds of little loose items. A bowl, basket, and hooks by the door cured the problem. We also had a junk drawer that was filled with old batteries, keys, spare parts, and other unidentifiable things. I bought a container from a fishing supply store that had assorted and adjustable dividers in it. It was small and flat and fit inside the drawer. Now everything is easier to find because it is divided up, labeled and the whole thing is portable. Yikes! I'm a left-brainer. I could go on, but you get the picture. Think big (everything is organized and somewhat orderly) but start small (your little things are sorted and stored safely and conveniently).

EMOTIONALLY ATTACHED TO *THINGS*

Author Stephen King says, "Books have weight and texture; they make a pleasant presence in the hand. Nothing smells as good as a new book, especially if you get your nose right down in the binding, where you can still catch an acrid tang of the glue. The only thing close is the peppery smell of an old one." Ahhh, books. When I say I love books I mean it. I LOVE books. I guess it is possible to get emotionally attached to inanimate objects. I realize we don't actually love the item itself, it's the feeling it invokes in us. I'm a sucker for old baseball cards that still have that sweet smell from the stick of gum (that tasted like cardboard dipped in sugar) they were packed with. They remind me of being a kid. They also remind me of a time when I sold off most of my collection for a few bucks. It pains me deeply every time I think about it. Here's my advice. Keep the things that give you a positive feeling and either give away or get rid of the rest. I clearly recall going to the fire ring at the beach to burn a bunch of painful papers (the first draft of this book, ha, ha, ha) and it felt great. If that's too tough, put all the stuff that makes you feel bad where it belongs—out of sight and out of mind.

IT'S ALL OR NOTHING

Where most people will dip their toes in to test the water, we will dive in and immerse ourselves. Hmmmm, let's have a spur-of-the-moment party. Hey, I think I'll surprise my wife and paint the walls today. Maybe I'll cook a new dish; now I need to buy a recipe book, ingredients, and a ton of pots and pans. We are always doing cool and creative things that many times make a mess. Hey, that's just the way we are. The solution is to make it easier to clean up and do it when we are still in our excited state, not when the euphoria of the "big idea" has worn off.

LAZINESS PAYS OFF NOW

Admit it. At one time or another it was too much trouble to put stuff away so you just left it where it was, whether that meant pulling clothes from a pile of clean, but unfolded, laundry or not putting your CDs back in their cases. This is normal. Many right-brainers prefer cutting corners. However, when you say, "I'll just put this here for now," what that really means is, "That's where it will stay." For many of us, if there isn't any immediate gratification we are not interested. It takes too long to see results so why bother organizing? We want to *I Dream of Jeannie* it—cross our arms, blink, and everything is magically done. I guess you could hire someone to work her magic on your mess. Or you could do it yourself. Many people know what to do when it comes to organizing; they just aren't making it happen. This book is full of ideas on how to make organizing easier. Pick a few and apply them to the areas that need your attention.

LIKE LEAVING THINGS OUT

Our mantra is, out of sight, out of mind. Closets and cabinets are for hiding things, we insist. It would be nice if everything was out so we could see it, but who has the room? The problem is, we only have enough room for the most important and pressing things to stay out. Even the most visual, right-brained people will have trouble if everything they own is left out. They end up with piles on top of piles. The answer is to set limits on how much stuff stays out and rotate items based on the season or usage.

LOCKED IN THE PAST

Jimmy Buffett sings, "Lust for the future, but treasure the past." This could be the theme song for the right-brainer. We want to hang on to every memory through things—photos, mementos, magazines, and a variety of other relics. Yes, we will yell, "Next," after we have lost interest after a short while, but we like visual reminders of where we've been and what we've done. However, when it's over, we should move on down the line looking for the next big thing that excites and touches us and save only the best memories. Another problem is we don't change with the times. Relax. I am sure you are fashion forward: what I mean is when our lives change because we get married or divorced, have a baby, or a child grows up and goes away to college, buy or sell a home, move in or move out, take on a roommate or kick one out, start a business or finish school. We may not organize to reflect this new reality. These life-changing events and the stuff that goes with them change, too. Maybe it was the death of a loved one, and we want to keep a part of him alive by keeping his things. That's fine if you are organized. But when you have piles upon piles, that's not so good. It's almost sacrilegious. If this person were still in your life, what would he want you to do? Be more in the moment and take a mental picture. Store stuff so you can find it when you feel the need. Keep a keepsake, not the whole kit and caboodle.

NO GOALS, NO GLORY

Organizing works best when you have a clear vision of what you want to do, where you want to go, and what you'll need to get there. This doesn't mean you have to decide what you want to do with the rest of your life, just what you want to do with your life right now, and organize things around that. This way you can limit what you acquire and keep based on it if it helps make your dreams come true or not.

NOT A PRIORITY

"Nothing is worth doing unless the consequences may be serious," said George Bernard Shaw. We would rather be working on something productive instead of cleaning up after ourselves. My mother-in-law is a hairstylist who admits to being too busy making money to stop to clean up after every client. She figures she can see one more person a day this way, which translates to thousands of dollars a year. (She does clean up at the *end* of the day.) Organizing doesn't stand a chance when the choice is doing something fun. There isn't enough time to do all the things you want to do, let alone the things you don't want to do—like organizing. We choose to spend our time and energy elsewhere. Finish the day with a "rush hour" of cleanup, paperwork, or other projects that need to be finished. Pick a day and come in and do a little spring cleaning—once a month.

NOT ENOUGH STORAGE SPACE

When we see space we want to fill it up. That would be fine if we didn't add anything new (and we all know we will) to our lives. There is no rule that says every drawer has to be used or stuffed, for that matter. Chances are we will misjudge the amount of storage area we have and try to cram an unrealistic amount of stuff into our limited amount of space. Maybe you were once organized, but life and all that comes with it have overwhelmed you. There is simply too much stuff coming into our lives, and we are too busy to take the time to tackle this problem. Before you know it, there are piles on top of piles. It's so overwhelming you don't know where to begin. Just the thought of getting organized makes you want to take a nap. Of course we need to slow down and decide what stays and what goes and then find creative ways to make it all fit. There are hundreds of ideas in this book that will show you exactly how to do it.

NOT SURE WHERE IT GOES

You might put an item away if only you knew where it went. We are afraid that if we put it away in the wrong place, we will never find it again so we leave it out. Undoubtably you have heard the expression "A place for everything and everything in its place." Having a permanent place to put things makes staying organized a whole lot easier. The secret is to make it as easy to put something away as it is to leave it out and to keep things where you need and use them.

PACK RATS

People who like to hoard will say, "I like to look at things," or, "Clutter makes me comfortable." Then there are the classic excuses like, "I may need this at some time," and, "It may be worth something someday." Uh-huh. *Antiques Road Show* is NOT interested in your stuff, nor is Christie's auction house. There is a limit to how many boxes, bags, and publications piled to the sky you can keep. What's worse, this isn't limited to physical stuff either. With computers, people tend to save every single thing they ever created or came across on the Web on their hard drives. Some spend their money on storage for stuff instead of buying food. This is a result of not being willing to part with anything—ever. The more stuff, the more challenging it is to get and stay organized. I devoted an entire chapter to this area because it's too important not to talk about and tackle head on.

PERFECTIONISTS

David Letterman once said, "Martha Stewart is going to show you how to take things you find dead on the highway and turn your house into a showplace." I'll say it, too: Martha Stewart creeps me out. Who is that perfect—or wants to be, for that matter? (It turns out that Martha isn't the picture of perfection, either.) Don't be a diva or let a diva set unrealistic organizing expectations for you. Barbra Streisand may have a voice "like buttah," but she is also a Diva with a capital "D." She wants to control everything, and it has to be just so. Don't drive yourself crazy trying to have a perfect home that is perfectly organized. (As if.) It's not real or ideal. Forgive yourself if you allow things to get a little out of hand because you put your family or career first, but get back on it before it's too late. Get rid of the guilty feeling that you are not organized enough by doing something about it. Maybe you can't organize everything, so organize something and build some confidence. Do the best you can with what you have. If something is worth doing, it's worth doing (badly). Cut yourself some slack. Contain the clutter, but everything doesn't have to be perfectly neat.

PROCESS ORIENTED

Why is it we would prefer to begin something new before finishing the old thing we started working on awhile ago? Well, isn't something new more exciting than something old? For right-brainers, it's not always about the goal, it's about the process; so when something is completed, the process ends. Subconsciously, some of us may work on something like mad and then seemingly run out of steam at the very end. The only problem with this is a lot of tools, materials, and half-finished projects lying around wreaking havoc on your attempts to get organized. Pack parts in baggies or containers or files so that you can stash them until you do decide to finish it. Confine your mess to zones, whether it be a corner, shelf, closet, or container. For projects in progress, leave them in a place that makes it easy to pick up where you left off when inspiration strikes.

SABOTAGED BY OTHERS

When company came over to our house, my mom used to come up with some clever excuses as to why people couldn't go upstairs to see the "boys'" rooms. One time I had to pretend I was ill with the shingles. I didn't even know what that meant. If someone insisted on seeing our rooms, my mother would open the door a crack and then say, "Alrighty then, tea anyone?" in a shaky voice and usher them away. My poor mom. Many of us (men and right-brainers) don't feel it's our "role" to organize or take care of the tasks that lead to being organized—bill paying, cleaning, shopping, and a lot more. Organizing? I heard one comedienne say, "I wasn't born a bitch. Men like you made me this way." Maybe you have the misfortune of living with someone (or a whole family) that is even more disorganized than you and sabotages your attempts to get it together. Or you simply can't sell organizing to your husband and kids, so you figure, "Why bother?" Establish clutter-free zones and allow them to make a mess in their own space and shut the door or put up a partition. Call it what you will, "the man pit," "the cave," or "the boys' room." Allow each person in the house to do what he or she likes best and/or just keep his or her own areas clean and uncluttered.

SIGN OF BIGGER PROBLEMS

One out of four of us is suffering from some sort of mental illness. If your three friends are all okay, then it's you. I know, this is no laughing matter. Madness takes its toll; please have exact change. (Sorry.) I promise not to get preachy, but being somewhat disorganized can be considered quirky or eccentric, but severe disorganization can be a sign of bigger problems. Like a lot of problems, it may start small but can quickly become an "issue." Clutter can be a sign of attention deficit disorder, obsessive-compulsive disorder, and depression. Some people let clutter hold them back from being all they can be. They may say it's more comfortable to be surrounded by chaos and clutter, but it may be an excuse to keep others at a distance. It can be a safety blanket that keeps them in their comfort zones, and that means not moving, traveling, dating, because they say they want to deal with the disorganization in their life first but never find the time. Even if an organizing expert comes in and gets it all together, these people will eventually resort to their old ways. Don't let your life get lost because of disorganization and clutter. Please.

TOO MUCH STUFF

With so much stuff all out of place and in piles it can seem a little intimidating to get started because you don't know where to begin. It's not all your fault. It seems like every day there is so much stuff coming into our lives it's hard to keep up. If you let it go for a week or a month, it can get out of control and you start to feel a sense of hopelessness. Take the Sunday paper, for example. It's crammed with so much information it weighs as much as a bag of trash. You would have thought they'd covered all the news during the week, but no, there is more bad news to stress you out on the one day your are supposed to relax. Start with something simple like your wallet, purse, glove box, backpack, or key chain. Then take it one drawer at a time. Just start! Do whatever bugs you the most. Do whatever you want whether it is entering a few new names in your database or fixing or finishing one thing left out.

TOOL TIME

Maybe you thought that when you bought the PDA, organizing software, planner, and all those containers you would finally be organized. Much of what you bought is more trouble than it was worth. More than likely you discover that tools don't organize you without you changing your ways, and you haven't yet. You still do the same things in the same ways, but now you have more organizing tools cluttering up your home or office.

UNREALISTIC EXPECTATIONS

Don't compare yourself to other people. They are more screwed up than you think. Just because some people put everything away when they are done does not mean they are more organized than you. You'll have unrealistic expectations if you judge yourself against others because if you can't compete, you'll quit. We aren't looking for an operating room. Just comfortable, cozy, and clean. Let's assume that you truly want to be more organized but somewhere along the way became discouraged, disillusioned, and went back to being disorganized. It could be that you began the new year fired with the enthusiasm a resolution can give you. Then, little by little, the resolve dissolves and the next thing you know it's New Year's Day again. What's worse, we kick ourselves for our lack of willpower and convince ourselves we are big fat losers for not being able to be more organized. That's normal. You can do it if you take it one day at a time. It sounds cliché, but it's true.

WHAT CLUTTER?

It's strange how some people just can't see what's right in front of their faces—namely, clutter and disorganization. It's called unconscious clutter. It's always nice to have a clinical term to throw around when my wife screams at me—"You left your stuff strewn around the house again," to which I reply, "Really, I don't see anything out of place." My parents were like that. They thought they were neat and clean, but they had all kinds of clutter out and about in the home. They were oblivious to the piles all around them. After a while I imagine we get used to seeing stuff in piles and in our path. We like to live in chaos and clutter. It's a little like living on the edge. It's when it starts to cause pain and problems that some are willing to try something a little more safe. I will not recommend stripping yourself of the things that make you feel anchored. The key word is "comfortable" and not crowded, chaotic, crazy. You need to find a way to see your space with fresh eyes. Look at your place as if it were a hotel, restaurant, or small store. Would others feel comfortable (or safe for that matter), or would they turn and run away? If you were a prospective buyer, would you want to purchase your home? Change your perspective by cutting a small square in the middle of a piece of paper and using it as a viewfinder.

ZEN ORGANIZING

Many of us practice what is know as "Zen organizing." What is Zen organizing? you ask. It's where you don't organize per se; you just think about it. One of these days is none of these days. Or put another way, the road to hell is paved with good intentions. No, you aren't going to go to hell if you don't get organized, but a little action goes a long way. First things first, but not necessarily in that order. The first step is always the hardest. "Begin it, and the worst will be completed," said Johann Goethe. Maybe we don't know where to start, but as Plato said, "The beginning is the most important part of the work." Start anywhere. Maybe you need deadlines to deal with disorganization. Promise to organize and put stuff away at the end of the week. Plan a party at your home and send out the invitations so you finally unpack from the move. Volunteer to carpool the neighborhood kids or your coworker once a month, and vow to clean out the car. Do something, anything, to build some momentum, whether it is the easiest, hardest, most logical, most fun, most annoying—or just close your eyes and point and pick an area to tackle. When we are in the middle of a project oriented or creating, we put everything off. We work in fevered cycles and then have downtime. Returning calls, answering e-mail, paying bills are put off while the project is a priority. That's fine, just catch up during the downtime.

MAKEOVER: BEFORE AND AFTER

I knew I was on to something whenever someone asked me what book I was writing next. When I told him or her the topic was organizing, almost everyone said the same thing, "Wow! I need to read a book about that." As you will see later in the book, I met with and in-

terviewed over one hundred people for insights and ideas on organization and disorganization. (It wasn't always pretty, but I learned a lot.)
Here is a sample of one of the problems presented to me, and my answers to it.

Before

Annie wastes too much time looking for valuable papers that sometimes
never turn up again. (Hint: They are in the same place as all those missing socks.) The reason these papers are missing in action is that they are
in random piles all over the place.

After

I had to tread lightly because Annie was very defensive about her piles
of paper. My suggestion was to put rubber bands around those piles of
papers to keep them together. (Ironically, she had hundreds if not
thousands of rubber bands saved from the daily paper.) She now piles
like papers together in zones. Reading material is piled next to her
reading chair. Coupons are tossed in a basket by the door, and she
scoops them up on her way out. I built her little cubbyholes underneath a cabinet above the desk, which she set up for paperwork and
bill paying. I labeled each slot depending on the action needed, and
she sorted her bills and papers accordingly. We added cork to the front
of the cabinets and made two bulletin boards, which she loves, for pictures as well as reminders. I set up an action file box for her most frequently needed papers. We also designated one of the drawers for her
to throw receipts into and another for papers she was not sure of.
When it's full she dumps it out and either does something about the
paper or tosses it. Little scraps of paper with little reminders and
phone numbers are stapled to construction paper and this serves as
her things-to-do list. She also puts a sticky note on top of each pile so
her husband has an idea of what is where. After we cleared a lot of the
piles of paper, she rediscovered that one of the previously paper-
covered tables was inlaid with shells.

PEP TALK

Even if you are misunderstood and ridiculed by those around you for your unorthodox ways of filing, organizing, and methods for getting things done, remember, you are unique, special, creative. It's not how you go about doing things that's important; it's the results you produce that matter. Embrace your uniqueness and know that your approach to doing things isn't wrong, it's just different. Yes, maybe you have piles of papers on your desk, but some are near the phone waiting for callbacks; others are near the trash waiting for one last look before being thrown away. There is a method to your madness. It's others who have a problem understanding it.

ACTION ITEM

George Bernard Shaw said, "People are always blaming their circumstances for what they are. I don't believe in circumstances. The people who get on in the world are the people who get up and look for the circumstances they want, and if they can't find them, make them." What specifically is bothering you about your current situation? Write these down. Be as specific as possible. Next to each challenge, write down what you believe you need or what needs to happen to make you feel better. Then write a first step you can take for each.

Part Two

WHERE DO YOU WANT TO GO?

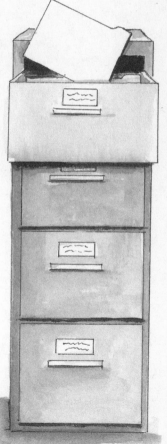

three

YOU CAN DO IT

The First Step to Being More
Organized Is Believing It's Possible

Everyone excels in something in
which another fails.

—Latin proverb

'll bet your parents berated you about your messy room. Maybe they thought it was a phase. Ha! Your boyfriend thought your clutter was cute—until you moved in together. Your boss probably accepted and worked around your disorganized ways because you are so darn talented, but secretly he or she wondered what to do with you. It's okay. Don't be so hard on yourself. Just because you haven't been able to control the clutter and chaos up until now does not make you a bad person. It's not as if organizing is taught in school, and you weren't paying attention. Even if you read the latest bestselling book on the subject, you probably came to the conclusion that some of the suggestions just didn't seem quite right to you. Chances are your parents may not have had a handle on this skill either. It could be that your boyfriend was a neat freak and nothing would be quite right in his little left-brain world. I bet your boss wouldn't trade your positive traits (creativity, grace under pressure, and the ability to juggle ten tasks at once) for a nice, neat (but uptight) small-minded, detail-oriented bore.

Have you ever wondered, "Who am I to be considered organized, together, and on top of things?" Actually, who are you not to be? William James said, "Seek out that particular mental attribute that makes you feel most deeply and vitally alive, along with which comes the inner voice which says, 'This is the real me,' and when you have found that attitude, follow it." You have what it takes to be organized. Organizing is a skill you can master. You just didn't realize it because you thought there was only one way to do it—the left-brain, logical, linear way. Not! Sing with me, "I'll do it myyyyyyyy way." Your approach can be new and unique. There may be no other system of organizing like yours. Good!

We will work on a simple organizing system that is based on your own ideas and insights and will take advantage of your natural tendencies instead of working against them. You just have to believe that it's possible. You can do this. There are lots of other right-brainers who were in the same boat—drowning under the weight of their disorganization. But they were able to bail out, right the ship, and experience clear sailing and calmer seas. I believe in you—now it's time you believe in yourself. You may feel like you were born with the organizing chip missing from your brain. Well, you're right. Nobody is born with these skills—they are learned. With practice, anybody can master them. Sorry, there goes your excuse for why you don't organize your stuff. There is truth in the idea that it comes easier to our left-brain counterparts, but it is possible for a right-brainer to be organized. Others have done it who were in worse shape than you, with more stuff and *without the help of this book*.

The major obstacle to becoming more organized is not external forces but internal ones. Our decisions (or indecision) cause us to make mistakes and make even more of a mess. You can't change who you are, but you can be a better, more organized YOU by making better choices. Step one is to accept some things as they are, not the way you want them to be. For instance, the past is just that—past. It's what you do now and in the future that matters most. The only good that comes from looking back at your messy ways is to look for clues about what *caused* the problem. To uncover what *didn't* work. Once you know yourself and how you like to do things, then you can put together a complete organizing package that will stick.

The best part is that you don't have to start from scratch. Look around and figure out what's *working*. Certainly you have had some success with organizing. You probably don't give yourself enough credit. Instead, you may say, "I am disorganized," but that blanket statement may not be totally true. One of my relatives claims she is a total slob, a mess, and totally disorganized, and yet her camera case is perfectly organized. That's the starting place. We can also learn a lot by finding the things that are functioning and build on them.

I realize that to a right-brainer, getting organized is like having to endure an IRS audit and root canal on the same day. We can organize when we want to. We just have to *want* to. Getting organized starts in our head. "We have free will. We can change our minds. We can have an open mind and heart. We can eradicate the darkness inside of us. You don't do it purely from blessings or reading a book. You've got to do the work," says Richard Gere. The problem is that some of you may not want to change. Maybe someone gave you this book as a gift. *They* want you to get organized, but you say, "I'm disorganized and proud of it. Clutter is good. Everyone should be like me." You don't want to conform. That's cool because that is NOT what this book will do to you. You can remain unique and unorthodox but also find a way to fit everything into your life without having it get in the way of your goals—whatever they may be. Organizing can help you whether you want to be a better parent, start a business, find true love, get out of debt, travel, be more creative, improve your grades, make a difference, or live with less stress. (This is good, yes?) Being a bit more organized will help, not hurt your chances of reaching those goals.

ACTION ITEM

If your current life were made into a movie, what would it be called? *Not Enough Office Space, Clutter of Titanic Proportions,* or *Clutter from the Black Lagoon*? What type of film would it be? A comedy? Tragedy? Disaster? Now, let's shoot the sequel. You are the star, screenwriter, director (and set designer) of your own life. What kind of movie do you want to make? One with a happy ending? *The Matrix Unloaded, It's a Wonderful Life,* or *The Secret of My Success*?

MOBY

Just like not all chaos is bad, solutions can come out of a sense of order. Not all clutter is good. Master musician Moby is quite content with a spartan twelve-by-twelve-foot zone in his lower Manhattan loft that serves as his recording studio. It is neat, clean, and uncluttered. There are computers, keyboards, and recording equipment, plus pull-out shelves and a bookcase filled with a library of samples— all within arm's reach. It's highly organized and still very creative.

WHAT ORGANIZING IS (AND ISN'T)

If a messy desk is a sign of a messy mind, what is an empty desk?

—Unknown

Some professional organizers can make you feel like a failure because you didn't clean off your desk at the end of the day or hang your clothes in a certain way. Whatever. The truest definition of organizing is this: if you can find what you need when you need it, then you are organized. If it doesn't *look* organized to others, it doesn't matter. If it works for you, that's what matters most. It's about function more than it is about form. It's creative, colorful, and comfortable, and not necessarily neat and perfect with everything put away. It isn't a cold, clinical environment devoid of any sign of life. It's more about controlled chaos. It's cozy and personal. It is also clean. There is a place for everything (even if it's a pile by the door) and everything is at least near that place. Things move and flow in and out of your life and your space based on need, want, and room.

If you have a box with a bunch of like things in it and it's labeled, what's wrong with that? I have lots of bins and boxes that I simply throw things into. I can pile, but with a plan and a purpose. Some left-brainers would say this isn't organizing. But it is. I put my bins close to where the contents will be used. The items in there go together, and I clearly mark the box. This makes sense, and there is a method to my madness. I can find what I need quickly and easily, which is what a well-organized space is—one that makes it easy to find what you need when you need it and with minimal effort. Most-often-used items are within reach and less-important things are put away. Piles of papers or unfinished projects are left out but are pushed aside so there is a clear and clean area for working. Memorabilia are shown off on shelves and the walls, and my personality and preferences are allowed to shine through. I feel comfortable but not crowded. Loose items aren't left floating around, and paper flows in and out of my life almost effortlessly. Everything helps me reach my goals (whatever they may be), and my style shines through.

Too many left-brainers are judgmental when it comes to organizing—and just about everything else. I was watching *MTV Cribs,* and drummer Tommy Lee had a purple room in his home. Not many people would want a room that looks like the inside of *I Dream of Jeannie*'s bottle. I say, if it makes him happy, then the heck with what others think. We all have different goals, but being organized will help you reach them. What we are going for is a strategy that *you* develop with the help of this book. A way of organizing that is organic (it feels natural to you) and will not only work wonders but will last a lifetime. When it is done right, you don't even have to think about it. Then you can concentrate on other, more important things without all the distractions. You'll have more open space in your life to allow new thoughts, ideas, and feelings in. There will be more room to roam. More time to laugh, love, and do lots of other fun and meaningful things. If clutter and disorganization get in the way of your happiness, success (and sex life), then there is a problem. Organized chaos is okay. It's *disorganized* chaos that causes conflict.

Since everything has a place (that makes sense to *you*) and it's in its place when not in use, you'll be amazed at how freeing this feels. Things flow in and out of your life naturally and effortlessly. You have space to breathe and grow. Everything in your life supports your goals. You keep things that are important and have meaning. You are surrounded by stimulating stuff and anything that brings you down is banished to storage. What's out is organized and orderly in a creative way. The key is that YOU decide what organizing means and you decide what stuff stays and is displayed. Things don't get lost, and that means less stress and more time for the things that mean the most to you. This is FREEDOM, baby! By lightening your load, you make room for new and better things to come into your life and get rid of roadblocks to your success and happiness. There's more life in your life now.

Organizing the right-brain way is an overall philosophy and a new mind-set that is actually more important than the tips. It's a creative endeavor and a chance to use your resourceful right brain. Apply the principles in this book, and put them into practice. Organizing is not something you do once and it's over. There will always be things coming into your life. There will be challenges. This is a way to deal with whatever comes your way. It's a new way of looking at things, a philosophy to deal with the day-to-day challenges of where to put things and how to find them when you need them, a system that you will continue to use and embrace. It's natural, comfortable, and workable and in tune with you and your way of working and living.

YOU CAN CHECK IN BUT YOU CAN'T CHECK OUT

As a speaker and author I travel a great deal, and I can tell you some horror stories about hotels I have stayed in. However, as bad as some of them were, most were at least organized and neat. (Notice, I didn't say "clean.") Pretend your home is a bed-and-breakfast and you are having guests next weekend. Would that help you create a cozy, but less cluttered, environment?

HOW YOU CAN DO IT

Don't fight forces—use them.
    —Buckminster Fuller

Many of us are searching for a system that allows us to be who we are but also to maintain some sanity amid all the things that flood into our lives every single day. Organizing creates smaller, more manageable streams and keeps things moving (whether that is to a holding tank or down the drain). It's impossible to survive and thrive without being at least a little bit organized. How organized is up to you, but I bet you would benefit by at least listening to how other right-brainers have found simple solutions to their challenges. Let's face it, life doesn't seem to be getting easier despite all the new technological breakthroughs of the last few years. It just seems to speed up and continue to roll over us, leaving us crushed under the weight of a thousand e-mails and a hundred voice mail messages. Some of us are keeping pace and are even able to race in front of this massive onslaught of information before it catches up to us, but without the basic organizing skills it would simply be impossible. We might as well just lie down and let it rush over us and drown us in a sea of unopened mail, past-due notices, and missed meetings.

What we need is the antidote. I think I know what it is. There are practical, empowering, and creative ways to become organized without losing who you are. These are strategies that turn right-brain disadvantages into advantages. "To me, life is questions and answers—the whole history of humanity has involved problems and solutions. Rather than just in some idealistic philosophical way, I get down to 'What can we actually do?'" says Dan Millman. Let's look at what we can do to get a handle on all the stuff that has a hold on us.

We make pledges to finally, once and for all, get our act together and clean up our clutter, only to fail and fall back into our old, disorganized ways. Why is this? Maybe it's because we see it as torture rather than a task that can be creative, empowering, and most of all an improvement in most areas of our lives. Everyone thinks that organizing is a drag, pure drudgery—and it can be. Kinda like math is. However, one savvy San Diego teacher made math more relevant by using baseball statistics to teach fractions, percentages, and odds. He started a fantasy baseball mathematics project that students could really relate to. "Math is fun," said one of his students. With organizing, if you get goofy or slip in a little silliness, it can actually be fun. Did I say "fun"? Okay, that's a bit too strong a word. How about palatable? How about making organizing into a big adventure. Be Indiana Jones and go through each room of your house searching for what doesn't belong there, rescue it, and return it to where it needs to go. Pretend to be on *Law & Order* and argue the case for each item as to whether it should go free or get put away. Put happy face stickers on things you want to keep because they make you feel good. Do it to music and dance your way to a new and organized you. Dress for the job. Wear something strange for your trip down memory lane. A friend of mine who works for a large newspaper says, "My suggestion for organization is a pretend game. Pretend you are moving and start stashing things in piles."

We have a natural ability to solve problems. It's one of the strengths of a right-brainer. Let's come up with some creative solutions using this strength. Look at it like any other creative endeavor—brainstorm with others, borrow ideas from existing solutions and adapt them, experiment and play around with possible solutions. Don't just think outside the box, draw on the outside of boxes to make them colorful and creative. Take unusual objects and make them useful. This way you can express yourself and your creative abilities. Many of us don't have the time to be creative, but now you can be more organized and flex your right brain as well. Do some simple, quick, or creative organizing projects every day—rearrange the furniture, turn a useless piece of clutter into a functional work of art, or relabel your computer files with fun and functional titles.

I don't want to hear any excuses about why YOU can't get it together. I have whiners who come to my seminars, and no matter what I say, they come back with, "But I tried that . . . ," or, "But I'm different. . . ." "But . . . (fill in the blank)." They think they are special and unique—*just like the rest of us.* I say no big "buts" allowed. This stuff works, but nobody can motivate you to organize. It's your life and your career, and you are the boss. If you don't feel like organizing, nobody will shoot you—but there is a price. Don't blame others or society for your circumstances. You are where you are because you chose to be. You are not helpless. Don't say, "Getting organized is hard for me because I am a right-brainer." Instead, try saying, "I am disorganized because I am too lazy to put things back where they belong." It hurts to hear, but it's the truth. If you say, "I've tried to stay organized, but it never sticks," keep in mind that it's not what you did, it's what you are doing now that matters the most. Disconnect from the past and project yourself into the future, a place where you are organized and stay that way. Then act as if you are there already.

FIND THE CLUES

Spend a day paying attention to what you do with your stuff. Every time you do something, ask yourself why. Where do you naturally put things or look for them first? Don't fight it; make it fit. Find a way to make these patterns work for you. When you are frustrated, ask yourself, is there a better way? This will give you some idea as to why you are organized or disorganized and suggest some solutions. Keep doing this every day for a month to try to develop a system—your own customized organizing program.

You have to know the way you think, act, and live to be able to organize. When you start to see patterns, pay attention and notice the reasons and the decisions behind them. Then we can begin to figure out what works. We are slaves to our past patterns. Some of us repeat the same mistakes over and over again. Maybe we take two steps forward, but inevitably we lose ground based on our old habits. These are subconscious things that sabotage us as we struggle to change. Just seeing that these patterns are a problem is the first step to a solution.

HALF-FULL?

We often complain about what we don't want. That's a start. What are you constantly complaining about as it pertains to getting organized? What is it that bugs you? Why isn't it working? Now, what would work? What action can you take to make it happen?

Find the solutions that make sense and will work for YOU. No book on organizing has all the answers, and even if it did, they wouldn't all work for you. I encourage you to explore new and exciting techniques for organizing yourself. Make them up as you go along. Discover what works well for YOU and stick with it no matter what others may say. Once you know the basic rules (covered in chapter 5), you can apply them to your own situation. Use your creativity to come up with some innovative ideas on how to be more organized. You are where you are because of the choices you have made up to this point in your life. You can change how you choose. Old habits die hard, but they do die. None of us come with an operating manual. We need to figure out what works from trial and error.

Could it be that you want to organize but don't know how or where to start? The place to begin is to decide you want to do it and determine why you want to become organized. Once you are motivated, you can hit the ground running. Maybe you don't want to do a complete makeover, but make a move in the right

continued on next page

direction to being more organized. That's a start and a good one at that. Small steps in the right direction are better than running in place. Pick one problem, break it down, and start looking for solutions. Use the suggestions in this book and try out your own innovative ideas. Then take some baby steps.

When you put something down somewhere, chances are it will stay there. If it had a home and you went to the extra effort to put it where it belonged, you would be amazed. Being organized begins with making better choices. Maybe you admire the clean, uncluttered homes you see in *House Beautiful* and *Architectural Digest,* but you don't have the discipline to do it. That's okay. Start with one room and work your way out. Keep that vision in your mind. Better yet, clip out those examples and save them as an inspiration. Start by organizing one small thing that will lead you to the life you are looking for. You'll be amazed at the difference it makes in your life.

This is a lot like a diet. It's not a crash course but a lifestyle change. That's why setting up an organizing system is so important or you'll revert to your old ways, and the clutter and chaos will come back. It's also about gradual change. Pick an area of your life to clean up first and finish it. Then figure out a way to keep it this way. Focus on the positive goal and avoid fixating on the problem. Just keep your eye on the goal, and make small steps toward it. Keep your head up, eyes forward, and pick things up as you go. With a vision, burning desire, and some consistent actions, you can change. Form a picture in your mind of what kind of environment you want to live and work in. You become what you think about. Adopt a mantra. This is an expression that you repeat to yourself to remind you of why or how you can be more organized. "Less stuff equals more life." Share these with those closest to you and ask that they repeat these sayings and slogans back to you if you start getting offtrack. Change your thoughts and change your world. Then act on it.

FUN FACT

In the January 1948 issue of *House Beautiful,* the question was asked: to clutter or not to clutter? Interior decorator Harry Gladstone was pro-clutter and said so. "I always have room for something new." He championed our right to collect and display clutter. Blanche Knopf was the vice president of a large publisher and her take was, "I need visual tranquility for mental tranquility." Her position was that of a purist, and she preferred clean surfaces and plain fabrics. The bottom line is, neither approach is wrong. It's what is right for you that matters.

four

A METHOD TO YOUR MESSINESS

A Plan to Tackle Your Biggest Organizing Challenges

Many of us are daydreamers who live in a fantasy world, acting on any whim, going through life with no rhyme or reason and collecting clutter along the way.

—Unknown

We know who the enemy is. It's us! We would much rather take random stabs at anything that moves than follow a rigid battle plan. However, when it comes to the war on disorganization, we need a strategy to succeed in our constant battle with clutter. If we just went charging off and tried to attack whatever was in our path, we could do more harm than good. The proper way to plan is to define your objective, come up with clever and creative solutions, get all the supplies needed, schedule or set aside some time, and *then* attack, attack, attack! Sometimes knowing what to do and when to do it are as important as how when it comes to organizing. Finally, you need the desire and discipline to see this thing through to victory. Are you with me? I can't HEAR you! Good. Dismissed.

Being creative people, we can come up with all kinds of wonderful ways to organize, but these ideas are all over the place, so to speak. When it comes to putting them into practice, a plan of action can be a godsend. Here are several unique techniques to form concrete yet flexible plans of action. These plans will hopefully help you break your traditional patterns of thinking, move you beyond your clutter and out of your comfort zone, and aid you in getting organized.

Planning is an important part of the process of getting organized and keeping things that way. YOU are in control of how you want your home or office to look, feel, and work. You need a vision to determine what's important in your life and what stuff supports that vision. Then decide what goes where. You can keep all you want, you just have to be able to determine what means the most and then put it where it's more accessible so you can either see it or get to it with ease. The planning stage is the perfect time to set limits about what you can and will keep. You can decide for yourself what you want to keep and where it will go. It's better than having others decide for you. In the movie *Pillow Talk,* Doris Day plays an interior designer who wants to get back at Rock Hudson's character for being a bit of a player. She decides to turn his apartment into a crazy funhouse, complete with orange walls, purple carpet, animal-print throws, beaded curtains, and all kinds of other crazy decorations.

If you want to make positive changes, it helps to be committed to change and then have a plan to pull it off. It allows you to look before you leap and map out what, where, when, and how you will organize before you begin the transformation. Planning also provides focus, motivation, and an understanding of just what needs to be done and how to do it. On the popular TLC shows *Trading Spaces* and *While You Were Out,* the designers follow this simple formula: plan, purchase products, prepare the room, and put the pieces together. It's a step-by-step process that has been proven to work.

Planning is something we can be great at. We can tap into our ability to daydream and see the big picture, plus use our powers of intuition and imagination to design the dream home and office environment that would make us and those around us happy. If you can see yourself living in your dream home, working in the ultimate office or studio, and having a relatively clean and uncluttered garage where you can actually park your car, you can then gather the courage, motivation, and focus needed to make it real. If you can see it, you can do it.

With all this talk about being more organized and clearing the clutter from our lives, I don't want you to think I've forgotten that happiness is found in the moment—no matter what kind of mess you're in. You can be happy right now. You don't have to wait until everything in your life is organized perfectly to be satisfied. However, being organized helps you to be clear and in the present, whereas being disorganized leaves you frustrated, frazzled, and stuck in the past. Maybe the word "organized" doesn't do it for you. Find the deeper meaning of what being organized could do for you. For example, to me being organized means much more than having a place for everything and everything in its place. It means freedom, peace of mind, contentment, respect, pride, and so on. These are things that give me inner satisfaction. Disorganization is no reason to be unhappy, but being organized is a worthy and important goal. Getting organized is hard with a plan; it's almost impossible without one.

FACT

One-third of American workers never plan their daily work. Almost half make a daily plan at least once a week. The interesting thing was the higher the income, the more likely the worker was to make a written schedule and prioritize tasks, according to a study by Day-Timer. Makes you think, doesn't it?

PLANNING TO PLAN

The best way to predict the future is to create it.
                                    —Peter Drucker

Take a few minutes to answer the following questions as quickly and honestly as you can. Your reaction and responses to these questions will be a big help in the actual planning process as you move from disorganized to organized.

"WHAT'S MY MOTIVATION?"

Let's look at *why* you want to be a bit more organized.

- What do you want people to think of when they enter your home or office? Does it reflect this now?
- What do you want out of life? Could being more organized help you reach these goals? How?

- How would being more organized improve your personal and professional life?
- If you were more organized, what would you do that you can't do now?
- How has being disorganized hurt you?
- Finish these sentences: My mission in life is to . . . To do this I need . . .

WHAT MATTERS MOST

There is a saying that goes like this: "You can have anything you want in life, you just can't have everything—at least not all at once." Let's take a look at what you value most and what you're finally ready to remove from your life.

- Look around your home for clues about what you want, value, or treasure. How do you decorate? What do you read? What hobbies do you enjoy? What items are featured prominently? What are you proud of? What are the ten most important things in your life? What would you like to eliminate from your life?
- For a minute imagine the worst, your home burning to the ground with everything in it. What would you miss the most? What would you replace if you could? What wouldn't you replace?
- Look around your home or office. What items do you use most? Are they easy to get to and put away? How can you improve this?
- What do you need more of in your life? What do you need less of?
- Name five things that would make you feel you "have it all."
- Finish these sentences: I am happiest when I am . . . All I need is . . .

SEEING IS BELIEVING

Let's look at how you want to organize and what it means to you. This is YOUR vision, so anything goes.

- Create a mental picture of your dream home and what you want this space to look like and how it is organized.

- After you have seen it in your mind, get it on paper. Draw, write, list, mind map, or find pictures representing what you want your environment to look like.
- The next step is to describe what it would mean to live and work in this new, organized environment. What feelings would you have from this new and improved you? Describe how you would live your life if your home was the way you have always wanted it—organized. What would an ideal day be like if you were organized?
- Describe in detail what you want your environment to be like. What areas would you like to improve? How would you like everything to look? Work? Feel?
- What do you need to make this happen?
- Finish these sentences: My ideal environment is . . . The place where I feel totally at peace and comfortable is . . .

WHAT'S STOPPING YOU?

So what's stopping you? Procrastination can be a fear of failure. This fear comes from looking into the future and allowing our insecurities to take over and convince us that we will fail. Having a clear vision of what you want drowns out the negative messages and attracts the positive things needed to make it happen. A plan also allows you to get lost in the process. If you just keep putting one pile in front of the other, you will make steady progress and build your self-esteem along the way.

- What do you perceive to be your challenges to getting organized? Draw them.
- Bounce a ball off the wall, and every time you catch it write down the first thing that pops into your mind regarding this question: I would be more organized if . . .
- Let's brainstorm some ideas about the problems related to organizing. Is it that there is too much stuff and not enough space? Is it that you never really gave any thought to where things should go based on how you live and work so that it makes sense? Is it too hard to put things away? Come up with ten reasons why you are not organized now.

- For the next few minutes eliminate any limiting thoughts or beliefs and write, draw, doodle, talk into a recorder, or discuss with a friend the following question: "If I didn't fear failure, I would organize . . ."
- Make a list of all the areas of your life that are disorganized, and for each one come up with at least one possible solution.
- Finish the sentence: "I'm glad I am not _____." This is much better than saying, "I wish I were _____."

WHERE TO BEGIN

Walk around your home or office and rate how frustrating certain things are to you on a scale of 1 to 10. You will likely find most things are mildly annoying and rank a 2 to 4. Tackle the things that rank a 6 to 10 (very irksome) first. Let some of the lower ones wait.

- If you could hire help, what would you want them to tackle first?
- If you could only organize one thing/area, what would that be?
- What are some supereasy first steps you could take to be more organized?
- What are some new habits you'd like to adopt regarding organizing?
- Study your home, office, car, and other areas for clues about why you do things the way you do and organize with these tendencies in mind. Take a look at what is working and do more of it.
- Finish the sentences: I hate . . . I want more _____ in my life. I would like to eliminate _____ from my life.

ACTION ITEM

Never say never. "I will never be organized" is a common complaint. If you remove one word from the sentence and reread it, it sounds so much better and is more accurate. "I will be organized."

CREATIVE WAYS TO PLAN

The painting had a life of its own. I try to let it come through.
—Jackson Pollock

A plan and goals are written descriptions of the overall direction of what you want to do. It can also be a picture, poem, collage, image, song, or sentence—as long as it has meaning for you. It's a philosophy to live by and organize around. I have always had goals. Always. When people first step into my office, one of the first things they notice is that my goals are up where people can see them. I have a dream board on the wall, with pictures of my main goals along with captions for each. There's an affirmation on my desk (which I also write out every single day). My goals are also in my planner, wallet, in my computer—everywhere. It sounds hokey, but it works.

Rank and File

Go through all the stuff clogging your home or office. Using index cards or sticky notes, put one item on each card and do this for everything you have. Then on the back of each index card, rank the item based on how valuable it is to you. If it makes you happy, put a smiley face on the card. If it will make you money, put a dollar sign. If you use it often, put a star. If you absolutely love this thing, put a heart. If you used it within the past few months, put a checkmark. Finally, rank it from 1 to 10 based on its overall value to you. Or write why you should save each item on the back of the card and make a case to keep it or toss it. Now sort the cards by ranking. Make two piles. One is what should stay, and the other is what can go. For the stack of cards containing what stays, sort these by priority. Try keeping only what's most important and find a place for it. To that end, you can get a big board and map out your house into zones (or by rooms). Put your index cards (or sticky notes) in the zone or room where each belongs. (This means the item is either used there or is not used very often and is stored out of the way.)

Movie Magic

Pretend you are making a movie about organizing yourself. The plan can look like a storyboard used for planning a shoot, with "scenes" representing each room or area of that room. Instead of dialogue, make a list of things you'll need to make the scene work. Put a big "X" through the scene when it's "a wrap." Give the "film" a title. You can actually film your surroundings and create a documentary of the before-and-after transformation from disorganized to organized.

Scrapbooking

Look at what your subconscious is telling you and discover your deepest desires. What your heart and your head say. Grab some magazines and catalogs and rip out any picture that triggers something in you related to how you want your space to look. Pay attention to any connections, patterns, or ideas. Then make a collage on a big board or on smaller boards representing each area that needs your attention. Write a caption underneath the picture about how it would feel to live like this and what your life would be like when everything is well organized.

Doodle Art

Doodle, freewrite, or mind map what you want from your space. What would be ideal? You can do this visually by drawing pictures (or cutting them out from magazines) and pasting them on a page. For instance, you could write down an area or item to organize like "Reading Material" and then map out all the different types of reading matter and possible solutions to deal with it. Draw, doodle, or list all the things you would like to change about your environment. (These are things that cause you trouble.) On the other side, make a list of the things you can control and leave off the things you can't.

Playback

Using a tape recorder, walk around your home and comment on what you see. What's working and what's not? Don't judge. Just observe and report. If you think of a solution or have a suggestion, say it out loud. If you want to add how you feel as you walk through each area, do it, but don't let it get you down. Play back the tape when you are done and make notes based on what you said. There may be a lot of useful ideas that come out of this exercise. Brainstorm for the best ones, and then integrate these into a plan. Another way to do this is to write a sentence that describes your ideal environment. How it would look, feel, and work. Then go for a walk with a tape recorder and start talking (to yourself) about what you want and all the possible ways to make it happen.

It's Linear, but It Works

Make two lists. The first list is everything you like about your environment and why. Then make a list of everything you *don't* like about your environment and why. Look for clues about what works, and now come up with some solutions for what doesn't. Go from room to room and make a list of all the things that are in there. To figure out what matters most, rank them as you would movies. Five stars for a hit down to a dog for something that really doesn't work for you. It's subjective and should be based entirely on your tastes and preferences. Ask yourself, how much time does it take to deal with this thing? Is it worth the effort? How much space does it take up? Is it earning its keep?

How and How Now

On the left side of a piece of paper, list the organizing objectives you are planning for. On the right, make two columns. At the top of the first column write, HOW. Call the second column, HOW NOW. To begin the planning process, write down all the things you can do, the "how" that will accomplish your objective. Do this in broad strokes. Let it sit for a while, then move to the second column and branch out from the "How" steps into more specific "How Now" solutions and action steps that are more short-term in nature. A "How" would be "Clean up sporting equipment." Connected "How Nows" could include (1) donate, sell, or give away old, broken, and unused items, and (2) get a good container to keep everything organized and out of the way.

End Zone

Draw a diagram of your home and determine what you do in each room and what stuff you need there to do it. Make notes of storage areas and write in what SHOULD go there based on what is used in or near this zone—not based on what fits. Move the related items to that area. Just doing that will help you get going in the right direction. You can divide rooms into zones as well and organize items based on where and when (how often) they are used.

Homework

Walk around your home and make notes about what really bothers you. Then use this book to find one solution for each problem area. Post this list up where you'll see it, and start working your way down it. (You can also do a mind map.) Make a list of EVERYTHING that you want to do and a first step for each. Schedule each area for a week or month.

Mind Mapping

This is a fast (and effective) way to formulate nonlinear plans using word and idea association. It works because it suspends judgments, naturally clusters like ideas, and gets your plan on paper. Start by deciding the essence of what you are aiming for and either write it or use an image to represent what you want in the middle of the page. (Turn the paper horizontally for more room to write.) Draw branches for each area you want to organize. Next, without passing judgment, write whatever comes to mind (using trigger words) with rapid-fire speed. These will extend like leaves from those branches. After you have exhausted all ideas, go through and eliminate any duplicate or unfeasible organizing ideas and cluster others together. Finally, using a different color for each, highlight your long-term, mid-term, and short-term tasks.

On a Mission

Turn your main vision for a more organized you into an affirmation. You'll review and write it regularly until it is internalized and drives your decisions and daily actions. An affirmation acts like a mission statement for an area of your life. It's a sentence or two that states your purpose. It could also be a poem you recite regularly or a song you sing all day long. By writing, reading, or singing your affirmation, you retrain your brain. Now you have a mind-set that's rooted in what's possible. You're now focused on the future and what you want it to be like. If you are burdened with negative thoughts all day, every day, you aren't operating at your best. You won't see solutions to your organizing problems because they are buried under a mountain of negativity. You can't get rid of these thoughts, but affirmations are the answer. The more you believe you will be and deserve to be organized, the more likely it will happen. When you feel better about yourself and your environment, you will worry less, make better decisions, and by feeling better, bring good things to yourself.

Dream Board

This is an exercise where you cut out pictures representing what you want your environment to look like and then paste them on a big board. I recommend adding a caption for each picture in the collage so that you engage your left brain, too.

You can plan as you go if that's more your style. If you do decide to just wing it, at least walk around your home or office, look for areas that really bother you, and make a mental note to begin there.

HOW TO MAKE IT HAPPEN

When you don't have some kind of plan, the end result is such that nobody can understand how it works and there aren't any clear rules about how to use it.

—Linus Torvalds

Since right-brainers are usually multitalented, it's easy to become overwhelmed with possibilities. So what we need to do next is cut down on the number of goals to get to the "need to's" and "want to's" and eliminate the "could do" and "should do" items. We want to tackle the most important areas—for now. A deadline can cause you to get going and keep you focused. Look at a calendar and pick a big event—like a birthday, tax time, a pending move, or a holiday—and focus on being organized by that date. Make a promise to yourself and keep it. That's what goals, resolutions, and plans are really all about. The only person you let down if you don't act on them is yourself. You're not rebelling against the system or making a statement, you are letting yourself down. If you bought this book, then obviously you want to make some changes in your life. Take responsibility. Stop with the excuses and get going. Break down the "whole enchilada" into bite-sized morsels that you can snack on every day. It will be from these simpler and smaller chunks that the big goal gets done. Now it's not so "pie in the sky" and certainly more real.

ACTION ITEM

Life will pull you away from your goals—if you let it. The secret of successful people is that they keep their goals in the forefront of their minds and make decisions based on what they want to happen, not what is happening around them. In a word, they are focused. How can we, as right-brainers—with our tendency to be distracted—stay motivated and focused long enough to organize everything and keep it that way? Simple. Post your dreams where you will see them. It's no good to make New Year's resolutions and not at least write them down. (This way, when you sober up on New Year's Day you will remember what you wrote.) Most people never commit their dreams and wishes to paper. That's mistake one. The second mistake is to put your wish list away and never look at it again. I know of what I speak. I can't help but come across my dreams several times a day. I know I am unusually obsessed when it comes to going after my goals, but if you just do one of the things listed below, you'll be better off.

- The first thing you should write across the top of your things-to-do list is your main goal when it comes to organizing. Then put one task related to that goal on your list and DO IT during the time of the day when you are most motivated or energized.
- Using a journal, a pad of paper, your planner, or PDA, write out a daily affirmation or your mission statement at least once. Get in the habit of doing this first thing in the morning. If you get bored, write with your other hand. (This connects to the other half of

your brain.) Draw a picture that represents what you want. Say it aloud ten times. You want to internalize this message to yourself and make it a mantra to live by.

- Make a wall chart with all the areas you want to organize. Each time you accomplish a step in each area, put a gold star next to it. Yes, it is a lot like elementary school, but we all need a pat on the back from time to time, even if it is from ourselves. Celebrate your success. Keep a victory log or a bowl where you post or put your past successes.

- Carry a reminder of your goals with you in your pocket, purse, or planner. This could be a picture of what you want your life to look like or a list of things you will do to stay organized. When you are faced with some downtime, pull out this piece of paper and read and review your goals.

- Post a picture of your dream environment in the room it represents. Put your dream board up on the wall or next to your desk so when you want to daydream (often, I'm guessing) you can ponder a time when everything in your life is organized.

- Put plans and goals in plain view (to you) and make it a habit to look at them often. Plaster them all over your walls. Turn them into a screen saver. Carry them in your purse or your planner. Make a coffee cup, calendar, or a sleep shirt with your goals on it. Create postcards of your goals and send one every week to yourself (or e-mail them to yourself every day). Paint or draw a picture of you living your dream. Record your dreams on a tape and play it in your car or while walking. Keep them at the forefront of your mind, and remind yourself to focus on them daily. If you are bold, you can even share them with others and ask for their help.

WHERE TO BEGIN

You can't build a reputation on what you INTEND to do.
                                                            —Liz Smith

- The first step is a doozy. Yet without this one, you will freeze up and panic. (Organizing is overwhelming, and it's tough to get going.) I have a simple first step for you on your way to becoming an organized person. Begin by writing the following statement down daily and telling three people who care. The statement goes as follows: "I will become organized and stay that way."

- Use your initial burst of energy to deal with what's visible. Make piles of stuff that go together. Put them in boxes (labeled) so when you burn out you can come back and pick up where you left off. Pick one room you will experiment on. Keep this room clutter-free. Make this an oasis, the calm and collected place in the middle of the storm.
- Start by removing the items that don't belong. Get rid of all the stuff that doesn't need to be organized—duplicates, dated goods, things you don't need anymore, items that no longer serve your needs or goals. Organize what's left.
- If step four is too much, just make a first pass at an area. You have permission just to take a stab at it. You don't have to do any-thing—unless you want to. If you do decide to start organizing, do things quick and dirty just to get the ball rolling. Start by sorting through a pile. You don't have to put anything away but toss what-ever you can.
- Organize an area you can complete in one sitting. This can be a bookshelf, box, or a backpack. Don't stop until you finish. Repeat this process over and over, and you will start to see some progress—one area at a time. It may take a long time to finish everything, but this is the way to do it.
- Schedule one thing a day at a time when you know you can and will do it. Maybe you can do it when you are most motivated or when you usually need a break from a tough task. Every time you touch something, make one small improvement.
- List everything you have to get done. Get help with as many of these tasks as you can. What a relief that is. Write down two things and follow up on what you had been putting off. Put down a start date, a deadline, and a first step.
- Get the gear. Be motivated by new containers. Sometimes just the act of getting started, even if it is just going to Wal-Mart, is the motivation needed.

FINAL THOUGHT

There is no one system or plan that will work for everyone. You have to pick one based on your preferences. That's why this book has several suggestions for every possible organizing problem. You should simply pick the solutions that make sense to you—ones you will embrace and stick with. I've read a lot of books on organizing and I have to be honest, half of the things I came across would only work for people who are already organized. Many of the other suggestions were good, but only a few really clicked for me. That's what you should look for—ideas that really speak to you.

ONE OF US: BECKY HAWLEY, GRAPHIC ARTIST

"I have a graphic design business and have a few main clients, each with lots and lots of both really small and really huge projects. One thing I have been trying to do is keep a small spiral notebook on each client. I get the little stick-on page tabs (like index tabs) and use a new one for each project. I take the book to all my meetings so that I can put all my notes in it (so I can find them later!). As I get quotes from printers or other vendors, I put them in the book under that project. As proofs go out and come back in, I put in the dates and any comments. As I go along I'm beginning to build a history of projects for that client."

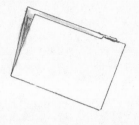

Part Three

HOW DO YOU GET THERE FROM HERE?

five

ORGANIZING RULES NOT TAUGHT IN SCHOOLS

Lessons Learned and Adapted
from Organized People

Rules are made for people who aren't
willing to make up their own.
　　　　　　　　—Chuck Yeager

ules are made to be broken," you say. Troublemaker. Henry
Wadsworth Longfellow said, "It takes less time to do a thing right,
than it does to explain why you did it wrong." Okay, let's compromise. I will share with you the forty most basic rules about organizing,
and you pick and choose which ones to use. Look at it this way. What
fun is breaking a rule when you don't know what it is?

In all seriousness, this chapter may be the most important one of all.
When you know the tried-and-true rules behind being organized, you
will be able to handle and gain the upper hand on any mess you en-
counter. These rules are actually more valuable than the organizing tips I
will share with you later in the book. (That doesn't mean you can skip
those chapters. It simply means you'll know the reasons why these organizing tips work and how to apply them.) Reading these rules will lead
to a new way of thinking that will help with decisions and keep things
looking good. It's an overall philosophy and a set of principles that have
been proven to work. These are the parameters within which you can
experiment and expound when organizing.

These rules are the "secrets" of organizing that we never learned—
until now. Now you have your decoder card. Organizing techniques that
come naturally to our left-brain counterparts, that we often wondered

about (or not), are demystified and explained in a simple way. You pick and choose the points that interest and apply to you. Once you know the overall concepts and the basics, you'll be able to organize anything and everything. You will also be able to engage your right brain and come up with your own clever method, approach, or system.

I learned a similar lesson in art school. The teachers continually drilled the basics of design (and how to apply them) into our heads until I was actually saying them in my sleep and applying them in my work without even realizing it. The reason I mention this is that as methods and mediums changed in the graphic arts—hand rendered to computer generated and brochures to Web sites—the same principles applied. These lessons have lasted a lifetime. To this day I can design almost anything using the basic rules I learned in school. I'm sure it's the same thing for interior design, fashion, and other art forms. I see this same thing on all the new makeover shows on television. The designers just *know* what to do based on the basics. It is THAT important in the organizing process as well.

Now you have no excuse not to get organized. After reading this chapter you will have the tools and techniques to decide what stays and what goes, where to put what's left, and how to develop and design a system to store your stuff so that you will stick with it. Some of these rules are like, duh, "I know I should put things away after I use them." "Of course, files are for putting papers into." "I shouldn't have to park on the street because my garage is overcrowded with clutter." Right-brainers don't want to conform. We're rule breakers, trailblazers, innovators. That's all fine and good in other areas of your life. But when it comes to getting it together and cleaning up our act, here are the rules to organize by.

1. **Don't put things where they fit, put them where it makes sense—where they are used; or if they are not used, store them out of the way.** Every time you put something away, ask if this is the best place for it. Is there a better place to put it? Put stuff where you use it. To do so means you may have to arrange or rearrange your storage—add some shelves, put piles in different places, or simply designate one junk chair for clothes that

you like to drop. (Clean it up when it's full or you run out of clean clothes.) Most of all, put things where *you* want them to go. Putting them where you think they SHOULD go is a mistake. Just because Martha Stewart says to put your umbrella by the door doesn't mean that keeping it in the trunk of your car is wrong. Nobody knows exactly how you live and work or what suits your style or your situation. The question that needs to be answered is this: Does the place where you put this item work well for YOU? The key is function, not form. If it works, it works (and it works the way you do). That's what matters most. Where you would look for something is where you should put it. If it's something that is used often you shouldn't have to get out a ladder to get it down. If it's an item you never use and only need once a decade, don't put it in a prime position; put it somewhere out of the way. For instance, being a visual person (like most right-brainers), I put things I need to take with me in my path so I have to trip over them on the way out the door. Few other organizing books recommend this, but it works for ME, and it will work for you, too.

2. **Things have a natural order and go together. Figure this out and you are well on your way to being more organized.** It is so much easier to decide what goes where and to find it again when you group similar items together, whether in a box, bin, or basket. Most things go together by type, category, use, project, energy, or placement. As a trainer I try my hardest to entertain attendees while I teach them, too. Over the years I have added props, magic tricks, and anything and everything to get and hold an audience's attention. It's so easy to pack for a talk or trip because I have plastic containers for each talk I do, with the related props and tricks as well as my notes. I learned this lesson and use it for everything—put things together that are used together. Sometimes this seems unconventional. For example, I tape instruction manuals to the back or bottom of the item each belongs to. I probably should file these, but this works for ME. The same thing goes if you like to pile. Just put like items together in the same pile. It may be easier to file than pile. Piling isn't a problem

when you use dividers, colored file folders, containers, racks, sticky notes, clips, tabs, a summary, quick review, or a list of what's in the pile on top, and add to it as you build your pile.

3. **Go with your natural tendencies. If you or your family puts things in the same place over and over again, don't fight it— fix it.** If your entryway is the place where you, your kids, and even the dog drop everything, don't fight it. Make it work for you by building, buying, or adapting something to organize the mess. Where there's smoke, there's usually fire. If an area is starting to be a nuisance, chances are it will be a full-blown problem before long. Create cubbyholes for each member of the household (the dog's space would be on the bottom) or have a hook or shelf designated for each "person." (Let him or her decorate it, too.) Life is trying things to see if they work for YOU. When they do, they flow in and out of your daily life easily and effortlessly. Organizing, when done correctly, feels natural and makes sense to you. That's why we put things where we would look for them or where we want them to go. Observe your patterns of behavior, come up with a plan to put things in their proper place (according to how you prefer to live and work), and then organize around that. This means you shouldn't have to make major changes to get organized. You may have to make some adjustments, but if you have to redo or rethink everything about where you want your things to go, you'll never stick with it.

4. **Create zones based on the activity that takes place in that area and organize accordingly.** Organizing is a lot like planning a town. You have a library (where your books go), there is the hardware store (for tools and supplies), the laundry area (where you wash, dry, and sort clothes), there is a Bed, Bath & Beyond (the linen closet), a restaurant (the kitchen and dining area), a sporting goods store, repair shop/car wash (where your automobile supplies are), office complex (a home office), a bank (where you pay bills and handle financial matters), self-storage (where you keep valuable, but seldom-used, items), and so on. Look at each room and divide it up into a grid for the activities that are done in each area. We already know we should store items close

to where they are used and keep like items together. The way to know what goes where is to decide what you do where and what things are required to do it, then organize accordingly. The remote, *TV Guide,* and your glasses are in a basket by the couch where you sit and watch TV, for example.

Each room (or part of a room) should have a purpose, and you should try to stick to it. The zones you create are entirely up to you. Perhaps you want a creativity zone. Of course this is where all your art supplies for creating are kept. Many parents prefer a kid zone for toys so that they don't end up taking over the whole house. Some people prefer a serenity zone where they limit what is allowed in. (This may also be a bathroom, so keeping it clean and clutter-free is important. Candles are okay, but clutter is not.) It's best when you don't let one zone bleed into the other. A linen closet is for linens and a clothes closet is for, well, clothes. They shouldn't share a space with office supplies. Once entering that space, you should be able to focus on the task at hand.

This is such an important point, I'd like to elaborate just a little more. When I recently moved, I had the chance to start from scratch and put this principle into practice. I began by deciding what I would do where. Then I drew a floor plan and cut out paper to represent the big stuff that went with these activities. That's how I designed my new office, music studio, and even the garage. Since I surf almost every day, I made it easy to just grab my gear and go. I built a surfboard rack so my boards are all together and easy to get to. Next to the boards are my wet suits with a specially designed area that allows them to drip-dry. Towels are on a hook nearby, and my gear bag is on a shelf with extra surf wax and ding repair supplies. Most of you won't have surf stuff, but you get the idea.

Maybe some of your clutter is from a temporary situation, and the solution is to create a zone based on a project you are working on. That's cool. My friend is working on getting his fixed-wing pilot's license. He's in a hurry so he's doing a crash course. Oops, poor choice of words. Anyway, his dining room table is covered with charts, books, notes, and equipment. Since nobody of importance is coming over (that includes me, I gather) and his wife doesn't mind, this makes sense since they eat elsewhere. Getting this class out of the way is a high priority and the mess is contained to one area—temporarily.

ASK A PRO: TERA ALLISON, PROFESSIONAL ORGANIZER

"Within your home or studio, create zones or centers of activity. If you create in a variety of ways (as most creatives do), store your tools and supplies according to the way they are used. For example, if you're a painter, create a painting zone. Within that zone, store all of your oil paints in one container, acrylic paints in another, as well as designating specific places to store your canvases and paintbrushes. Do this same type of organizing for each creative activity that you are involved in. Discipline yourself (OUCH) to put things back into their designated homes after each work session, or at least every couple of days. The few moments you spend on maintaining your organizing systems will pay big dividends in the long run. By creating and maintaining creative zones, or centers of activity for each of your endeavors, you will always know that the materials, tools, and supplies that support your craft are ready and waiting for your creative touch!"

5. **Set some limits to live by or else your clutter will get out of control.** What if you chose just one area to keep clutter-free—like your desk? Then there would be an oasis amid all the chaos. It could be that you want to make a good first impression so you organize the entry area and keep it clean. How about setting a height limit for your piles? When you run out of room to store stuff, institute a "one in, one out rule." (For every item you take in, get rid of one. Or if you get rid of one piece of clutter, you can keep one.) You probably have a finite amount of space to display and store stuff; that can be the deciding factor about what stays and what goes. What if you only keep and display the most recent kids' drawings and treat them like an art gallery? Have month-by-month showings and celebrate the work, then let

someone else enjoy it. Send some artwork to grandparents, for example. Decide that two sets of bedsheets are enough. All catalogs not dated this year are recycled. Once the inbox is filled with over fifteen e-mails, you will go through and either respond, file, or dump them. For instance, actress Wendie Malick says, "My little mantra is 'Every time I buy something, give something away.' It helps me keep the crap out of my closet." This way everything flows in and OUT of your life and only the best stays. Maybe the only things you allow into your life are items that enhance you and help you reach your goals. Ask yourself, "Does this item bring me closer to my goals or farther away? Does it enhance my life? Is it worth the space it will take up to store it?" Keep the best and store or get rid of the rest.

6. **Assign parking places for your permanent stuff.** I realize that we (right-brainers) like to wing it, thrive on change, and don't like being tied down. Fine, live like that in other areas of your life. Life is so much easier when we have a designated place to put things. Items usually stay where they are first set down so try to put things in their place. As soon as something new comes into our life/house that we intend to keep (that's just about everything, right?) we should decide on a space for it. To make decisions about where to put things, limit the choices by creating slots, spaces, and dividers. When something new is added to our life (loose-fitting clothes), this is a good time to get rid of something we no longer want or need—for me it was my "skinny" clothes. Oh well, at least I'm a realist. Things need to have a home where they "live." If they float around they are hard to find and we won't put them away as easily, if at all. Remember, keep the things that you need to get to frequently the most accessible; otherwise, an organized system may look neat, but probably won't stay that way for long. Things don't have to be put in their proper place all the time. During the day leave things out until you're finished with them. When on a deadline, getting the job done is more important than how it looks doing it. However, the old saying "Pick a place for everything and put everything in its place" is a rule that actually works—even for us

right-brainers—as long as we limit the number of places an item could and should go.

7. **Don't love anything that can't love you back.** Antoine de Saint Exupery said, "The meaning of things lies not in the things themselves but in our attitude towards them." Many things will catch your eye, few will capture your heart or mind—keep those. Only we can decide what is important and how much of it we should and can keep. I will tell you this. I know for a fact that storing all sorts of useless stuff won't make you happy. I have traveled the tropics sailing and surfing, and one thing became very clear. Some of the happiest, healthiest, and most content people had next to nothing. This proved to me that we don't need a life of goods to live the good life. Besides, it feels freeing to give/sell some of your things. It's good to give—*almost* as good as getting. When my wife and I moved into a beach house that was smaller than our previous place (did I mention it's steps to the sand and surf?), we realized that we could, and should, part with a lot of things that we no longer needed, wanted, or were willing to pay to store. So we sold some (and used the cash for new furniture) and gave the rest away (making many people pleased in the process).

I'm big on books and research material. I had more information in my files and piles than my local library, but then I lightened my load. I came to the conclusion that I didn't need half of this stuff and neither do you. Most research material also is available online or at the library. You'll also be happy to hear that you know more than you thought you knew. It's all in your head—literally. It's information that's been internalized. You don't need half of the material you have on hand. You don't have to save every single thing you see. It's in your brain; you just need a better way to access it. Work on improving your skill at reading and retaining. Instead of highlighting a reference or business book, read with index cards and take notes on what matters most. Then organize these index cards by topic.

8. **Think big, start small.** Think in units of "one"—one space at a time, one surface at a time, one pile at a time, one piece of paper at a time. Everything we do is done one step at a time. That makes it

all possible. To borrow a baseball analogy, take it one pitch at a time. Wait for "your" pitch; and when it looks good, take a swing at it. Taking the first swing at a small area of clutter and getting it under control is like your first hit. Admire it, enjoy it, celebrate it, learn from it, build upon it, and, of course, keep swinging away. Players get in trouble and strike out when they try to hit a home run. It's the same with organizing. Start small. Begin with a drawer, purse, or shelf to build some momentum and see some success rather than burning yourself out on a big organizing project that could take weeks to complete. The first true step is to figure out what's wrong. I know what you are saying—"EVERYTHING!" Chances are some things are working and some are not. Look at what you don't like, what doesn't work, and start there. Go into each room and storage space and ask yourself what is right or wrong with this. What do I use this room for? Am I happy here with the way it is now? What would I like to change? What could I do without or move? Designate a purpose for each room or drawer, eliminate as much junk as you can, and then find a home for what's left. It sounds so simple, doesn't it? Well, it is easier than trying to tackle the entire kitchen in one attempt.

9. **Rather than buying something new, use your creativity and right brain to come up with creative solutions to your organizing problems.** This book is filled with creative solutions to chronic organizing challenges, but don't stop there. Come up with your own. Be creative with how you store stuff. Look up, look down, look all around for hidden and not-so-hidden places for storage. Make the most of your space through innovative ideas. When it comes to clutter, come up with new uses for old objects.

10. **Organizing isn't all about getting rid of things. It's about having the right stuff in the right place for a right-brainer.** I am sure you have heard of the 80/20 rule at some point in your life. Applying it to organizing isn't such a stretch. Think about it. You probably use 20 percent of your stuff 80 percent of the time. Aw, come on, you know it's true. Truly organized people recognize this and store the stuff they use all the time in prime spaces and archive the rest. Look at all the obsolete things lying around your

home and office. Do you use pencils anymore? If you said, "No," then why is there an electric sharpener taking up valuable space on your desk? Think of your space as a retail store—it's all about location, location, location. There is prime space on the shelves in a store. The end cap is where seasonal items are displayed. On the shelves in grocery stores items on the top shelf are usually slow sellers or overstock (rarely used); things used (sold) most often are at eye level. Ever notice how kids' cereals are down low at eye level with their target market? Big and heavy items are on the bottom. Items near the cash register are called impulse items. You can quickly grab them on your way out. Items that go together are displayed together or at least in the same section. Slow sellers are stored out of the way, and overstock is stored in the back (or returned). It's the same with organizing. Don't put rarely used items in prime positions. Keep key things in a prominent, permanent place and move unimportant and rarely used things out of your way. Most frequently used stuff is stored where it's easiest to get to. Leave items out if they're used daily and in your path if you don't want to forget. Most stores track sales. We can track usage. Mark things when you use them so you know what you use most or what makes you feel good when you see it. Something with a strong track record gets the best spot in your home.

NONTRADITIONAL LIST MAKING

A traditional things-to-do list is a convenient place to make notes to yourself and eliminate a lot of excess paper from your life. There are other (nontraditional) ways to do it, too.

- A stack of phone messages, reminders, and sticky notes can also be considered a to-do list. Whatever works.
- Make an anti-things-to-do list: things that you do that are either a complete waste of time, you hate doing, should and could be done by someone else, or that you can live without doing. Post this and add to it whenever you feel that you are in over your head or spinning your wheels.

- Have fun when making your things-to-do list. Turn your list of tasks into a poem. Draw all the things you need to remember. Invent your own font while writing them out. Heck, paint them if you want. Do them with crayons, colored markers, create cartoons, or use stickers.
- Post all your scraps of paper on a corner of your bulletin board (designated as your reminder zone) and remove them when done. You can also tape or staple little loose scraps of papers with scribbles on them to a large piece of paper.
- Write out your list of things to do with your nondominant hand.
- Maybe it all begins with what we call a very effective but boring-sounding tool, a "things-to-do list." How about a "things-to-create list" or "exciting-challenges-to-engage-in-today list" or "potential-accomplishments list" or "opportunities-to-excel-in-this-week list."
- Make a daily to-do list that matches your energy cycle. Make a curved line with peaks and valleys. Put your creative, more difficult tasks along the peaks and your less-creative or errand-type tasks in the valleys.
- Make a wall board or fold a vertical piece of card stock into three sections so that it is a freestanding (accordian-style) display. Write TO DO, DOING, and DONE at the top of each section and move your sticky notes around or write your tasks on it. Or make three columns on your paper, MUST DO NO MATTER WHAT, SHOULD DO, BUT IF I DON'T CAN DO TOMORROW, and THINGS I WANT TO DO FOR ME.
- Make your things-to-do list into a game. This is one of my favorites. You compete against yourself. List all the things you have to do. Assign a point value to each one. (Keep it simple—1–10, depending on its importance or degree of difficulty. I add in bonus points for exercising.) At the end of the day total up all the points for the tasks you completed. Then total the points for the tasks you didn't finish. Which total is higher? At the beginning of the day, I write down some small prize I'll give myself if I "win." I have found that just by playing, I'm winning.
- Make a time-line list. On the left is the time you wake up. For instance, noon is near the middle, and whatever time you go to bed is on the far right. (Turn the paper vertically.) Your things to do, calls to make, appointments, meetings are plotted along the time line either with sticky notes or by writing them in.
- Make two lists, one a right-brain list of all the fun stuff you want to do and the other a left-brain list of the things you must do.
- Make your things-to-do list into a board game. I play against my assistant. We each make our list of things to do, calls to make, etc. We then have little colored pieces that move along a board game we created. As you complete a task you move your piece, depending on the difficulty. (Difficult 3 spaces, tedious 2 spaces, easy 1 space.) There are places on the board that say draw a

card. Some of the cards give you fun things to do, while others challenge you to do more (pick up one of other player's tasks). Create your own game to play with a coworker. It makes the day go by faster, it's fun, and the winner not only gets a little prize, but both players get a lot more done!

- Write your things to do on a stack of index cards, shuffle them, and do whatever comes up. Add in "wild cards" that allow you to take a break or do something fun for a while. Shuffle and choose throughout the day. Add in new cards as things come up. Or pin the cards to a wall or bulletin board in the order you think things should be done. (Write urgent things in red.) Move them around as your day changes. (I use different-colored cards for calls, meetings, and urgent items.)
- Take a sticky note and fold it along the glue mark and you can create little standing reminders. If you turn a typical sticky note on its side it makes for a little things-to-do list that can be affixed to just about anything.

11. **If it's not on a list, it doesn't exist.** Of the estimated ten million great stories told over a beer, around a fire, or as bedtime stories, literature only consists of roughly five thousand that are written down. Your brain can only hold roughly seven items at a time. After that, important things to do, places to be, and good ideas start falling through the cracks, never to be seen again. Do not rely on your memory alone. If it's not written down, it does not exist. Your brain is busy thinking about other things, especially right-brainers whose minds run like a CD player on shuffle play. It's easier to know what you'll need for the day when you have an idea what you'll be doing. Less brain clutter and stress make you more efficient. This book comes with a lot of tips on creative ways to capture your ideas, things to do, and reminders. Put at least one of them into practice. If all else fails, use sticky notes.

ONE OF US: MARK GOLIK, WRITER

"I don't know about you, but as I grow older and more established in life, I find myself confronted with the requirement to retain more and more information and address more and more responsibility. That can be hell for those of us with a creative bent, right? After all, where do we get the storage capacity to accommodate all that information? Unless you can properly manage the influx of data in your daily life, your brain—much like a computer—will crash. I find the best course of action is to simplify the mundane. Clear your mind of the things you *have* to know and free up some gray matter for the stuff you *want* to think about. The best part of any system—paper or PDA—is that I feel more completely in control of the information I need to retain."

12. **The easier you make something, the more likely you are to do it.** This is so true. If you make something easier to put away than not, you will probably do it. Everything should be made simple, easy, and natural. If it's inconvenient, you won't do it and you'll likely bail the organizing process. Eliminate any obstacles, steps, and barriers to staying organized by simplifying the process. For projects in progress, I use clear plastic baskets to throw things in until I'm motivated to work on them again. If you pile clothes in the bathroom, put a hamper there. Keep all the supplies and equipment handy to both back up your computer and synchronize your PDA. If things are poorly designed, it makes organizing ten times harder. Think about a CD case. First, when you buy the CD you have to try to unwrap it and remove the sticker/label on top. Good luck. Even when all that junk is removed they are almost impossible to open (and close) and will break if you breathe on them. How about that little booklet with the liner notes? It barely fits back where it came from, and the little plastic tabs that hold it in place break off faster than you can say, "Poor design." No wonder nobody puts their CDs away.

13. **Make better use of space.** Maybe the problem isn't that we prefer to pile, it's that we don't have enough room to do it correctly. Let's clear some space. Hang the phone on the wall. Switch to a small laptop computer rather than a big and bulky desktop computer. (The best part of a laptop computer is, it doesn't matter how much you stuff into it, it never gets heavier.) Hang another bulletin board to get a lot of those loose little papers up off your desk. Then use dividers to keep your piles neater.

It often helps to subdivide storage spaces so that everything doesn't slide back into one big disorganized mess of "stuff." Make big spaces into smaller ones with dividers, containers, cabinets, shelves, or bookcases. Be smart about how you use your space. Use drawers that are shallow for small stuff and deep drawers for bigger items. Buy the right organizing products and you can double your storage area. Clear containers are great because you can see what's inside without opening them.

BASKET CASE

"Put all your eggs in one basket, and watch that basket!" said Mark Twain. Baskets are a beautiful and practical way to organize almost anything. They look good (many baskets are works of art), and they work wonders whether you need to corral lots of little items or just tote the laundry. The possibilities are endless.

14. **Not everything needs to be left out for all to see.** The key to keeping a lot of clutter (and your spouse/boss/roommate off your back) is concealment. Stash stuff that accumulates in very public areas or is simply in the way. Maybe you can dedicate one room that remains messy, but you close the door when company comes. Designate a drawer for junk and throw in things when you have no idea *where* they should go. Decide to keep the entryway of your home clutter-free so that you make a good first impression on visitors. Stash stressful stuff in a box until you can find the time to deal with it. Get it away and out of sight if you can. You can write a note to yourself about what is where if you are worried that something out of sight will never be seen again. (Just don't lose your note.)

15. **Piling papers will work when there is a method to your madness.** This is covered at length later in the book but let me just say, piling can be an effective way to deal with paper if you have a system that makes sense to you, keeps it moving,

and you have the room to do it. The general rules of organizing still apply when you would rather pile than file. Divide your desk into zones based on the activities that are done there and pile accordingly. Keep like papers together and find a creative way to keep them from getting loose and lost. Keep out papers that are in progress or are often referred to and move the rest out of the way—throw away, throw in a marked box, or file them.

ASK A PRO: LAURA SCHRONEN, FOUNDER OF SPACE GRACE

"Keep your focus. Organizing chaos or clutter can feel overwhelming, especially if it's yours. Choose one area to start with and try to stick with it until you've made progress. If you finish an entire area, section, or room, it can serve as an inspiration for the rest. I like to go back and take another peek at a recently organized space. It usually feels so much better than it did previously; it motivates me to do more!"

16. **Variety is the spice of life, except when it comes to organizing.** We are intuitive people and make many of our decisions based on emotions. We are also divergent thinkers and tend to make all kinds of seemingly random associations between unrelated things. We prefer new and exciting to safe and secure. We love to come up with creative ways to do things. What am I getting at? These tendencies (and several more mentioned in chapter 1) make it hard to come up with consistent patterns for putting things away. It's almost impossible to find papers if you file intuitively or randomly. Make changes when things aren't working; but if it ain't broke, don't fix or fiddle with it. It's okay to be all over the place in other areas of your life where it won't matter. When it comes to organizing, stay the course.

17. **Things do not get easier to organize with time.** The best day to get organized is any day ending in "y." (Ha, ha, ha.) There is a lot less clutter when you take care of simple things right away. Open your mail over the trash and thin it out. Do something as you need

to before it piles up. Staple a business card to your Rolodex or add names to your mailing list as you get them. Back up your computer at the end of the day. If a task takes less than two minutes to do—just do it. When you do something when you think of it, you don't have to remember to do it later.

18. **Leave important things out where you can see them.** The basic rule is, out of sight, out of mind. Things need to be in plain view in closets, storage bins, and on shelves—even in the trunk, glove box, and toolbox. Since we are visually oriented, we like to leave things out where we can see them. When we can't, we fear we'll forget where they are or act on them. You can still store your stuff, but you want to be able to know where it is at a quick glance. Clear containers are GREAT! Containers with a space in front to put a picture or make notes on work really well. This clear container system is very efficient when you don't want to leave stuff lying around but still want to know it's there. Not everything has to be put in some kind of container. Put the important things where you'll see them and less urgent, current, or important things keep out of the way. Later in the book there are several solid ideas about how to remember things visually. For now let's just say that a sticky note on the door, a hook for your keys, and place to put the things you need to take with you work wonders for the right-brainer. When you do leave things out, the rule is, *never put a larger item on top of a smaller one.*

19. **Don't put it down, put it away.** Keep moving things closer to their final resting place. We want stuff to flow, not start to pool and then stagnate. Don't say, "For now," when putting something down. Instead, don't put it down, put it away. If you pass it, pick it up. Never go from one room to another empty-handed. Put things in the room where they are used as a way of getting them closer to their final resting place. If you're not sure where that is, have a box for the "I don't know what this is or where it should go" items. Patterns may form or after a while you may realize you really don't need to keep the items. Make paper and information flow in and out. Don't let things coagulate, stagnate, and procreate (they multiply). If you don't need, want, use, or love

something, then what the hell is it doing on the floor? This clutter is a drain on your energy and your creativity.

20. **Containers, planners, PDAs, and other organizing products won't make you organized.** I read somewhere that 57 percent of people polled purchase organizing products to make them feel like they have more control of their lives. In my experience many of those same people will never use those same organizing tools. This creates even more clutter and a giant case of the guilts. They can help or they can hurt your chances to be organized. They could just mean you have more clutter if not used or not used properly. Tools are not a silver bullet, and there is no such thing as pixie dust to solve your problems. Some organizing tools take more time than they are worth. Are you skeptical that there is any tool out there that could actually make organizing any easier? Good. Nothing can completely organize for you, but there are several types of baskets, bins, and other accessories that are easy to use and don't cause you to completely change the way you prefer to organize.

21. **Life is mostly maintenance.** It's not *get* organized, it's *stay* organized. When it comes to organizing, it's an ongoing project that includes some less-than-thrilling things to do. Still with me? I thought I may have lost you there. What makes organizing bearable is that when it's done right it feels so freeing, and the feedback is so positive you will want to keep it that way. The challenge is to make some of the maintenance tasks a higher priority. The answer is to make the mundane organizing tasks go by faster by getting things done and having fun. Have some friends over for a "best of" contest to help you determine what you should keep or toss out. Hold up an item and have them give you a thumbs-up or -down. (Nice if you can have a third as a tiebreaker.) Music makes terrible tasks go faster. Now you are distracted in a GOOD way. When you need a break from more challenging tasks, take on a simple one related to organizing. Keep some things to do in a basket by the phone or TV and do them during the commercials or while on hold. Whenever you pull a book down from the shelf, straighten up the others in that row.

22. **When you absolutely, positively hate to do something, hire someone to do it for you.** Do what you do best and write a check for the rest. Especially organizing the big stuff, like your computer or your closets. Doing it yourself is not always easier or cheaper. I used to change the oil in my car myself. This took tools, time, and trying to find a place to dispose of the old oil. Sound like a pain in the neck? Well, it was. Now I gladly pay to have it done. If you are short on cash, trade your talent for help with cleaning up the messes in your life.

23. **Expect the unexpected.** Leave room for growth and change. We want to be flexible and adapt to what's next in our lives. Things change. You change and your life and home should reflect those changes and who you are NOW. Systems to stay organized should be able to expand and contract based on the ebb and flow of your life. Don't hesitate to rearrange that drawer or system of organization if your initial try isn't working for you.

ASK A PRO: PAULETTE ENSIGN, PAST PRESIDENT OF THE NATIONAL ASSOCIATION OF PROFESSIONAL ORGANIZERS (NAPO)

"Continue to review your systems no matter how organized you are. Organized people maintain their systems because they are consciously or subconsciously reviewing those systems to be sure they still work for them. That monitoring usually happens in small increments, so a massive overhaul is not typically necessary. Right-brain people can save themselves a lot of angst by noticing and modifying a system in small increments to avoid a massive redo."

24. **Perfectly organized doesn't mean perfect.** Don't wait until everything in your life is perfect to get organized. There is no perfect time. No perfect system. No perfect place to put things. Do the best you can with what you have. The secret is to do it now. Just start and things will literally fall into place. You can't possibly be prepared for every imaginable possibility. If you believe that all those things you save and hang onto will prepare

you for any problem that may arise, you'll be (unpleasantly) surprised.

25. **Things you buy, keep, and store should help you reach your goals.** Becoming organized begins with better choices. If your goal is to spend more time with your children, then why would you want to subscribe to ten different magazines that you'll never have time to read? You desire peace and tranquility, but you have a home filled with useless clutter. That makes no sense. If your dream is to sail around the world, but you can't afford to because you have several storage units filled with stuff that costs you a lot to keep, you could sell some junk to finance your trip. If you want to start a business, you need to learn how to deal with paperwork. We need to show some restraint and say, "No," more often than, "Yes." When the cute kid comes to the door selling several subscriptions, just say, "NO." When a friend or family member asks if you could store some of her stuff, what do you say? Not just no but heck NO. When your birthday rolls around, ask for what you really want and *need*. So you don't end up with useless junk. For the holidays just say, "Ho," and instead of exchanging gifts, celebrate in other ways. You need to have goals in your life. That way you'll know what stuff is supporting you as you try to reach these goals. It's easier to decide what to keep when you know what's in the way of your getting where you want to be.

26. **Most things are only valuable when they are used.** A lot of books about becoming organized will say, "If you don't use it, lose it." That's a little too harsh for many of us. Let's take reading material, for example. I keep back issues of graphic design magazines like *Before & After, Dynamic Graphics,* and *How* from five years ago. There is room for them. They are organized in holders by year, and I thumb through them quite often. I also know that my library does not carry copies, and I can't find back issues online. Since I use them, they are valuable. However, I don't save past issues of *TV Guide* or *US Weekly*. Why would I? The information would be dated, and besides, I don't have the room. If I needed to look something up, I could find it archived elsewhere

or I'll tear out an interesting article and file it away. Author Julie Morgenstern says, "Keep the source, toss the paper." Most information is a mouse click away. That's why a forward-thinking friend of mine put computers in more places in his house and has a lot less need for paper. He's connected to the Internet for recipes, coupons, movie reviews, and so forth.

27. **Learning to organize is a skill anyone can master—even a right-brainer.** It's like learning a new language. It takes time and it takes practice, but it's doable. First, you must believe you *can* be organized. Keep in mind that others have been MUCH MORE MESSY than you and are now organized and can find what they need when they need it. They have control over their lives and their clutter. If they can do it, you can do it! "If you act like you know what you're doing, you can do anything you want—except neurosurgery," says Sharon Stone. This book is so full of information on organizing it's like a college course. Read the rules, try the tips, and take it one pile at a time, and you'll be fine.

28. **Your home or office should express your personality and fit your own way of working or living.** The look and feel of your space should reflect who you are and what you *want* to be. Think about that last statement. I never said you have to create an environment that is based on what others think it should be. You can be organized and still uniquely you. However, if you see yourself as needing to be surrounded by ten years' worth of unread newspapers, enough canned food to fill a bomb shelter and feed the entire town, then there may be bigger problems at work than how to be more organized. If you want to create a space that is fun but functional, cozy and less cluttered, easy to maintain, and allows you to live your life, I say, "Bravo." You can do that without changing who you are. The right organizing system should fit you like your favorite pair of jeans.

29. **Simplify your systems.** Keep organizing systems simple and a match for your own individual requirements. That's the only way you can sustain your organization and your sanity. It's almost seamless. I always hear how marriage is hard work. Not

mine. It's like breathing. I married my soulmate, and we complement and complete each other. It just works, and we don't have to work at it. Similarly, how you handle what comes into your home and office should not be a struggle. "I must create a system or be enslaved by another man's; I will not reason and compare: my business is to create," said William Blake. The key is to eliminate steps and roadblocks to getting organized by simplifying your system.

30. **Being messy and disorganized does not make you more creative, unique, or special.** It just means you are messy. Yes, some clutter can be inspiring and helpful in the creative process, but like your mother probably told you, "Everything in moderation." A cluttered mind or enviornment is NOT always the best for coming up with ideas. Be orderly in your life and chaotic in your art.

ASK A PRO: KEVIN HALL, COFOUNDER OF CLUTTER NO MORE

"Creative people can be overwhelmed by the amount of things sitting or lying all around them (like that other horizontal surface—the floor). Some feel that this creates a sustaining stimulus to be more creative. However I find that too many things left lying around leave people overwhelmed. Finding 'homes' for items helps you gain control of your surroundings. Labeling shelves and drawers makes it easier to find those items."

31. **Less stuff is easier to organize.** Putting a cap on clutter and compulsive saving is a tough sell, so I won't even try to tell you what stays and what goes. I will simply say organizing is a LOT easier with less junk. It's also hard to be cluttered *and* clean. It's hard to scrub surfaces that are covered with stuff. Bugs love little piles of stuff to nest in. (I know, nasty.) I speak from personal experience. I was a pack rat, and now I am just a rat. (Ha, ha, ha.) I asked myself some simple questions like, "Do I really want this? Need it? Will I use it? Is it still current? Is it earning its right to stay? Can I get it elsewhere when I need it? Could I rent rather

than buy this item when I need it? Will it matter in a year if I tossed it?" The things that stayed in my life were items that made me feel good (photos and fan mail), helped me build my business (marketing materials and speech notes), made me more productive (computer software and power tools), made me look good (clothes that actually fit and were flattering), and improved the quality of my life (music and musical instruments). Getting organized started with gaining control over the clutter that was crowding out my life. With the clutter out of the way, I could see the light at the end of the tunnel and that light was happiness, fulfillment, and creative freedom. By letting go of a lot of my junk from the past, I was able to look to the future and, more importantly, live in the moment. Now staying organized is a breeze.

32. **Being organized simply means you can find what you need when you need it.** It's okay to have (a little) more stuff than the average bear. Just be able to get to it and still function. Even if your desk is full of things that look like clutter it does not necessarily mean you are disorganized. If you are able to find what you need when you need it, get the right things done when they are due, and it's not causing friction with those around you, you may want to leave it alone. I bet a friend I could find anything in my house in under ten minutes. Anything. Let's just say I enjoyed a nice big steak dinner on him.

33. **Time is money.** Actually time is more valuable than money. When you waste time, you waste a piece of your life. Losing time looking for lost items is no way to live. Having to fix, clean, move, and manage a bunch of crap is a waste of your LIFE. When you spend money to rent extra storage, you have traded your time (which again means you gave up a piece of your life) to earn the money to pay the rent. What a waste. More on this later in the book, but it's worth repeating. All you have is your time, which is your life. There IS a real cost to clutter. What's more important, the people in your life or the things you are hoarding? I hope you know the answer to this question before it's too late. (Put people first.)

34. **Label everything.** Label boxes and bins so you can quickly see what's inside. (This includes disks, DVDs, and CDs.) This book contains several creative ways to do this.

35. **Think multipurpose.** I have made an effort to buy things that have more than one function. When you are short on storage space, it really helps to have a bench that opens up to reveal a place to put a lot of loose items. Using a laptop computer means any flat surface can become a work area. If you collect cool stuff from your vacations, try to make them memorable and practical—a coffee cup can become a pencil holder or a decorative box that holds and hides your many remote controls.

36. **You can never have too many trash cans.** Make trash cans easy to reach and put them all over the place.

37. **Buy quality not quantity.** This rule works on three levels. First, if we buy inferior products chances are they will break down. Then we have to either fix them or find a replacement. Since we keep everything, we will end up with two or three of the same thing and only one that works. That's where some of our clutter comes from. Second, if we buy a cheap filing cabinet that is hard to open or is broken, then filing becomes difficult. That's all the excuse we need not to put papers away. Aha! More clutter. Finally, when it comes to clothes, it is better to have less of the best than it is to have a bunch of cheap things that fade, fall apart, and are fashion faux pas. (At least that's what my wife tells me.)

38. **Some stuff simply refuses to fit nicely and neatly into a category and will always be out of place.** Thus, the junk drawer was born. It's been said there is no such thing as "miscellaneous," but I disagree. There are often random and unrelated items that only go together because they are *all* "one of a kind."

39. **You don't have to reinvent the wheel.** I have borrowed organizing ideas from restaurants, retailers, bars, bands, and Mother Nature. I have also learned a lot from watching left-brainers. Pay attention to how others get a handle on organization and go ahead and steal the ideas that would work for you.

40. **Make up your own rules so they suit you, your style, and your life.** "Things like 'touch a piece of paper only once' are

unrealistic rules whether left-brained or right-brained. Do a large sort and then do a refined sort of paper or possessions. THAT is realistic," says organizing guru Paulette Ensign. I agree.

The same rules that apply to organizing your everyday stuff work just as well with your computer clutter. Oh, you don't believe me? Let's try to solve some standard computer-related challenges with our basic rules and see what happens. Problem one, a failure to back up our files. Make it easier to do by keeping CDs near the computer and by keeping all of your current projects in one place. We are overwhelmed with software and all the manuals and disks that come with them. Simplify. Go with quality software that does more, which means you need fewer little programs floating around. Focus on software that helps you reach your goals. Lost and missplaced documents are constantly wasting our time (and it's frustrating). Put things where YOU would look for them. Use only one calendar or sync your PDA calendar with your computer's calendar. There are all kinds of accessories that go with computing—scanner, printer, copier, fax, and so on. Think multipurpose. They make all-in-one machines that will do everything, including make a latte. When it comes to computer clutter, keep in mind this rule: group like items together, organize by zones, archive outdated documents, keep things moving to their final resting place (a CD or DVD stored in a safe place). Let your personality come through and customize how your computer files, icons, and aliases look and work. Make it personal, visual, and functional.

six

PILE, DON'T FILE YOUR PAPERS

Putting Paper in Its Place—the
Right-Brain Way

What the world really needs is more
love and less paperwork.

—Pearl Bailey

efore we begin, let me please say this to those of you who would
rather pile than file your papers—it's okay. No, I'm serious. There
is nothing wrong with leaving papers in piles as long as you can
find what you need when you need it. See, getting organized isn't going
to be as bad as you thought. The truth is, there is no right or wrong way
to deal with paper. There isn't a Paper Police that will issue you a cita-
tion (yikes, more paper) if your papers aren't nice and tidy, filed away in
alphabetical order, and cross-referenced chronologically. We are constantly apologizing for having our papers *organized* in an unorthodox
manner—even if they are working for us. Face it, we are right-brainers
living in a left-brained world. "Excuse the sticky notes and piles of papers, I'm gonna get to it soon," we say meekly to those who ridicule and
reprimand us for our unique way of working. Well, I'm here to tell you
that it's okay to be who you are. There is no shame in being a right-
brainer who by nature is visually oriented and likes papers out where
you can see them. What this chapter will do is show you how to make
sure that the paper in your life keeps flowing, and that when it does
come to rest, you can find it again.

You are not alone when it comes to paperitis and pack-rattedness.
There are people from all walks of life who have the same symptoms—too

much paper coming into their lives and no effective system to deal with it. The desk that is piled high and deep can belong to just about any one of us. Does it make you a loser? No, not unless it gets in the way of getting what you want out of life. If it holds you back, then you have a problem. Let me give you an example. Our band had this amazing lead singer who had so much going for her except for one thing—she was a flake when it came to paper. We would give her the set list, the song lyrics, and even lend her CDs to make sure she could practice and prepare. When we had a gig, I would make sure I gave her a sheet with the date, time, directions, and other details. After she failed to show up twice and did not know the words to songs on several occasions (because she constantly lost the paper with the lyrics), we fired her—talented as she was. She made US look bad.

You would be surprised to find that many people with the nice, neat, everything-is-in-its-place style can be disorganized, too. (Heaven forbid we ever open one of *their* drawers.) Having a neat desk does not make you more productive. In fact, it may mean you don't have enough to do. Yet society in general frowns upon the everything-out philosophy and looks favorably on the clean-off-your-desk-every-night-before-you-go-home crowd. You don't need a clean desk, just a *clearing* is all. What you *do* need are right-brain techniques to tackle paperwork and keep it moving in and out of your life naturally and effortlessly.

If total chaos reigns, things can get out of hand. Many right-brain people simply will not organize their paper. Period. They believe that to stop the chaos just for the sake of neatness is a waste of their precious time. They are opposed to filing papers away or even straightening up their desks on principle alone. So papers pile up, things get lost, appointments are missed, bills are left unpaid, all of which can add up to even more time wasted in lost business, bad credit, strained relationships, and time spent worrying about all the problems I just mentioned. What we are going for is a balance between what we would like to do (just leave all our papers out and shuffle through them from time to time) and what the world wants us to do (file, file, file).

My very first (paying) job was as a part-time janitor in an office building for scientists. Since they were paying me fairly well, I wanted to go the extra mile and do a thorough job. My job description called for me to dust, empty the trash, and vacuum the floor of each office. It was a pretty easy job, really, except for this one guy's office, which nobody had ever tried to clean before because it was so crowded with stacks of papers. You couldn't even make your way to the trash can. (The whole room looked *like* a giant trash can.) And when I say there were stacks of paper, I mean he had stacks upon stacks. When piles would reach critical mass and topple over, he would stack more papers on top of the fallen heap. One day, I decided to make a good impression on my boss by straightening up this guy's office and then giving it a good cleaning. I spent several hours neatly organizing his papers into small piles and then moving them around until everything looked orderly. You can probably guess the rest of the story. It was at that young, impressionable age I learned what the words "organized chaos" and "you're fired" truly meant.

Since that episode, my philosophy has become, If it ain't broke, don't fix it—just tweak it a bit. When it comes to papers, a case can be made to pile not file. But if all those piles are creating gridlock, we can work on that. If most of what's sitting around is just "gubbish" (garbage mixed with rubbish) and all you do is shuffle it and move it from pile to pile, there is a better way. I will show how some minor modifications to your piling or filing can create a fun (maybe that's too strong a word), flexible, visual, easy-to-use-and-maintain filing system that will let you put your hands on any piece of paper in under ten minutes without having to change your ways—much.

WHY WE PILE

I live on the fringe of society, and the rules of normal society have no currency for those on the fringe.

—Tamara de Lempicka

There are many sound reasons why right-brain people prefer to pile. Here are a few of them to consider.

Decisions, Decisions

It's likely that indecision is causing you to keep paper around longer than you probably should. "Where should I put this? Oh heck, I don't know, I'll decide later," you may say. Over a period of months of doing this, these papers pile up. Then there is the classic fear that you just might need this piece of paper someday and you couldn't possibly throw it away (even though you could easily get it off the Internet, from a colleague, or at the library). A paper-processing system starts at your desk, where paper comes in. It then goes to an action sorter or to storage. The only other option is the trash.

It's Positively Stimulating

Seeing a pile of papers can actually enhance your creativity. An illustrator friend explained it to me this way: "I like to pile papers. For the most part I can find what I need, even if it takes a little time. But the advantage is I see things on my search that spark new ideas and approaches to a project that I never would have thought of otherwise." It's a little like a brain dump. It's everything you collected in one place. Pretty soon connections are made, and the pile begins to take shape and have meaning. This works—up to a point. It can also be incredibly distracting.

Seeing Is Believing

Right-brainers are by nature visually oriented. Aha! That explains everything, doesn't it? That's why having papers out where we can see them provides us with a visual reminder, and we feel, for good reason, that things filed away are out of sight and out of mind. (There's a lot of truth to that, too.)

What a Hassle

The easier something is to do . . . (go ahead and try to finish that sentence). If you said, "The easier something is to do, the more likely it is I'll do it," you are correct. Many filing systems are a hassle to use and hard to understand. Having things within reach can be considered easier. Eventually, having everything in your "swivel zone" (where you can swivel your chair and put your hands on it) can catch up with you.

"My Boys Need a Home"

Many times paper piles up because there's no home for it. Not having a clue about where to put paper could be a result of the paper not having a home—a clear-cut, final resting place. After a piece of paper has served its usefulness, find a final resting place for it. (Hint: The trash. Or, if you believe in the afterlife, recycle it.)

Comfort Zone

Believe it or not, being surrounded by papers can act as a security blanket for some. As strange as this sounds, clutter equals calm. I believe it's due to an emotional attachment to printed material. (Who knew?) For a reason we can't explain, we simply can't let go.

Justification

"See, I am busy. Look at all these papers and files lying around," some will say, as if their immense amount of paperwork equals productivity. But leaving too many papers out can have the reverse effect. Yes, key or current papers have a place on or around your desk—ten-year-old copies of *Sports Illustrated* (swimsuit editions) do not. Or do they? It's too bad others who aren't as enlightened see papers piled all around us as a sign of flakiness.

Someday Isle

"Someday Isle" is a place I like to call P-R-O-C-R-A-S-T-I-N-A-T-I-O-N. You know, someday I'll . . . We truly are "Big Picture People" and not good with details—like filing. We probably would like to clean up but don't know where to begin. Maybe we really are too busy to get to it. (Not that we would want to do it anyway.) Besides, it's not in our job description. That's why I recommend a "Spring Cleaning Day" every month (regardless of the season) to catch up.

Rebel Yell

Society (and hundreds of books on organizing) tell you, in no uncertain terms, that you must clean off your desk and file everything away, or else. (Or else what?) So the natural response for a rebellious right-brainer is, "Oh yeah, then I'm going to do the exact opposite." This is out of spite and to be different. "I'm a creative person; see my mess!" we shout. I agree, don't ever lose your originality. (Hopefully, it's not buried in a pile of papers somewhere.) Repeat after me, "As long as I can find things, I don't care where they are or what my work area looks like. I have my own way of doing things, my own style, my own system, and it works, so leave me alone." Ooooooh, that may be a bit harsh. But fight for your right to pile papers and/or file them however you want—within reason.

Booooooring

Right-brainers like fun and games, and filing papers is the antithesis of that. It's work, it's logical, it's linear, and above all, it's boring. It's anything BUT creative. Since preventative work—like filing—offers little in the way of immediate gratification, it isn't all that appealing. So we have to find ways to make it interesting and light.

We Thrive on Chaos

Let me repeat that. Creative people seem to thrive on chaos. What can be more chaotic than a blizzard of papers lying around? Grab at this, flail about, and yet, eventually, everything falls into place. In the words of Lin Yü-T'ang, "Besides the noble art of getting things done, there is the noble art of leaving things undone. The wisdom of life consists in the elimination of nonessentials."

The Rat Pack

Oops, I meant Pack Rat. Right-brainers are savers—maybe not when it comes to dealing with dollars, but when it comes to anything sentimental or useful, we'll save it. A case could even be made for us being born with a genetic predisposition to want to hoard things, like paper, for instance. Right on, T'ang.

I Know It's Here Somewhere

Maybe at some time in your past you filed something away and were never able to find it again, and to this day you remain traumatized. Files can be like a black hole that things fall into. Once papers go into a filing cabinet, they are never seen or heard from again. Probably because you forget the headings you chose for them. With all that creativity, you can come up with several things you may have put them under. "I know I filed it, but I can't remember under what." Filing is a left-brain function: Linear, orderly, and logical. Divergent thinkers can come up with all kinds of subtopics that keep branching out. (This is good for brainstorming, bad for dealing with papers.) I have the solution to this filing fiasco, and it is this: Use your right-brain and ask it, "Where is the first place I would look for this paper if I need it again?" It only has to make sense to YOU.

File This!

Sometimes filing and putting papers away *are* a waste of time. It is so much easier to keep things out until they are done. But when projects that were completed when the Dodgers played in Brooklyn are still hanging around, it's time to start thinking about taking steps to control your paper-related clutter.

Know How

It's quite possible you never learned the three "r's" in dealing with paper. They deal with how to read, retain, and then recycle it. Some of us never learned the proper way to read/skim things so that we can determine what to do with the document when we're done. If we decide to retain paper, where should it go? Some of us have never learned how or found a system that works when it comes to paper—that one is no longer true. This chapter is loaded with suggestions, so read on.

FAST FACT

A survey of top-level executives at *Forbes 1000* companies found that the stock of messy-desk companies rose an average of 3.5 points while neat-desk stocks fell by one point.

PAPER PUSHERS

The problem with paper is that like a weed left unattended, it breeds, spreads, multiplies, and will cover all available space. It never lets up. Sure, to some a dandelion, which is a weed, is a thing of beauty. To others it is, well, a weed. Paper is relentless, it never lets up. As soon as you get rid of one piece, several more are there to take its place. The longer you wait, the worse it gets, and the longer it takes to get it under control. It grows, multiplying at an alarming rate. It seems like we spend more time than ever handling paper. Worse yet, we are making copies of it, spreading it around to others as well as hoarding it. It would seem the mantra for today is: "Do unto others, and leave a paper trail."

QUICK QUIZ

There's nothing wrong with your system if it works. Take this quick quiz. You know you have a problem when . . .

1. You can't put your hands on a piece of paper you are looking for in under ten minutes. (You can't find papers when you need them.)
2. You know you filed something, but you can't remember what you filed it under and you can't locate it anywhere. (This happens weekly.)
3. You know you may need this piece of paper someday, but you aren't sure where to file it, so you add it to the pile on the floor. (Which is now creating a fire hazard.)
4. You had to rent additional storage space to hold your papers. (Or, for the home-based business person, you can't park your car in the garage because it is being used for storing your papers.)
5. You have been passed over for promotions, lost clients, or were fired because of your lack of organization. (Or your chronic disorganization hinders your ability to function.)
6. Others have complained about lost papers, missed deadlines, and misplaced papers more than once in the past month.
7. You no longer feel in control. You're stressed out by your work environment.
8. You had to pay a fine or penalty because you either misplaced or were late paying a bill, invoice, or your taxes.
9. You're finding things weeks later that should have been done yesterday.
10. Others have given your piles of papers names like Mount Everest and Kilimanjaro.
11. You spend entire mornings shuffling papers from one pile to another but not really accomplishing anything of significance.
12. You have a reputation for losing things, not following through, and being inept.
13. People leave notes on your chair for fear that if they left them on your desk you'd lose them.

14. You have to go elsewhere to do your work because there is no "open space" in your office or studio. It's an uncomfortable environment that affects your peace of mind.

How many "Yes" answers did you give? More than a few and this chapter is really gonna help.

A TRUE STORY

Amy, a comedy club manager, complained that although she performed her job effectively, the club owner continually insinuated that she was a slob, disorganized, and that her office was a disgrace. No laughing matter. (She cracked jokes about it to me, but inside she was hurt.) While we were talking, her boss walked in and let her have it. She had had enough. With me there for support, she defended herself. "Ask me to find a paper. ANY paper. Go ahead," she challenged confidently. "Okay," he smugly replied. "Find me the letter from the American Cancer Society I asked you to follow up on." He winked at me as he stood there, arms crossed, smirking. Effortlessly, Amy reached into a giant pile of papers and pulled it out. The expression on his face was priceless. After he sulked away in silence, I said, "That was amazing. How did you do that?" (I was prepared for her, like any magician, to keep the trick a secret.) "It was easy," she said. "Since I was waiting for a call back from them, I knew it was in the pile near the phone with other paper awaiting a call. I also knew that it had been about a week since I had called them so it had to be about halfway down. Then it was just a matter of finding their letterhead color. Simple." She had a system, and it worked. Not all "messy's" are that efficient, though.

FAST FACT

It has been estimated that the average American worker has thirty-six hours' worth of work on his or her desk and wastes three hours a week just sorting through it.

THERE IS A SOLUTION

Creative clutter is better than tidy idleness.
                    —Unknown

Okay, it's time to talk about fixing our paper problems. When I say, "Fix it," I'm not talking about a major overhaul, just a minor tune-up to make things run a little smoother. It won't take much effort on your part, and the rewards of implementing some of these ideas alongside your own system can really help. First and foremost, a good paper-management system saves time and aids in your creativity. You won't have to crazily search through stacks of papers every time you need to find something. You won't lose things as often, and you won't be seen as forgetful and flaky. (As a bonus, others will be blown away.) You'll make fewer errors and be able to deal with details. Besides, it actually feels pretty wonderful to be organized, in control with some sense of order. You'll be the king of the hill (paper mountain). Paper will flow through without stagnating on the floor, credenza, and desk. When paper is moving, it encourages action, and action enhances creativity. If your system isn't working, don't be too hard on yourself. Nobody was born organized (or disorganized for that matter), and I know this isn't easy, but it's worth the effort. Thumbing your nose at this information (and at organizing in general) can feel good in the short run, but it eventually catches up to you in the form of unpaid parking tickets, missed opportunities, stress, and that nagging feeling that you are always forgetting something.

   It's also come to my attention that the reason filing was such a fiasco for me was that I had TOO MUCH paper to begin with, and it was bogging me down. I started by asking myself, "Is this paper replaceable?" (Most paper is replaceable, I have come to realize.) Is it relevant to what I want to do with my life? Some papers that others would say should go I saved because I know that some of these things are research and resources for my writing. Others I knew I had to toss. Consider this. Most of the papers that you are clinging to are obsolete and unnecessary. I know, I love to save paper, too. I have also come to realize that there is newer and better stuff available online, and the information I have saved is dated. "I'm feeling lucky" isn't just a phrase. It's a shortcut to online search success. Google allows you to find out almost anything in a matters of minutes. If you Google something, you have searched it. End of story. That's the goal of Google cofounder Sergei Brin. The beauty is that we don't need to save so much stuff. It's all out there when we need it. In less than half a second you can find almost anything, anytime, from anywhere in the world. It's amazing. I still go to the library, but the Internet is probably the most important tool a writer has at his disposal. There are a dictionary, phone book, newspapers, catalogs, and maps. I can find images, do special searches for products and quotations. It's the Yellow Pages, encyclopædia, and Social Registry all rolled into one.

ONE OF US: JANIS ISAMAN

"I used to have random papers all over the place. I bought a 9 × 12" clear Steralite box. Now when I get mail, information packets, and catalogs that I don't want to/don't have time to deal with, I put them in the box. Once a week I sort through the box and file the papers into various categories, including the recycle bin. It lets me spend time organizing when I have time and focus but keeps things clean if I don't. A big benefit is that if you need to clean up in a hurry, all the extra papers can be put into the box to create the illusion of cleanliness and control, but allow you to easily make sense of it after your visitor has departed!"

WHAT IS IDEAL?

What you do with a piece of paper is not nearly as important as doing it consistently.
                                                    —Barbara Hemphill

The ideal system to manage your paper flow and filing needs is visual (a few piles are okay), functional (you can find things quickly), comfortable (it feels natural and works the way you do, so you'll use it and maintain it), and it doesn't scare those around you. It allows you to get your work done, keeps track of those pesky little details, keeps paper moving, and allows you easy access to information, plus one other important aspect: it saves you time.

If you use your natural tendencies to your advantage, you have an edge over the so-called paper pushers. Neatniks can claim to be superior because they clear off their desks every night before they go home, but can they manage several different projects simultaneously, all in different stages, different areas, while thinking up two new ones, and chew gum? I think not. You are special, unique, so use this to your advantage when it comes to paper management. Here are some quick tips to help you get *started* taking control because once you've begun, you're halfway done.

1. Don't know where to begin? Choose the area that gives you the most trouble and concentrate your efforts there first. Or organize something easy and quick, like your purse or wallet. Win the battle with your desk, and you win the war with paper.

2. Break these things down. Right-brainers have a tendency to be all-or-nothing types. Do a little at a time rather than try taking on your whole office or home in a morning.

3. Cut paper off at the pass. Don't even let it into your life if you can help it.

4. Most of us know how to pay bills, write letters, sort mail, and file papers. The tough part is finding the time to do it consistently. Schedule a time to do it, and mark it in your calendar.

5. Try to make it more fun. Buy new and colorful supplies, ask a friend or coworker to help you get started. This way you have some support, and you can turn it into a party.

6. If you are really buried in paper, have a left-brain friend or coworker help get you started.

7. Allow yourself to do it quick and dirty at first. Don't force yourself to make too many tough decisions early on. It doesn't have to be perfect. Keep it simple and flexible at first.

MAIL STORM

To get more organized I need to write my appointments down. I don't have anyone's addresses. I'd like to send out Christmas cards, but I need addresses to do that.

—Claire Danes

We spend eight months of our lives opening junk mail. Even though e-mail marketing (spam) is growing, we still get a lot of unsolicited mail—and it's not going to let up anytime soon. According to the Direct Marketing Association, catalog sales in 1991 were just under $50 billion. (Yes, that is BILLION.) In 2001 catalog sales exceeded $100 billion. Paper skills are needed now and in the future. There are, however, several things you can do, in combination, to stay on top of all the papers that come your way.

1. **Dump it.** Junk mail accounts for 3 percent of landfills. That's where most of what is delivered to your house and office belongs. Get a big trash can and a shredder and get rid of as much useless paper as possible. Ask yourself, "Will this paper make me wealthier? Happier? Wiser?" If not, see ya.

2. **Strip it.** Forty percent of junk mail is never even opened. That's the ticket. Don't even let mail in the house. Strip it down to the bare essentials over the trash or shredder. For example, when you get an invitation or notice, make a note on your calendar and toss everything but the details and directions. Keep a report summary but toss the report itself after you have read it. Put a stamp on a bill and note the date it's due. Better yet, simplify. Begin by only using one credit card, one checking account, join fewer clubs that offer newsletters, and *try* to choose medical plans that won't bury you in paperwork.

3. **Recycle it.** Look for creative ways to eliminate paper from your life. Recycle as much as you can. A classic organizing tip is to write a reply on a letter or memo and send it back. My friend Mike Metz reused the front of a cool greeting card I sent him for his birthday as a thank-you card. He simply cut off the cover and wrote on the back sending it to me as a postcard. Clever.

4. **Do it.** Act on a piece of paper right away if possible. Don't put it down if you can deal with it in a minute or two. If you set it aside, before you know it you have a pile that lives there for months. Don't waste time thinking about where to put it; take the time to tackle it.

5. **Post it.** If you have a big-enough bulletin board you can pin bills and things on it that need a reply. Set a section aside for things to do by the end of the month and another for reminders of less pressing papers.

6. **Collect it.** Do you get easily distracted and leave mail scattered all over your house? Are you losing letters and having problems finding bills that need payment? Do you simply leave mail wherever you open it? Go postal. Emulate what they do at the post office. Deal with the mail daily, and don't let it pile up. Carry it from the box and walk it to the trash, sift through and thin out the junk mail, and then sort out each family member's mail and put it in a pile for that person. Make a mini post office in your home, complete with all the tools needed to handle mail, including stamps, a scale, envelopes, paper, a trash can, plus any other supplies you need. (Make the place where it piles up the place you deal with it.)

7. **Pay it.** One Orange County man was caught in an automated speed trap that measured his car's speed using radar and photographed his car. He later received a ticket for forty dollars and a photo of his car. Instead of payment, he sent the police a photograph of two twenty-dollar bills. Several days later he received a letter from the police that contained another picture—a pair of handcuffs. How about this? Andy Rooney finds the junk mail inserted in with bills so distasteful that he puts garbage (coffee grounds, orange peels) in with the check when he mails it—he writes, "Could you throw this away for me? Thank you." If you can, pay bills as they come in. The interest you would have earned at today's rates isn't worth one late payment fee.

8. **Stop it.** The best way to get a handle on paper in your life is to have less of it to deal with. Get off mailing lists and cancel subscriptions for publications you don't read. When you receive an unsolicited catalog or offer in the mail, send the label back along

with a form letter demanding they remove you from their list. (By law, they must reply.) Don't encourage others to write reports that you will eventually have to read, file, and respond to. Instead, ask for a verbal summary, e-mail version, or a recording you can listen to in your car.

9. **Read it.** File less of what you read. The goal is to read and retain, then toss it or send it to a friend.

10. **Don't do it.** As strange as this sounds, there are actually people out there who enjoy doing paperwork. Find them and ask for their help. Get an intern or assistant to help you with mundane paperwork or to go through and sort mail and respond to routine requests. Do what you do best and delegate the rest. Eliminate worthless, duplicate, or pointless paperwork now. Be an advocate for simplifying your company's paperwork. Always ask yourself, "Is this the best use of my time and talents?"

11. **Download it.** Internet access can reduce the amount of mail you have to deal with. Read the paper, pay bills, and answer letters online.

12. **Limit it.** When doing research, realize going in that you can't possibly get it all. It is easy to get off-track and collect more information than you need or could ever use. Decide on a cutoff date, page count, or pile height to decide when enough is enough.

RECYCLE AND SAVE A TREE

The other day I got a chain saw in the mail. Now I have to send chain saws to ten other people. The postage is gonna kill me.

—Brian McKim

Maybe you can't completely eliminate paper from your life, but you CAN eliminate *unnecessary* papers. Get rid of papers that aren't relevant to what you do, who you are now, who you want to be, and what you want to do in the future. Paper costs you money to store, time to shuffle or file, and your sanity when it gets out of hand. So ask yourself, "If I throw this paper out, what's the worst thing that could happen?" If the answer is "Nothing," then freakin' do it because paper, unlike wine, does NOT improve with age. If this sounds difficult to you, enlist the help of a nonjudgmental friend to encourage you to toss, toss, toss. Start by getting rid of dated and duplicate stuff. Then try to get some of this information into your computer or on disk. Toss the old business cards you entered in your mailing-list program, or scan receipts you need to save but don't have room to file. Before you give me your excuses, let me assure you, I get it. I'm "old school" and prefer paper to many forms of communicating, transacting, and, especially, reading. Thinning out my piles of paper was the most difficult, but also the most rewarding, thing I did to get organized.

PHAT IS WHERE IT'S AT

There are really only four things to do with paper. Here's the skinny (which I call "PHAT"). You can PILE/FILE, HORDE, ACT, or TOSS paper. PILE/FILE = Have a pile for things that should be filed. HOARD = These are papers that you can't part with, but you probably won't need. Archive them in a (marked) box somewhere out of the way. ACT = Have separate piles for things to pay, do, read, or give to others. TOSS = A nice big circular file (trash) nearby. If you have any papers that don't fit into any of these four categories, start a junk drawer and throw in the papers you aren't sure what to do with yet. Every couple of months deal with it or simply dump it.

DEAL WITH IT

Changing the way you deal with paper means going outside your comfort zone. It's a little scary. Give these ideas some time before deciding they are or aren't working for you.

* Notice where papers seem to keep piling up. It happens so subtly at first. Take your purse, the car, or any countertop as an example. Before you know it, your wallet is bulging at the seams with old receipts and scraps of paper with questionable phone numbers, the glove box is crammed full of napkins and expired coupons, and the counter is lined with unopened mail and various take-out menus. How did this happen? It doesn't matter; deal with these first.

- Adding more space to accommodate more paper isn't the answer. It's just like people who say, "If only I made more money, I'd save more." We all know what happens. The more they make, the more they spend. Same with paper. The more room you have to hoard it, the more paper you will save. I got rid of a four-drawer filing cabinet to force myself to get rid of old papers that truly were outdated. It's quite freeing, actually.

- Be realistic about how you deal with paper clutter. Neat is not the goal, nor is perfection. What you want is organized—and what that means is an individual thing.

- Take five minutes a day to deal with what has accumulated on your desk. Pick the perfect time for you—whether that is morning, noon, or night. Just make it a (good) habit to tackle your piles of papers once a day.

- Do two things at once. Sort the mail while on the phone, read reports while in line at the coffee shop, or sign off on papers while waiting for the printer to warm up. While talking on the phone, go through your in-box. Many paper-related tasks don't need your best effort. Just do it quickly without concern for neatness, creativity, the perfect font alignment, or punctuation. Just keep moving that paper along.

- The 80/20 rule applies really well with paper. It seems that we never look at 80 percent of what we file again. So when deciding whether to save and file a piece of paper, make certain it is in the 20 percent of paper that has lasting value.

- Make additional copies of papers that others always seem to need. After the third time someone asks for a copy of that report on the many uses for elephant dung, print out a dozen more. It's easier than making a copy each time you get a request. Also, when things are in two places, place a note in the pile or file that there are more and where they are filed.

- Date and put notes on paperwork when you first look at it. Note where you would look for it if you filed it (if that's where it'll end up). Note any action that should be taken. Do all this on the first read through and it will save you time later when you come back to the paper again. Highlight areas of key points; or if you think of something related, mark it in the margin (not on another piece of paper, puleeze).

- Match your mood. After completing a big project—like writing a book—it's (almost) a pleasure to deal with paper-related problems. Take a day or two (when you won't be interrupted) to catch up on paperwork.

- Color-code the paper with a colored dot. A red dot could mean urgent, a green dot file, and blue do not file when done.

- Keep that paper moving in the right direction. Dealing with paper isn't about activity, it's about results. Just moving a piece of paper from one pile to another is not necessarily progress, unless you are moving it closer to its final destination. Eliminate it, sort it, file it, act on it—whatever needs to be done—but try not to let it hang around too long.

- Try jotting things to do, remember, or research on index cards. I find working with index cards preferable to paper in many cases. This book was researched, outlined, and written using 5 × 8" index cards that were sorted into piles and eventually filed by chapter and category, using divider tabs in an index card file.

JEEPERS KEEPERS

What papers should you keep? Resources: Keep what you WANT. Records: Keep what you HAVE to keep.

YOUR MOST VALUABLE ASSET

Success comes down to who you know, and who knows you.
                                                    —Unknown

Mailing lists are full of people who can make your dreams come true, so get your "ACT!" together. Contacts are what your business is all about. Family and friends are what your life is about. Staying in touch with them is so important. Organize these names and addresses in a meaningful way, using contact management software, a Rolodex, or whatever method works for you. If you don't get a handle on this valuable tool, you won't get the benefits. The key is to keep track of everyone in your personal and professional life. Your mailing list is one of your most valuable assets, and you should treat it as such. The problem is it's a pain in the neck to keep current. There is nothing right-brain about entering in names and numbers. Find a way to force yourself to update (and back up) this important asset.

TRUE STORY

I made a wall chart for frequent flyer programs. I travel a great deal as a lecturer, many times on a different airline. So I listed all the airlines I hold frequent flyer cards for, how many miles I have accumulated (in pencil), and how many are required for a free trip. Now, with a quick glance I can see how I'm doing, and it takes a second to update.

STRANGE FACT

Dr. Lew Begley, a retired physician, has "collected" an unbelievable four hundred thousand back issues of *National Geographic* magazine.

WHAT'S BLACK AND WHITE AND READ ALL OVER?

The next best thing to knowing something is knowing where to find it.
                                                        —Samuel Johnson

A mom and dad found an S&M magazine under their eleven-year-old son's bed. After debating over the punishment they should give the kid, the father said, "Well, we sure can't spank him, can we?" If we kept all our reading material underneath the bed, we would be better off. Not counting books, I bet you have publications all over your house and office. My wife "reads" several different periodicals, and I find them everywhere. (After scanning some of these women's magazines, I am no closer to understanding them than I was before. If anything I'm more confused than ever!) It's a myth that having a ton of articles around makes you smarter. I will say, if you read (and retain) the information you are ahead of the game. But when I say retain, I mean in your brain. I don't mean keep the reading matter around.

My wife was "encouraged" to buy several subscriptions from her boss's daughter to help raise money for some cause. So we are now responsible for the cutting down of three trees a month for the privilege of receiving magazines with articles on how to be better hosts, get more from our love life, and learn the curious details of Jennifer Lopez and Ben Affleck's wonderful life. At first I designated a drawer to hold the overflow, but the onslaught of these advertisement-laden women's magazines quickly consumed us. I then started stacking the current issues on the coffee table only to discover some of my male friends engrossed in articles about how to please a man. Disturbing to say the least. We have since canceled a couple of these subscriptions because my wife (and friends) felt obligated to read them even though they had no redeeming value. We finally had to buy a magazine holder for all these "positive" publications.

I think it's easier to find what I need when I need it online or at the library. I no longer feel the need to save as much research and reading material. Most of the things I used to squirrel away are rarely looked at ever again. Information becomes obsolete so fast now. How much time would it take for you to read all the publications you have piled up? Is it worth it? Will you honestly ever find the time to read through all that old and outdated stuff? Wouldn't you rather read what's new? Why not just keep the current and previous month's issues? Newspapers are fish wrap after a few days.

I don't know about this so-called paperless society stuff. It seems to me there is as much paper as ever. If not more. Maybe someday there will be no need to use money, have business cards, or write checks. Maybe we'll all have our own bar-coded number tattooed on our foreheads, and they can scan it for everything. Fortunately, this day isn't around the corner. There's a lot of paper out there, and more on its way. Here's how to handle reading materials.

Be Selective

Right-brainers have millions of interests, thus there is more we want to read. Let go of your need to know everything about everything. You can't possibly read or retain all the information that you receive. If you miss something, don't worry that you'll be left in the dust. Chances are you won't. Don't feel guilty. How much room do you have in your head and house for this stuff anyway? Stay current only in areas of interest and importance. Take yourself off lists for free publications to resist temptation. By the way, the three magazines Americans read most (according to *Adweek*) are: *Parade, Modern Maturity,* and *Reader's Digest.*

Ditch Duplicates

If you find it hard to part with your old publications, start by getting rid of duplicate magazines, papers, reports, and printouts. Then get rid of items that you haven't looked at in years. Pass old magazines on to others. Give back issues to the library, doctor, dentist, a school, friends, a retirement home. Recycle the rest.

A Page a Day

Try to set aside a little time each day to do a little reading. Take reading material outside. Faxes, newsletters, and memos can be read in a hammock, coffee shop, boat (unless you get seasick), by a pool, at the park, while waiting, working out, before bed, or the most common time of all . . . in the bathroom. Create a "to read" box, file, or basket. Put it by the door and grab something to read as you leave.

Daily Briefings

I was in the market to buy a big-ticket item and my buddy had read all the reviews and kept all the catalogs from when he bought his. So I had him brief me on what was best. Have you ever considered letting others do the research and reading (and keep all the clutter) and then have them give you a synopsis? Try it.

Online News

Read the paper online and download info to a file on your hard drive if you have to. This eliminates a lot of paper (and ink smudges in your home).

Create an Index

When reading, take notes and highlight as you go. This saves time having to go back and read everything again. Better yet, make notes from the book you're reading on index cards and create a cheat sheet of the top points (along with the corresponding page numbers). That way, when you want to refresh your memory or review what you've read, all you have to do is read the cards instead of rereading the entire book. (The card also serves as a bookmark.)

Rip and Read

Consider that 60 percent of magazines are ads and are worthless. Rip out good stuff and toss the rest.

Look Sharp

With a Sharpie write on the magazine cover the page numbers of the articles you want to read. If the cover is too cluttered with busty women, attach a sticky note. Put an expiration date on the magazine.

Mass Media

Instead of saving entire articles with reporters' e-mail addresses and contact information, I cut out the address or e-mail address at the bottom and staple or tape it to pages in a binder to create my own media guide. I also started a sheet I call my activist list, with people I can contact to help me clean up San Diego. I enter their name in my contact manager, staple their card in my Rolodex, or just write down their contact information on a page in my resource binder.

Nice Rack

Magazine racks are the answer for long-term storage. Group the same kind of magazines in the holder and label the side facing out. Stack back issues in piles based on the periodical.

Out with the Old

For most catalogs I keep the current one and toss the old version.

Block Buster

When I am looking for new ideas, I like to look through my old magazines for inspiration. Having a well-stocked library can be very helpful.

MAKE A MAGAZINE

Buy an expanding file for sorting and saving articles. Tear out what you want to read and file it under "To Read." The other pockets and tabs can be for "Recipes" or "Design Tips" or "Health and Fitness" or "Sex" or whatever categories you can come up with. In a way what you are creating is your own "Best Of" magazine with you as the editor. You can also have an advertising section where you keep coupons and things to buy. Keep movie reviews and recommendations in one section. Carry your expanding file with you when you are on the road or (and this is a big if) keep it in the bathroom if that's where you prefer to read.

MANUAL MADNESS

One of the weaknesses with my filing/piling system was manuals. I wasn't consistent. Some were with the item (taped to the side of the washer or underneath the stereo) and others were in the box the thing came in, receipts were filed away for tax purposes, and still others were, well, I wasn't sure. Then I created a binder with clear pockets to hold the manuals and was able to divide them up by room and stapled the receipt to the manual and warranty information. This was also effective because it was portable. Saving all this stuff has helped me to sell everything from my old laptop to my home gym. Without the manual they would have been harder to use or assemble.

GOT PAPER?

While holding a piece of paper in hand, ask the following questions. Hang these questions where you can see them.

- Do I really need to keep this? (Is this something new that I don't know? Is it current and relevant? Is it easy to replace? Is it stored somewhere else? What's the worst thing that would happen if I toss it?)
- What's the next action I need to take with this piece of paper? (This tells you what to do with it.) Where would I look for this? (This tells you where to put this.) What is the first word that pops into my head related to this paper? (This tells you how to label a file.)

"PILING" CABINETS: FOR PEOPLE WHO PREFER
TO PILE PAPER

A filing system based on intuitive logic: Old letters from Mother are filed under
CATASTROPHES, and old love letters are filed (naturally) under IMPORTANT
DOCUMENTS.

—Lorraine Bodger

A friend bragged to me that he kept his most important papers in a safe and accessible place. I had to ask, "Where is that?" His reply surprised me. "I keep them on the floor, of course." If you want to look busy and appear important, make sure your office appears swamped. Your desk should look like you are engaged in a project of the utmost importance. The difference between controlled chaos and just plain disorganized is having the papers on your desk arranged in stacks and the ability to explain your piling system when pressed. For a final touch put your glasses on top of a pile.

When it comes to a system to take control of paper clutter, the easier the better. This will probably entail some piling of papers. Here are some simple guidelines to help you get a grip on this area of chaos so that you know what paper is where (whether it's in a pile or a file). What's important is that you are able to put your hands on a piece of paper when you need it. Think about it. When it comes to paper, if you don't know you have it or you can't find it, it is of no value to you. Some people can't find things that they have filed away, so who is to say making piles isn't preferable? (Certainly not me.) Having a system (any system) to manage your papers means you keep most of it moving and save the most relevant, important, and valuable papers and put them in a place that makes sense to you. So it stands to reason that less paper equals less stress. Then organize what's left in some system that you understand and will embrace. Urgent, current, and important papers are out, and the rest are kept out of the way (but still organized so you can find things quickly and easily). This will likely be a combination of piling and filing (with an emphasis on piling).

We have to focus on the most important papers and be willing to let go of the rest. We can't get ahead if we treat all papers equally. Put a higher priority on important papers. It's partly about geography—put papers that matter most or are most pressing near where you use them. Old and less important papers go elsewhere, and junk paper goes in the trash.

Piles can work when there is a method to your "madness." (It may look like madness to others, but if you know what each pile has in it and can find what you need, then it's fine.) You probably should start by looking for common themes among loose papers and group them together by category and priority. For example, "hot" piles are for items that you must do or should have done yesterday. Keep these close by. "Warm" piles are for papers you should do, but that can wait till later. These stay visible and nearby. Then there are "cool" piles for projects that are waiting for inspiration or information from others. There are the "cold" piles for papers that need to be filed or tossed. You may also have a pile for things to read that you will scoop up and take with you. Make piles per project or per person. What you don't want to be doing is pushing paper around from pile to pile. It's a waste of your talents and energy—plus the paper never leaves.

PERFECT PILES
Here are some creative ideas to make piling an art form. Check off the things you want to try out on your piles of paper.

Focus on the Positive   □
A pile of papers on your desk can be a distraction as it gathers dust (especially when they are unfinished or unresolved). Here's a great idea. Put some kind of positive reinforcements on the top of each pile.

Get a Spine   □
When you have stacks of paper and files for various projects and purposes, wrap a large piece of paper around each grouping and create a spine. Now you can label each area of your pile and with a quick glance get a clue as to what's in the stack.

Clipped   □

For a lot of loose pieces of paper, use a clipboard. You can have one for each area of your life or each project you are working on. Label each clip so you know which is which and hang them on the wall. Underneath the various (but related) scraps of paper clipped together can be a pad of paper that acts like a master list of things to do and remember.

In the Zone   □

Divide your desk into quadrants and pile by zones. For example, a pile on top of a filing cabinet is folders and papers waiting to be filed. This way the pile is in a place that makes sense, and it has been moved closer to its final resting place. (Of course you keep spare folders and a Sharpie nearby to make filing and labeling easier.) You may also want to designate different drawers to throw papers in. Label and limit each to one topic or type of information. You can control the chaos by setting some parameters for height and space designated for each pile. Maybe you keep piles limited to one table, for example. When it starts to spill over, go through and thin out, throw out, and straighten up the piles. One thing that works for me is to designate one space for unfinished projects and the papers that go with them. Everything that goes there isn't hanging over my head this way.

I Can See Clearly Now   □

Put piles in clear containers. This works because you can see what's inside, they are portable (take papers with you to tackle at home, at the beach, or the park), and piles don't topple over when you put the lid on. With containers you can sort papers by action, project, priority, or whatever you want, and left-brainers honestly believe we are neat and clean. Ha! A clear plastic rack on the wall puts papers up where you can see them and clears off counters and other surfaces. You can also achieve similar results by placing wicker baskets on top of your desk or on the floor.

Think *Inside* the Box   □

Author J. K. Rowling (Think: *Harry Potter*) puts her papers in open boxes and marks the outside (with a numbering system) so she knows basically what's inside. Rowling likes this system because she still has to shuffle through the papers in each box to find what she's looking for, which will usually trigger an inspiration or idea. Anyone can use boxes for managing overflowing papers. Put projects in progress in a series of bins and boxes; do the same for things that are completed and need to be archived—just be sure to label the outside. For current papers an open box close at hand is best. For long-term papers create a dead storage like the police have for old case files. The papers are still there if you want to "reopen a case," but they are not taking up valuable space "in the precinct." Only "open cases" are kept in your office. I boxed up my notes and research from my older books and put them in my garage. I put an expiration date on the outside of the box and after a few years tossed them because the information was dated.

It's a Sign   □

Take a piece of letter-size paper, fold it in half, and make a tent that will stand out on top of a pile as a label. This way others can see what's where, and it forces you to group like items together—both of which are important points. If you don't do that, having a cover page for each pile works almost as well. Some other ways to make things stand out in a horizontal format (piles) is to label the bottom of a file folder so you can see it when it's buried in a pile. Try flagging important files with a bookmark that sticks out and stands out. Use construction paper to indicate its level of importance or area of concern and/or label it. You can use this bookmark also as a checklist of things to do, a notepad/brain dump, or include key information on it for fast reference.

Hot, Hot, Hot   □

Active papers belong in the action pile. This includes things to read, sign, copy, enter, discuss, pay, write, respond to, and so on. The active pile is not the place to keep papers that have exceeded their shelf life by being completed or becoming irrelevant. "Hot" piles are for active projects. When you add a reminder in your calendar to tackle these unfinished tasks, you have a pretty polished system—no matter what it looks like to others. The advanced version of this idea is to pile according to project and then prioritize within the pile. Some people use bright-colored paper as a type of cover letter to indicate where a project is in its cycle. For instance, I print drafts of my books on different-colored paper so that I quickly know if the papers are a first draft (yellow), second draft (cream), or a final draft (white). Also, use different-colored folders for different projects so you can see a file at a glance.

The Basics   □

The same rules apply to piling as they do in the rest of the book. For instance, when making a pile, put the larger stuff on the bottom (book or binder) with the smaller stuff (disk or sticky note) on top. Group like things together with everything related to a person, project, or thing in one place (a pile or file). If you are overwhelmed by the sheer amount of paper piled up around you, tackle it one pile at a time.

Stay Close   □

Pile papers where you'll need them—recipes in the kitchen, coupons in the car, art ideas in your studio, computer-related papers near the computer, and bills where your stamps, checks, and envelopes are. If you use something once a week (papers, directories, instructions), pile it within reach. If a project or paper is done, move it closer to its final resting place. Keep papers that contain a possible solution close at hand in a big pile near you so you can rifle through them from time to time.

Hold It Together   □

Something as simple as squaring-up piles can make your office or home look more presentable. To keep them that way try using supersized rubber bands. They are perfect for keeping piles of papers and publications together. Rubbermaid makes a visual organizer called the "project keeper" for loose papers. It lies flat and has pockets that allow you to label them. They overlap so you can see them all at a glance. Of course you can simply staple and fasten relevant papers together so you can grab and go. Try putting a colored ribbon around your piles, suggests interior designer Kristine Porter. To reduce the amount of little (read: lost) pieces of paper, copy your small scraps onto one single page. How about shrinking papers down on a copier and doubling up?

Pad the Pile ☐
I read that at HP you could leave projects out so others might shuffle through them and offer suggestions. I'm sure you don't want others peeking at your papers (so why leave them out?), but a notepad on top of each pile is for YOU to add ideas as you think of them or to create a "table of contents" for the papers in the pile. If your boss insists that you clear your desk, put a pad of paper on your desk and write down where you put everything for the next day. If you want even less paper in your life, enter this information on a sticky note *inside* your computer.

A Treasure Chest ☐
Seretta Martin, a poet, wrote me saying she has a large file box where she likes to toss all those scraps of paper that have the potential of becoming a poem or story. She calls this box her "treasure chest." To her it's an important place she can turn to when she wants to rekindle the moment when the "muse" struck and an idea was born or to give herself a lift or "kick start." In her treasure chest is everything from random papers to snippets of poems that are unfinished.

Put Your Piles on a Diet ☐
Go through piles every day. Pull out folders and papers that are most pressing and put them in prominent positions. Or try this: one weekend pretend that you are moving and clean out and organize each pile by breaking big piles into mini piles. It's easier to manage paper piles when you divide them into subpiles and sort them by category. For instance, you have piles of papers you are currently working with. Keep these piles close by. There are probably papers that are there for reference purposes. These papers are not used daily but frequently and should be piled nearby but out of the way. For the person who loves to save everything, there will be papers that are rarely needed but could come in

handy *someday* down the road. These should be boxed up or filed away and kept elsewhere. Mine are in the garage with an expiration date on them so I know when to toss them. Label these boxes and group like items together so you can find what you need without too much trouble. Finally, there are papers that are a waste of space (you'll never need them) and these go in the "circular file."

Undecided ☐

In publishing, editors create what is known as a "slush pile." This consists of unsolicited manuscripts (those not sent in by literary agents). Every once in a great while these manuscripts are read and a bestselling book is discovered. Anyone can create a "slush" pile. This is where you throw papers you don't think you will want again, but you aren't absolutely sure yet. Keep a box near the door—which is one step closer to the trash. Go through it from time to time and pull out anything of value, but basically this is where your junk papers go to die. If you can't part with some of these papers, put a mark on each piece of paper every time you look at it. At the end of the month you can decide whether papers with no marks are worth saving. You may also want to do this with papers you can't decide what to do with or don't know where to put. (Throw them in a box and review the contents regularly.) To determine file categories, go through these papers and see what comes up. You will quickly notice categories like things to pay, people to call, papers to save or file.

The Pending Pile ☐

Here's how to have a clutter-free desk the right-brain way. Using a box or a big drawer, drag everything on your desk into it at the end of the day. Put the most important stuff on top to begin the day with. If that seems too crazy, leave papers out on your desk, but keep them in file folders so that you appear to be living with less clutter.

Gone, but Not Forgotten ☐

One well-known writer was sued on several occasions over the years and has prevailed each time because he saved all the paperwork related to each of his nonfiction books. I have been audited by the IRS three times and was able to prevail because I could produce all my past paperwork related to my deductions. I put all of my receipts with my returns and used a variety of storage solutions over the years including shoe boxes, various containers, giant envelopes, accordion files, and bankers boxes. The key was to keep everything together and archived by year. I keep the past two years close by and save several years' worth in the garage. Set up a long-term solution for papers and projects that are not active but that you need to save. This could be a filing cabinet in the garage or file boxes out of the way. Label and put an expiration date on the boxes or file and toss them when they expire.

To File or Not to File? □

Good question. Although this section is about piling, I have to confess that there also good reasons to file paper in conjunction with your piles. A filing cabinet is still the best place for loose papers that are not needed on a regular basis and aren't currently in use. I know, you would prefer to put paper in a pile or in a drawer in your desk. This works with a small amount of paper, but if a blizzard during the busy season brings in a bunch of paper, it can easily overwhelm even the best piling system. I discovered that the problem with piling is you may reach a point where it's not working, mostly because too much stuff is out. This defeats the whole idea of a visual system. That's why I bought a couple of top-quality filing cabinets and just did it. There are hanging file folders clearly labeled with logical categories and subcategories in each drawer. That's right, I file. I know, it seemed impossible a few months ago, but when it came to this very book, I bit the bullet. It would have been almost impossible to gather all of the research and then retrieve it without the filing cabinets.

ASK A PRO: EVELYN GRAY, PROFESSIONAL ORGANIZER

"Can't see all the files on your desk because of the clutter? Smile and pile. Here's a hint to see a file ten feet away (but you have to have your glasses on if you need to see distance). Crease the bottom of the manila part of the folder (½") and write the name of the folder with a Sharpie (no pens or pencils—can't see). Stack each folder horizontally on your desk, and you can see exactly what you want at a glance. (Of course, organizers prefer files standing vertically so they're easily viewed.)"

FAST FACT
No piece of paper can be folded more then seven times.

SINGLE FILE
It's not how fast you can file it, it's how fast you can find it that counts.
                                            —Unknown

After John was awakened by his wife hitting him on the head, he screamed, "What did you do that for?" His wife replied, "I found a scrap of paper with the name Mary Lou on it." John quickly replied, "That's the name of the horse from the races last week." "Oh, I'm so sorry," his wife said. A week later John's wife clobbered him again. "What did I do this time?" John asked. With her hands on her hips, John's wife screamed at him, "Your horse just called!" This is why you don't want to leave everything out in the open. The answer is (don't cheat on your spouse and) file important papers away. It's almost as easy to file as to pile if you have a system set up that makes sense to you. I know, easier said than done. We have tried and the results are fragments of several different filing systems—none of which worked. Why is this? We are afraid if we put paper away, we will forget about it. The truth is, we probably never look at 95 percent of the stuff we save. Another reason we don't file stems from indecision and fear. We aren't sure where to put paper and fear we will put things in the wrong file and they will be lost forever. The result: Papers pile up. All your papers can't be kept in clear view. A few items out in the open are okay, but eventually your office becomes cluttered and overcrowded.

You would think filing would appeal to us. We love to squirrel away paper and this is a pretty effective way to do it. Right-brainers can set up a filing system. I have seen it happen. "If one man can another man can!" screamed Anthony Hopkins in the film *The Edge*. I believe that. The secret to a successful filing system is to think of it as an extension of your brain. When you do this it will work as well, if not better, than piling papers. You will be able to find papers quickly and easily; and with less stuff lying around, you'll have room to move. When we are honest with ourselves about which papers will help us reach our goals (and which ones won't), we can better decide what's valuable and worth recalling. So we save only the best and forget the rest. Your files are not trash receptacles or recycling bins. Want fewer things filed? Try this. Either act on a piece of paper, put it in a file folder, or throw it out.

HOW TO FILE

Step one, get some file folders, a pen or label maker, and file boxes or a cabinet. Next, brew a pot of coffee. If you are afraid of what you'll find, invite a friend over to help. One woman and her friend decided to make the process more fun, so they dressed up as superheroes before diving in to save the day. If you are alone, turn on the radio or television for company. Ready? Okay, here we go. Dump everything out and weed through it. So the first step is to ask yourself if you should even file it. If you decide to keep it, ask yourself where you would look for it if you needed it again. What is the first word that pops into mind or your gut reaction to where you'd look for it if you needed it? Or ask yourself when and where you might need this and under what circumstances. My rule of thumb is if paper goes in more than one place, put it where you would look first. File stuff according to how you'd use it. Premark files with sticky notes so you can change your mind without ruining a folder. Avoid setting things aside. (You may have to put some papers aside that don't fit a category and soon they will form their own.) Devise a simple sorting system that uses baskets, containers, files, piles—whatever works. I put papers into bankers boxes, which equal about one drawer, so you can see what you'll need in the way of file cabinets. Sort into broad categories. When piles get too high, create subcategories. Then sort papers into workable piles based on these categories. These categories can include papers related to your everyday life (household) and include finances, bills, medical, warranties, etc. There are papers that are more for fun and these include plans, recipes, decorating ideas, hobbies. Reference-related papers and booklets include information and tips on fitness, catalogs, manuals, travel, maps, computers, kids' stuff. Business is for your career or business. Organizations for associations, charities, clubs. You may have a separate file for your spouse to keep these things separate. Old and dead files are for things you think you may need when pigs fly and hell freezes over. For example, you may need to keep papers of importance but not important enough to clog up your regular system: old tax returns, receipts, correspondence.

Don't Reinvent the Wheel

Saving resources for future reference is as simple as A, B, C. Since decisions about what goes where can be overwhelming and paralysis by analysis sets in, maybe we don't need to reinvent the wheel (even though that's what we do best). Creating an A to Z filing system still works for filing papers. A friend of mine proudly showed me her filing system for source material. Creativity materials are arranged so she can quickly find stuff where before she would go through piles of papers looking for a font, graphic, or layout idea. Now she skims magazines and catalogs and pulls pages with ideas she wants to save and sorts them alphabetically ("Fonts," "Colors," "Layouts," "Illustrations," "Photos," and so on). She can quickly locate the inspiration to bust through a block without breaking her creative flow. Some old rules about filing ("Rules—we don't need no stinkin' rules") are there to help not hinder us. Take straight-line filing, for example. I tried to do it the staggered way, but if I made one change the whole pattern was screwed up. I learned the hard way, so you don't have to. I can now highlight a key file or section by setting it off to the left. I also used to cram my files into the drawers of my filing cabinet. I created custom-colored tabs to divide them up. A professional organizer friend insisted that hanging files are the ONLY way to go. As much as I hate to admit this, she was right. Keep file folders handy so you do it as soon as you start a new project and add a file for tabs and filing supplies.

I'm Seeing Red

Howard Meyer contributed this organizing tip. He suggests color coding your files, saying that color coding is one of the easiest ways to make a good paperwork system better as it speeds up filing and retrieving documents. It's much easier to spot files on a messy desk. Colored folders and folder tabs help to quickly identify and find documents when they are in stacks, and it helps him recognize where to put them when they need to go back into a filing cabinet. Color coding your files works because you can quickly and visually know what the red file means and where it goes. Use colored files for each area of your business or home. These may be broad categories, but you should be able to instantly identify which category a file goes into by its color. Make a cheat-sheet chart with a swatch or square of each color and what it represents and hang it from one of the handles of your filing cabinet. You can also use a marker to put a colored dot on a piece of paper so that you'll know where it goes when the time comes to put it away.

Toolbox

My brother Scott does not have neat penmanship. In fact, he created a new font without even knowing it. It's called, "Huh?" For him using a label maker was a necessity. Filing cabinets are an investment for a lifetime and worth every penny so get a good one. As for what goes inside, get products that apply to your way of working and the types of things you need to file. If you have a lot of bulky information, deep files are best because everything can still stay in one folder. If you need to travel or take papers with you, a hanging, expandable file will work. It fits in a desk drawer or standard file cabinet, plus it's portable. If you have a lot of loose things, go with box-bottom files with pockets for small papers or disks. Think how you file and what you'll need (and use) is a personal preference. There are other filing systems for smaller papers like a recipe box or a 5 × 8" index card box with dividers for birthday cards, thank you cards, and blank cards. A fireproof safe for important papers, valuables, photos, disks, and for jewelry is almost a necessity.

Let's Travel to the "Topics"

Think of files like a grocery store. They have aisles with categories that are as simple and broad as possible. Within those rows are related items. What I'm saying is don't overorganize, and for once don't get too creative and make it confusing. (Do use colors to code each section.) Here's how to do it. Broad categories like "Insurance" will have subcategories like

"Life," "Health," or "Car." You will have a hanging folder for your car labeled "Ferrari" and everything related to that car goes in its own file
folder. There would be one for registration, another for repairs, and a
third for financing information. You may have a broad category called
clients, but you'll divide that up (alphabetically) for each one. I make a
file for each group I speak to and inside are my notes for the talk and
anything worth saving, so the next time I have to call or follow up I have
a record of past correspondence, calls, e-mails, and things to do. You can
also sort by category. "Hobbies" is a hanging file with manila folders for
crafts, gardening, music, Web site design.

Outside the Lines

Write frequently needed numbers and info on the outside of a file folder.
Put a list of things to do right there, too. You can add stickers or color on
the file folders for quick reference. Tabs can be artful, too. Make the
names of the files more enticing. The same person who said you can't
color outside the lines likely said that the outside of a file folder must
stay clean and free of writing. What's wrong with writing notes to yourself right on the file folder? That way when you pull it, key information
is handy and visible. Put sticky notes, ideas, sketches, things to remember, mind maps, phone numbers, access codes, whatever you want on
the folder.

Go with Your Gut

If you file by gut instinct and intuition, the key is to continue to do so.
Be consistent. Title your files based on how you will look for them, not
how you store them. Organizer Karen Roehl says, "Use titles that speak
to your soul." For instance, she suggests using "Creative Contacts" rather
than "Networking." Sounds a lot more enticing, doesn't it? When unsure
where paper or a file goes, set it aside and keep going. Later it will fall
into place or more stuff will collect that creates a category.

It's like a Lawn

If you don't trim your files, they quickly become overgrown. You don't
have to burn a weekend thinning them out; but when you pull a file, try
to get rid of anything that is no longer relevant, is duplicated, or doesn't

belong. Dead files are archived to a place out of the way and maybe even off the premises. This is stuff you don't really need but can't part with. Put theses papers or files in a marked box and get them out of the way.

Lost in Space

Put a marker in files when you remove something. These markers are kept on top of your file cabinet, making it easier to mark the spot where a file came from. Inside the files the marker says "Where I am" and you simply write where it is in the blank space.

Filing for Dummies

Just get a few boxes and label them "Things to Pay," "Things to Do," "Things to Read," and "Things I Don't Know What to Do With."

ASK A PRO: JUDITH JOSEPHSON, AUTHOR

Writer Judith Josephson battles piles of paper daily. "One thing that works for me," she says, "are clipboards for different areas of my life—work, children, household, financial, etc. (Clipboards capture pieces of paper before they become part of the muffins you're baking.) I hate dealing with paperwork, so I invented the 'one hundred minutes', where I turn into my own secretary. I set a Krups timer for ninety-nine (okay, it's not quite one hundred) for my filing/sorting sessions. If I'm on a roll, I reset it. Hearing that 'beep-beep-beep' when the timer hits zero gives me a feeling of accomplishment."

ACTION FILES

Don't be a slave to your in-box. Just because something is in there doesn't mean you have to do it.

—Malcolm Forbes

Action items may include papers that need to be entered (mailing list, business expenses), paid (bills and invoices), read (newsletters and articles), things that need to be done (correspondence), and finally, papers that need to be filed for future reference. If there is no need to reference them in the future, they go in the trash. (Wink.) The best action file system is like a good novel. It's a "page turner" and keeps the paper moving. It also calls for you to keep your most used and referred to files on your desk. These should be at your fingertips.

The everything-out system works if you keep like items together (rubber band them) and divide your desk into quadrants based on some sort of system that makes sense to you. (Papers piled near the edge of the desk where the trash is are waiting for one last look before being thrown out.) Or simply sort these piles by priority. (Put sticky notes on them with important deadlines and flag key papers so they stand out in the crowd.) The other way to manage important and pending papers is with a desktop filing rack so you can see what's pressing without cluttering your desk. This allows you to keep pressing papers within easy reach. The best action piles can be category-based with piles for ASAP papers, piles for one to eight, nine to fifteen, sixteen to twenty-three, twenty-four to thirty-one, and a pile for anything that doesn't need to be done in these dates or this month. This is your future pile. When you move from week to week, act on or do what has to be done and shift the rest to the next week's pile.

My system is pretty simple, but it works. I keep folders with frequently referred to resources in a divider on my desk. My calendar, to-do lists, pads of paper, and forms are all there, too. Then in another rack are box-bottom folders with things to pay, read, file, act on, or on hold (pending), invoices due, mailing list entries, and other pressing appointments and commitments. I also have a set for my wife.

One action or "inaction file" can be a drawer in your desk. This is a drawer for papers that don't deserve a place in prime time (the top of your desk) or rerun status (a file) but aren't ready to be canceled (thrown out), so this is where they can stay until the new season begins (the first of the month) when you dump everything out and evaluate what's worthy. Much of what you saved is obsolete or has worked itself out. A "things pending" in a wicker basket can work if you go through it often.

TICKLER FILES

To get started using a tickler file, throw two twenty-dollar bills into it, one ten days from now and one twenty days from now. When you find them, spend them on yourself.

—Paulette Ensign

A tickler system is perfect for papers that don't deserve a permanent place but also need to be saved temporarily. Since a general file that says "To Do" gets too fat too fast, the tickler is the answer. Of course I invented my own system but it is based on a basic principle—you sort papers according to the date they are due. It works much the same as a calendar that you put your appointments in according to the date they occur. In a drawer near your desk you can use hanging folders for the days of the month (one through thirty-one) and for the twelve months of the year (January through December), or you can use file folders and/or an accordion file. Here's how it works for me. The birthday card for my nephew is first put in the monthly slot when the birthday falls. Then when the month rolls around the card is moved to the slot a couple of days before the big day so it can be mailed in time. The only way this won't work is if you don't put items in the monthly folders and then check and move them into their daily slots (and check these slots every day). For this reason make it so you can't miss making it a part of your daily routine. Otherwise it is simple, easy, and VERY effective.

BINDERS

Arrange whatever pieces come your way.

—Virginia Woolf

Screenwriter Ron Bass prefers to use pencils and three-hole paper when working on a script. His rationale is that he can move the paper around as needed. He keeps a binder for each script. I agree. Binders are flexible, portable, and better than a pile. If you want to keep things in order yet have them visible, use a three-ring presentation binder. Label the spine of the binder with the name of the index tabs in alphabetical order of the contents within the binder. (Use tabs that stick out past the binder so you can see the tabs when the binder is lying down in a pile.) This system keeps the clutter off your desk so you can work on one project at a time.

Dividers are the key. You can make a tickler-type binder by using pockets or sheet protectors divided with daily and monthly tabs. You can sort and save photos, records, plans, things-to-do lists, articles, mailing lists, manuals, notes. One thing a reader of a previous book of mine suggested was to make a binder for each decade of your life. Or, you can have a different binder for each area of your life and keep clippings and documents. Keep owner's manuals along with the receipts by stapling the receipt to the manual or adding an envelope to keep receipts by category in the same binder. The advantage is that you can keep it all together and it's portable. Use binders for cooking tips, recipes, craft ideas, creative dates, gardening ideas, this book. Make your own cookbook from recipe clippings. Get a binder and tape or staple them to paper and put in categories from desserts to dinners. Family members can sort through and put a Post-it note on the page of what they want for dinner. Tear out pages from magazines and create your own cookbook, decorating guide, fitness guide.

BULLETIN BOARDS

When I was working on Fire Lover, *I had many thousands of pages of court information inside these walls. I got a big roll of butchershop paper and covered everything. They became my bulletin boards to get everything in chronological order.*

—Joseph Wambaugh

Brad Pitt was in a panicked state when he couldn't find his favorite photo of wife Jennifer Aniston. The last time he'd seen the photo it was on the crowded bulletin board inside their Santa Barbara mansion. It turns out the image was merely covered up by another one. Sound familiar? In addition to piles and files, a bulletin board is a great tool to put papers that aren't ready (or need) to be filed. These are papers you want out as a visual reminder (but out of the way). Thus the bulletin board was born.

Most people have one or two bulletin boards (made of cork) in their home or office. These are such effective tools, I think they should be everywhere lots of little, loose pieces of papers pile up. Put them where you (and others) will come into contact with them on a regular basis. This way you can tack up announcements, computer shortcuts, dry cleaner slips, FedEx tracking slips, goals, greeting cards, key phone numbers, messages, notices, passwords, pending papers, photos, post-cards, receipts, reminders, schedules—anything, really. Better yet, use a dry-wipe board for reminders and notes and you can cut down on paper. They don't even have to be corkboards. A bulletin board can be magnetic, a chalkboard, or just a wall full of push pins with papers under them. Whatever works.

Bulletin boards are also very valuable when it comes to the planning process. When I am designing a Web site, having a big dry-wipe board or putting index cards on a bulletin board is invaluable. By putting up plans I am able to see patterns, make connections, and chart a project's progress or multiple projects. Author Janet Evanovich follows the progress of her novels with a huge whiteboard on one wall, where she keeps track of her book chapter by chapter. Many writers put up several bulletin boards to post pictures of places in a book, character descriptions, outlines, deadlines, quotes, and phrases.

I like to dedicate one of my bulletin boards to motivational images and messages. Bestselling author Evan Hunter (aka Ed McBain) uses a slightly different approach. When he was in college and writing stories and sending them out to magazines, he papered an entire small bathroom with rejection slips, filling every inch of the wall. He had confidence that his writing was good and one day it would sell. He was right. Bulletin boards make a great miniart gallery for kids and their handiwork. You can also post ribbons, report cards, and photos of their friends.

What better way to remind yourself than a big message stuck to a bulletin board hanging right by the door or over your desk? Post daily routines and reminders so you don't get sidetracked. Things like go to gym, work on book, make the bed. Weekly rituals and reminders like Monday band practice, Tuesday girls' night out, Wednesday date night can also be posted. It helps others know where you are or will be. It can also be an extension of your brain. That's why it's handy to have a small whiteboard near your computer so you can jot down a quick note to yourself and clear space in your brain for the task at hand.

The possibilities are endless. If you are always running around town, try this. I have a map of San Diego on the wall where I pin my appointments, errands, and regular meetings. I can group things together (geographically) this way. It saves a lot of time by not having to backtrack or run around. Make a map of your home and what to do in case of an emergency. For example, if water overflows, where do you go to shut off the water and who do you call to fix the problem? Also, emergency numbers and important people like the plumber, electrician, baby-sitter, copier guy, landscaper, people you use frequently. Key people's names can be stapled or business cards taped on a bulletin board. How about a brainstorming wall at work? Hang a piece of paper on your office door and pose a question at the top. You can get help from others or you may just need to bring an issue to the forefront of your consciousness. Have others share their thoughts or add a comment or two when they walk past. Create a communications center for the family. Designate an area for each person. Now you know where to put messages, mail, and reminders. In the middle put a calendar that everyone can look at to see who is supposed to be where and when. Or divide a board into the different areas of your life and label it accordingly. There could be a space for things pending, things to do, things to remember, and people to call. A bulletin board can also be divided by project or you can make what looks like a giant mind map. In the middle is your goal and pinned in clusters are papers and Post-it notes that will help you reach your goal.

In researching this book, I have come across all kinds of different types of bulletin boards. Here are just a few of the best bulletin board ideas. How about a big roll of butcher paper that you pull down for notes, things to do, or just to doodle on? One rap artist painted an entire wall with chalkboard paint where guests can write a message or sign their name. What if you don't have any wall space? One woman hung a clothesline with memos and mementos attached with clothespins. An actress "borrowed" a spinning rack from the diner where she held a day job and attaches bills to pay, things to do, and ideas to remember to it. A speaker uses a flip chart as a bulletin board. Make a page in your binder a mini bulletin board using photo album paper or just attach sticky notes and tape scraps of paper there. You can turn any wall into a bulletin board with cork squares and some adhesive. What if you had a Velcro wall? How about a room divider that allows you to write on it, pin things to it, or hang a wall organizer on it? Many of these have transparent pockets that display papers in color-coded frames for easy reference. It can sit on your desk, or you can attach it to the wall. When on the wall it frees up some desk space. Perfect for reference material, take-out menus, computer codes, key numbers, price guides, schedules, lists, procedures, postage rates, and so on. Create the most multipurpose organized wall with a chalkboard, corkboard, photo display, letter bins mounted to the wall for mail, and items to remember to take with you, hooks for your keys or coats, a whiteboard calendar (that's also magnetic).

EMERGENCIES

Expect the best, but plan for the worst.
　　　　　　　　　　—Unknown

Renowned jazz vibraphonist Lionel Hampton lost a lifetime's worth of memorabilia when there was a fire in his Manhattan apartment. He lost a vintage record collection, sheet music, photographs, letters from past presidents. The mayor of New York presented the jazz great with copies of several photographs and city proclamations that were lost in the blaze. Most of us aren't that lucky—or well connected. "It will never happen to me" is the catch phrase among people who haven't been a victim of a robbery, fire, flood, mud slide (and, if you believe what you see on TV, a meteor or alien abduction). There are only two kinds of people when it comes to a disaster—those who have had it happen to them and those who will. Your passport, social security card, insurance, stocks and bonds, certificates, deeds, bank account information, medals, service records, degrees, citizenship papers, tax returns, your will, collectibles, photographs, jewelry—anything you don't want to lose—should be kept in a safe place. Keep anything you may need to prove to an insurance company that what you lost due to theft, fire, flood, mud slide, alien abduction, meteor, or any other disaster really was lost. Making a video of all of my stuff seemed about as exciting as watching a friend's vacation videos. That's right, BORING. But then I decided to have fun with it and videotaped it all as if I were Martin Scorsese. I added commentary while I described each item and what it means to me. Believe it or not, I enjoyed this. I hope I never need it, but I am sure the insurance adjuster will get a kick out of it and it will make it hard to deny our claim.

TRUE STORY

Every year Pam, a dancer and dance studio owner, cleans up the papers that have been accumulating for the past eleven and a half months. It's a ritual, and one that works for her. "By December, my office is cluttered with piles of magazines, unfinished projects, things to file, an overflowing in-box, and a bulging file of things to do. Not to mention my Rolodex is in complete disarray," she muses. So during the holidays she will spend an entire day alone organizing her office. No calls, no interruptions, and no excuses. She calls it her "Day of Atonement." She'll sift through the papers, file some, toss others, and get everything in order. She's well aware that one month later things will go back to the way they were before, but she likes this system for the following reasons: "I like to do it this way because it's my way to look back on and review the previous year. Seeing what got done and what didn't is very enlightening. It's sort of like therapy in a way. I celebrate the successes and examine the failures and then move on." It's very liberating to toss out the bad reviews.

ONE OF US: RACHELLE NONES

"I reserve the top drawer of my file cabinet for storing all of the receipts and canceled checks that I'll need for itemizing business deductions at tax time. During the year, whenever I have a receipt or canceled check that I need to save, I simply open the drawer and drop it in. When tax time rolls around, I scoop up all the papers, organize them, and head off to my accountant's office."

THIS FITS THE BILL

Now my credit cards pay each other. I've stepped out of the picture.
                                        —Kelly Monteith

On our list of favorite things to do, paying bills probably doesn't make the top twenty. Being more organized won't make it more fun, but it will make it go faster and a little easier so you can get to more enjoyable endeavors. Or you can have someone else in the family handle the finances. I read somewhere that three out of five women say they are responsible for balancing the checkbook and 56 percent say they pay the bills. Most of us have no patience for the mundane and maddening task of bookkeeping because it is both boring and a burden. The only way I have found to deal with it is to make it as quick and easy as possible. Come up with some way (it's okay to be creative with how you force yourself to do it but not with what you write) to add what you earn or have coming in and subtract what's going out. Maybe you just staple receipts into pages of a notebook or stick receipts into a shoe box and add them up once a month. Fine. (Try using an accordion organizer and just drop receipts into the month or category they fall into. It works!) Even a basket by the door (or wherever you tend to drop the mail) will work. Keep some bill-paying supplies in there (stamps, calculator, checkbook) and sort through the bills twice a month while watching your favorite show or talking on the phone. It's okay if your system for doing the books is to write down everything you buy and sell on the wall—if it works, it works. Whatever system will help you get a handle on your books is a good thing. Without a good bookkeeping system you will have a tougher time with taxes, forget to bill clients (or double and triple bill), you never really know how you are doing, suffer cash-flow problems, and worse. If your money matters are a mess, this may be the most important area to begin organizing.

Be a Regular Guy

Some people prefer to pay bills as they come in. Others do it once or twice a month. Once a week pull out all the receipts you have collected in your pockets and purse and put them in a basket or bin. When the credit card statement comes, compare the receipts to the charges and then staple them to the paid bill and file it. Place bills in a basket with all your supplies you use to pay them—stamps, checkbook, pen, stapler, envelopes.

Stop the Insanity

Simplify and consolidate to one bank or credit union, one credit card, one money market. I know you should be diversified, but if that causes you strain and stress, not to mention an avalanche of papers coming into your life, you have to decide if it's worth it. Make it easier by automating as many payments and transactions as possible (automatic investing, direct deposit, bill paying online). Online banking and bill paying are not for everyone. But if you are comfortable with this medium, it can be a no-brainer each month to have all of your bills paid on time and automatically.

Tool Guy

There are a few cool products available at Target and Wal-Mart that are basically bill sorters. There are slots that are numbered according to the days of the month, allowing you to organize your bills by the due date. You could make your own version of the above system or make a weekly bill payment reminder with folders labeled week 1, 2, 3, 4, 5.

Quick Draw McGraw

"The first thing I do when I get a bill is open it and immediately write the date the bill is due and the amount I plan to pay in the far left corner below my return address. I keep a small red basket on my desk and file the bills according to the date they are due, and then I check up on them daily," says designer Michelle Downey. I also find it easier to write transactions as they happen rather than let them pile up. It takes discipline, but it's really simple. It only takes a second, and I do it while I am on the phone. I still have to force myself, but these pesky tasks have become habits. To make it easier, create a stationery store or correspondence station in your house and keep it stocked with cards, stamps, letterheads, envelopes, return address stamps, or stickers.

Move It Along

The key to dealing with bills (and mail) is to have a place to put it but that moves it closer to its final destination, whether that means pay, file, toss, or wherever its final resting place may be. It's like your bills are on a conveyer belt. Picture the bill arriving in the mail; that's where it begins. You open it and remove and retain the key information and put it in a tickler file, action folder, an inbox for a family member, pin it on a bulletin board, put it in the "To Pay" pile, add it to your desktop organizer, or put it in a file folder. To make sure it moves, enter the date to destroy, pay, or deal with it in your calendar or on the envelope. Set up a tickler system to remind you to check back. Drop the invoice in the month or day slot it's due. Or write the date in your day planner.

For Fun

I finally stopped fighting my natural right-brain tendencies and manage my money in an unorthodox and creative way. I created colorful wall charts for sales and expenses that include stickers and symbols instead of plain old boring and mind-numbing numbers. I color in as I go; and when I reach certain benchmarks, I set up little rewards. I know this goes against conventional thinking, but if it works. . . . How can that be a bad thing? Find ways to make bill paying more fun. Use a new type of software or balance your checkbook with a colored marker or even a crayon.

Copy That

Carbon copy pads are great. When I get an order I will write it once and then pack and ship it and put one copy in with the order, one to enter into my mailing list, and one in a to-pay folder. These are also great for phone messages. Use one for things-to-do lists and save a copy.

Go Kramer

My friend Scott Kramer prefers to scan and then toss receipts. He says it's easier to access information this way (he organizes his scans by topic). He has eliminated a LOT of paper, which is now contained on two disks. Of course he makes a backup of each disk and keeps it in a safe place.

ONE OF US: LESLIE RAY, PHOTOGRAPHER

"For bill paying I keep two large three-ring binders with twelve pocketed, tabbed separating pages (January to December). In each section is a 5 × 7" envelope for smaller receipts (anything too small to be three-hole-punched effectively) to be kept for taxes, etc. When I sit down to pay bills monthly, I three-hole-punch every receipt or statement and file it in the binder. Whenever I need to refer to a bill or statement, I know right where it is and taxes are a breeze. (This was particularly handy when I was locking horns with the telephone company. . . . This system as well as my stubborn persistence paid off!)"

WHILE YOU WERE OUT

Make a preprinted pad at Kinko's. Put it next to the door. It can say, "I went to_____. I will be back_____. The number there is_____." You can make one for the baby-sitter, too. "Our address and phone number are_____. You can reach us at _____. In case of an emergency call_____."

seven

ORGANIZING FOR THE "PACK RAT"

Clutter Control for the
Person Who Has Everything

Moderation is a fatal thing.
Nothing succeeds like excess.

—Oscar Wilde

T he reason why many of us can't get organized is simple—there is just too much stuff. It's overwhelming. I believe that is the biggest single obstacle to some sense of organization. We are pack rats. Since our minds see connections in, and creative uses for, just about everything, we want to keep it close by—just in case. To us, this is perfectly normal. To others, we have "issues" and need to get rid of a lot of our "junk."

How do I know this? I've been on both sides of the pile of clutter, so to speak. I admit, I have a tendency to hoard stuff. That said, my father is like the Yoda of clutter. A real "space" invader, if you know what I mean. To him, I'm a traitor who went over to the dark side because I now live happily with a lot less clutter. To my dad it's been a battle between good and evil. I just realized that the force is in me, and I forced myself to live with less. I discovered that I didn't need half the stuff I was storing. It took two moves (and a bad back) to figure this out. I look back and wonder what I was thinking. Who needs ten Phillips screwdrivers? Why was I schlepping all my outdated reference books from home to home? Was the IRS really going to go back twelve years to review my receipts? The answers to my questions were, "No," "I don't know," and "Not likely." So I got rid of half of the "stuff" I was storing in my garage and closets. Don't panic, but the truth is we can live with half of what we have. You will end up with more room and a better (lighter) life. Hey, if I can do it, so can you. Let's do it together. You'll end up with the best of the best of your stuff and feel good about donating, discarding, or selling the rest.

You don't have to save every single thing that comes into your life. If you need nails, Home Depot is NOT going to run out. Rubber bands are cheap. Information usually doesn't get better with age; and when you need it, the library and Internet have more than enough to go around.

So how did we end up having to park on the street because our garage is overflowing with clutter? Why do we have to pay for off-site storage for our stuff? What led to a life of goods instead of the good life? It's like a forest fire. It probably began as just a flickering flame and then grew and spread through your home and office until it was out of control. We need to douse it now and not throw any more fuel on the fire. The first step is to admit that we may have a bit too much stuff. Then promise not to add to it for a period of time.

Clutter seems to multiply like a weed. I have hung onto stuff for years—YEARS! Somehow it has become overgrown and ugly. So I yanked some clutter out by the roots and other stuff I just trimmed back. Knowing that, left unattended, it will take over, I don't delay. I make decisions and then do something about it. I get it out of the house before it sticks and then stays forever. Whether I returned it, sold it, gave it away, loaned it out, I got it out.

Look around you. How did you acquire all this stuff anyway? Much of it you bought because you needed it at the time. Other stuff you inherited, borrowed, or received as a gift. Chances are some are things you bought when you were upset—the ad for it was enticing, your friend had one so you wanted one, too, or you bought it because it was a good "deal." Creative people can be a bit impulsive at times and in a quest for instant gratification will buy things they never really needed in the first place. They then become attached to their possessions (even those they borrowed from others and never returned). Some things may be kept around as a visual reminder of something that is waiting for a bolt of inspiration (okay) or an unfinished project that they never seem to get around to (not okay). It could be physically hard to put it away. Insecurities can be the reason behind wanting to keep all those old trophies, ribbons, and grade-school report cards. It's too big and awkward to fit anywhere, even if there was room for it. Or, it's easier to just leave it out because you have to move the car, get out a ladder, and shift several boxes before you can put it away. You are undecided about where it should go, so you leave it lying around or chuck it into a "holding" pile, which will likely become its permanent home. (Waffling on decisions is a key reason why things begin to pile up on us and cause us trouble.) Before you know it, that "holding pile" has multiplied to the point where it becomes too overwhelming to deal with.

Maybe the word "decluttering" would have the same effect on you as fingernails across a chalkboard. Don't worry, I'm not suggesting that to be organized you have to live like a monk. I am enlightened to the fact that we need a certain amount of "stuff" around to feel comfortable and creative. I wouldn't think of taking that away. Furthermore, I believe that most books and seminars that stress being neat and tidy (to the point of sterilization) are a waste of your time. These cumbersome approaches are ineffective and unnatural for the right-brainer. "A place for everything and everything in its place" is just a saying, not the word of God. *Everything* in its place? Not gonna happen. Total organization isn't a reality or a necessity. Life is messy and there isn't always time to clean up. A person's life should be rich, filled with fun and interesting things to do—the least of which is organizing and cleaning up. I am not suggesting that you drop everything (no pun intended) and make everything perfectly neat and orderly. Besides, neat does NOT equal organized. You can be neat and orderly and still disorganized. On the other hand, too much of anything, especially clutter, isn't healthy either. As writer Karen Mynatt put it, "Clean enough to live in, dirty enough to be happy." Devise a system that will work for you—and those around you.

Instead, I'd like to propose a compromise. You can squirrel away your little chochkas (a Yiddish term for "trinkets"), keep that oddball stuff on your desk, and continue to toss your clothes over a chair if (and this is a big "IF") it isn't a problem for you or those around you and doesn't get in the way of your health, happiness, or career aspirations. The bottom line is this: you need to be able to get things done when you need to. Be honest now, has your clutter been the source of an argument with a spouse, coworker, or roommate recently? Have you "misplaced" something in the past week, only to find it buried under a pile of other misplaced things? Are you finding the clutter in your life to be a distraction, stressor, or burden in any way? If so, maybe all you need is a little fine-tuning. That's all I'm saying.

FAST FACT

In a poll I conducted through my Web site (www.creativelee.com) only one-third of the people polled throw away rubber bands. Half of those polled reuse aluminum foil and two-thirds save and reuse gift wrap.

LEARNING TO LET GO

Until you make peace with who you are, you'll never be content with what you have.

—Doris Mortman

Think of shedding clutter like shedding clothing. To get more comfortable after work, don't you strip off the layers of formal wear and slip on your favorite sweatpants, T-shirt, and slippers? It doesn't matter how it looks to others, it feels great, free. In the same way, your space (both at work and at home) should feel free and comfortable without too much concern for what others think. If you want to feel even freer, you can strip to the bare essentials. For some this is liberating; others feel, well, naked. For this reason it's a good idea to take it slow and do it at your own pace, in your own way, with a little coaching and consulting from us.

Clutter consists of things that you don't benefit from having around. Things that don't make you feel good or bring you joy. Items that take too much time to deal with. Things you don't use or need or even want. Stuff that you keep because it was given to you or bequeathed to you and you feel obligated to save it. Anything that doesn't make your life better and that keeps your space from being soothing, stimulating, and sanitary. Clutter consists of scattered and disorganized items that no longer serve our needs now or in the future. The past is the past. "Have nothing in your house that you do not know to be useful or believe to be beautiful," said Henry David Thoreau. So what is clutter? That which is rotted, rusted, busted, or crusted over. That which is dated, faded, duplicated, or dangerous. Also consider tossing it if it is ripped, chipped, wrinkled, or a burden in any way.

ARE YOU A "PACK RAT"?

To begin with, the words "pack rat" don't have the nicest connotation to them, do they? (You probably picture a big, ugly rodent digging through junk and then dragging it back to its nest, leaving little droppings along the way.) Is it all that bad? I guess it depends on who you ask. Answer a simple "That could be me" or "No way!" to the following scenarios. Two or more answers could mean you are a "Pack Rat." Some of the signs include:

- When the blue light at K-Mart starts flashing, you feel all funny inside and rush to buy whatever's on special, whether you need it or not.
- You've had an argument with someone about who has more junk, and you won!
- You had to rent a storage unit to hold all your junk, er . . . "valued possessions."
- A well-meaning friend inadvertently threw away a piece of your clutter, and you are still mourning the loss two years later.
- Others in the neighborhood are sent to you any time they need a spare part.
- The local library frequently calls you to look up articles from *your* magazine collection.
- You have coffee cans filled with more fasteners than Home Depot.
- People call you before they hang their "garage sale" signs, knowing you'll buy them out.
- When shopping for a home, your first priority is how much storage space it has.

(More than one "That could be me" answer is cause for concern.)

THE COST OF CLUTTER

Stanford University researchers developed a drug to cure compulsive shoppers. No matter what you buy, it makes your butt look big.

—Jay Leno

1. **It could cost you your life.** A Reno, Nevada, man was found buried under a large pile of old newspapers in his home (which was overflowing with hundreds of papers in piles). He kept huge volumes of newspapers and kept paths cleared where he walked. My dad has a shed that is like a graveyard for old and broken stuff he is saving for the spare parts. My mom joked that when she passes away my dad will put her in the shed in case he needs the parts.

2. **It could cost you money.** You have to store it (rent extra space), maintain it (wash and repair), and move this stuff. It costs you to keep it all, in more ways than one. My brother and I have held onto our baseball card collection in the hopes that it would be worth more someday. Well, we missed the boat. If we had sold it a few years ago we would have cashed out. Since we couldn't part with it, we are stuck with a bunch of cardboard with photos on them. Other hidden costs of clutter include not being able to find a bill, video, or library book lost in the shuffle and having to pay late fees. You may not be able to sell your home for top dollar if the clutter ruins the "curb appeal" or scares off potential buyers who focus more on the mess than the master bedroom.

3. **It could cost you valuable time.** Clutter can be a form of procrastination. It wastes your time and gets in the way of your dreams. That's a tragedy.

4. **It could be robbing you of your life.** The most expensive vehicle to operate, per mile, is . . . the shopping cart. When you think about clutter, keep in mind the cost of every item you buy (and pay to store). You had to work to pay for it. When you work you are trading your LIFE for a few bucks. To spend your life/money on storing a bunch of stuff is insulting. It's wrong. But, but . . . I don't want to hear it. I have been there. Your life could be better. Think about it. If you make twenty dollars an hour and some-

thing costs one hundred dollars, you traded five hours of your life for that item. I don't care if it was on sale. Was it worth five hours of your life? When people are clinging to their last bit of life, I'll bet they would gladly give up their worldly possessions for just a few more days. Whenever I ask people what they would do if they had more time, they almost always say they would travel or spend time with family and friends. Pay down debt. Man, get a hold of yourself. You can. Sell off what you don't use and spend that money on more rewarding things.

5. **It could cost you your job.** Creative, right-brain people are always portrayed as being unkempt, uncaring, disorganized, and out of control. It's a bum rap. You do have to admit that if your clutter causes you to lose things, you might lose your job. Yes, they praise and pay us for the same right-brain traits that end up teeing them off.

6. **It could cost you your reputation.** David Bowie said, "Tidy became a discipline word for me when I first kicked drugs. Before that, the only time I put things away was if there was a knock at the door." What do you want others to think of when they see your place? If it's a mess they assume you are disorganized, undisciplined, unreliable, and out of control. Left-brain people (the majority) look down on us when we are untidy.

7. **It costs you space you could use for more important things.** Clutter robs you of space that could have been used for better things that are a better fit for who you are and what you want to do with your life NOW.

8. **It could cost you your creativity.** Clutter can interfere with creativity, be distracting, constantly diverting thoughts, which author Stephanie Winston calls, "Visual noise." How can you "clear your head" when you are suffocating with paper, clothes, toys, broken appliances, and souvenirs?

9. **Costs you relationships.** How can you get romantic with clutter everywhere? If you want (and need) to make a good first impression on a date, clutter isn't going to cut it. It causes embarrassment with clients, bosses, the mother-in-law, your dates, friends, and neighbors.

10. **Robs you of your peace of mind.** Most clutter is a permanent reminder of a temporary feeling. It litters our lives and clogs our minds. You'll be overwhelmed and under pressure. You can't find anything, which is stressful. You no longer feel comfortable in your home or office. It's no longer cozy, just plain messy. How can you relax when you look around and see things that make you feel guilty because you never finished or followed through on them? These constant negative reminders of unfinished business and the guilt can be very discouraging.

11. **Costs you your health.** Clutter causes strained backs if you have to move it around. It's a stressor when you have a strained relationship (there is all that nagging to deal with), plus it's a major turnoff in the bedroom.

KING OF CLUTTER

Have everyone in the house go through with trash bags and see who can collect the most clutter in under an hour.

ACTION ITEM

Repeat after me, "I have enough stuff. There is enough. I need no more."

THE CARE AND KEEPING OF CLUTTER

Clutter is anything that does not enhance your life on a regular basis (spouse excluded).

—Pam McClellan

Some of us have so much old stuff we could open a museum. Granted, it will be filled with every fool gizmo and gadget ever invented, none of which still work, but there they are taking up valuable space in our closet, crawl space, and cupboards. That said, my dad could look at a bag of rusty old nails and ask me, rhetorically I think, should we keep that? Many times these strange items have helped. Most times they just add to the clutter.

Stephen Hofer boasts a collection of over three thousand copies of *TV Guide*. The good thing is he will display his collection at the Philo T. Farnsworth Center for Television History in Indiana. I read about this pack rat professor in *TV Guide*. Another guy I read about saves everything. He loved his cat so much he saved her fur balls for ten years and kept them on his nightstand. That's what we call a "collector."

If someone tries to get you to part with your clutter, you can get very defensive and come up with all kinds of excuses for hanging onto things. (It's akin to trying to take heroin from an addict.) Do any of these sound familiar? (We are creative people, thus it stands to reason we can come up with some pretty clever rationale to hang on to things.) Carmen Electra says that since she was raised in a lower-middle-class family that was taught to keep everything—she does. "I feel like someday I'm going to wear something, but most times that day never comes. So I've been forcing myself to get rid of stuff." The thing is, her closet is beautifully organized and spacious. The lesson is this: if you have the room and are willing to spend the time to stay on top of your stuff, go ahead and pile it on and stuff it in. Just keep in mind, organizing is a LOT easier with less clutter.

I am not judging here. I have not and will not do that. But I have seen homes where you could not get around because there are layers and layers of litter. (The need to hoard is not always healthy.) You may think that you are in control of the mess because you know where everything is. There is still a price to pay. One man saved hundreds of empty plastic soda bottles and apparently slipped on one and killed himself. One woman slept on top of a five-foot pile of magazines. She rolled off her "bed" and died in her cluttered home. She wasn't uncovered for weeks. Ironically, among the rubble were old copies of *Good Housekeeping*.

KINDS OF CLUTTER
"Valuables"
Everyone thinks that stuff from the sixties will make them rich. The *Star Trek* salutation is "Live long and prosper." It doesn't say anything about collecting anything and everything you can get your hands on.

Useless
It's time to toss keys that do not fit anything you know of. (Also toss keys to things that you no longer own.) Odd socks. (Like the other one is gonna turn up. Get real.) Dead batteries and dried paint and crusty brushes beyond rehabilitation. (These are toxic, don't leave them lying around.) Dull razors. (Most are disposable, so do it.)

Little
Why save things that are cheap to buy when you need them—aluminum foil, string, rubber bands, pens, bags, boxes, twist ties, and coffee cans filled with nuts and nails? Trust me, more will come into your life.

Outdated
Do you have instruction manuals for things you no longer own? Are there party invitations pinned to your bulletin board from people who have already passed away? Do you have parts for products you no longer own and may never have owned in the first place?

Hobbies
"I've been working out lately—it's my new hobby. I thought I already had a hobby, but apparently going out, getting stinking drunk, and giving creepy guys phony phone numbers is not actually a hobby, but a lifestyle,'" says Andi Rhoads. I probably don't need to point out the obvious: hobbies usually equal clutter.

Mystery Stuff
Chances are you have some loose screws (not screws loose) that do not fit anything you know of. Steve Poltz, the singer-songwriter who cowrote one of Jewel's biggest hit songs ("You Were Meant for Me"), was interviewed in the *San Diego Union-Tribune,* and the reporter wrote a lot about his apartment. It was strewn with all kinds of clutter—an award invitation, cover art, audition tapes, paperwork of all kinds, cash, Vegas chips, and travel itineraries secured with an empty can of soda.

Don't and Won't Use

The Ab Blaster or Thigh Master you no longer use and probably never did can be sold and the proceeds used to buy a gym membership.

Big Stuff

Don't overlook the big stuff, like cars clogging the yard or a boat with a hole in the hull.

Clothes

Apparently there are regular pants, nice pants, good pants, dressy pants, and comfy pants—and only women can tell the difference. Many men have no trouble parting with clothes that don't fit or aren't fashionable. And if we won't, the women in our lives will do it for us. The sweater our ex gave us for a gift—gone. The Members Only jacket still taking up closet space—gone. The shirt that's too tight—see ya. Women, on the other hand, will keep everything, even if they will NEVER wear it again.

Extras

How many vases do you really need? Do you have enough pots and pans to furnish a mess hall for the entire U.S. Army? How many pens are enough?

Gifts

We all get gifts we don't want or need. We call these "shuvundahs" or, said more slowly, shove-unders. These are things you shove under the bed and scramble to display in case the person who so generously gave you this utter piece of *$%# comes over.

Reading Material

I realized I had been saving guidebooks from places I hated. I also had an atlas that was so old Texas was still a part of Mexico. Old magazines? We won't even go there.

Music

Have you ever bought a CD because you heard a song on the radio you had to have only to discover that the rest of the CD stinks? After a while your music collection begins to add up. Compilation CDs (that you create using your favorite songs) are one answer.

Career Clutter

Creative people can come up with some strange clutter in the name of creativity and our careers. An actor friend of mine picks up props and outfits from thrift shops from periods ranging from the fifties, sixties, seventies, and formal and business looks from those eras, too. The best part is it's all tax deductible. Almost everyone has career clutter, which includes old résumés, textbooks, tools, seminar notes, software, and, of course, office supplies pilfered from a previous employer.

CLUTTER AND WHAT TO DO WITH IT

- "But I paid money for that!" (It's costing you even more to store it. Cut your losses and sell or give it away.)
- "That was a gift from my late aunt Bess." (How will she know if you toss it?)
- "I might need it someday." (Could you even find it again when you need it?)
- "The leisure suit might come back in style." (Disco is dead; didn't you get the memo?)
- "It's a collector's piece." (Is there really a market for used Atari games? Will you live long enough to see it become really valuable?)
- "That magazine has good information in it." (Go online or to the library.)
- "It's hardly been used; it's like new." (*That* should be your clue. Give it away or sell it.)
- "It doesn't belong to us." (Return it to its rightful owner.)
- "I'm saving this for our grandkids." (Will they even *want* your junk?)

- "That catalog could come in handy." (Go to www.catalogs. google.com instead.)
- "I'm going to fix that." (Would it be cheaper to buy a new one?)

I'm sure there are several more that I missed. Remember, you can't take it with you when you go. As Don Henley points out, "There are no luggage racks on hearses."

FAST FACT
The most traditional wedding gifts are clocks, china, crystal/glass, appliances, silverware, and linens.

SORTING WHAT YOU'RE SAVING
Have more than thou showest. Speak less than thou knowest.
—William Shakespeare

A Little at a Time
The tendency for a creative person is to try to do it all at once. This approach doesn't work, mainly because we will burn out before we finish, quit, and never go back to it. The better approach would be to do a little at a time, a closet here, a drawer there, and before you know it, the whole room is done. The owner of a card shop I frequent says she gets up an hour early and tackles an area of her home before she comes in to work. After doing this for several weeks, she got her entire home in order, without any stress. Do a little at a time, perhaps during TV commercials. Make it fun and easy to do. Do it with your favorite music playing. Hold a reward for yourself until you finish a room. (The biggest reward is that once you do a little, you will want to do more. It feels great.) Approach one area at a time. Start in a room you don't use. Start with the stuff on the floor. Think small. Be realistic. Break it down and do a little at a time. This boosts your confidence when you can step back and see the fruits of your labor—a clean living space. Establish a schedule and

set aside some uninterrupted time. The message here is, as much as you want to; don't try to do it all at once. Do one room at a time. Go through one box at a time. Don't pull everything out of a closet. It's too much to tackle at once and then you are left with a mess if you can't finish.

Bigger Isn't Better

The hardest part is where to start. Organizing your office is too big a task. So is your filing cabinet. Break it down to the point where you truly believe you can begin. Take the hundred writing instruments you have in your home and get rid of the ones that don't work, whether they are out of ink or just not your style. Then sort the pencils, highlighters, markers, and pens into different containers. Duplicates must go. Do the same thing for pots and pans, linens and towels, and so on. Focus on one tiny area then start. Make an appointment with yourself in your calendar. Write down the area to tackle. Start with the room that means the most or the easiest place to organize and freakin' do it!

Timing Is Everything

The best time is when you are ready, willing, and able to make a change and take control of your life. Other good times to tackle clutter include: after doing taxes, changing jobs upon completion of big projects, major milestones (retiring, graduation, birthdays), long weekends, holidays, and especially when you are moving. Go for the worst areas first, while your enthusiasm for organizing is highest. Start with a pesky problem. Do one nuisance a day. Look for areas where clutter "nests" or the area that bugs you the most.

Quick and Easy

We struggle between perfection and possibility. Just do a little more than you do now to be more organized, to make your life work better. Some professional organizers do more harm than good. They create systems that are impossible for right-brainers to attain or maintain. We are lucky if we remember to clean out the fridge or our files once a year. Go for the easy kills first. Bail the obvious junk. Just do something you can finish and rack up a small victory. Use a junk drawer or box for things you can't seem to throw out. Every six months, dump it. No questions asked, just throw things away.

Make It Fun

Put on some relaxing or motivating music. Get a rhythm going. Sing as you go. "I'm throwing away my tie, it's ugly, I can't lie." Eulogize each item you are (finally) parting with. Play Jenga with the piles of clutter, and if you can pull an item out of the middle, go ahead and keep it. Make sculptures out of the clutter you are tossing. Put on a fashion show for friends and family with some of the ugly/dated clothes that don't fit and haven't been in fashion for YEARS. Do an improv skit for each item—*that's* your "motivation."

Sticky Situation

Go through your home, office, or storage area and tag things with a big sticky dot or a sticky note and indicate whether the item in question should stay, go, or go to storage. Your system can vary. One woman used a number-based rating system. I just used happy faces, sad faces, and other icons based on how these thing made me feel. Then I tagged them with a destination. You can go through your stuff and mark if it is relevant to your life today or how you want your life to be, with symbols. Go through and mark things with a heart (sentimental), a star (a favorite), a check (useful), a "ll" if it's a duplicate, or an "x" if it's outdated or expired. A circle with a line through it means it goes for one reason or another. Write in the circle where it goes (sell, store, shelve, give away, donate, recycle, or throw away).

Take Stock

Inventory everything in your house. Withhold all judgment. This is just to see what you are dealing with. When I owned my retail stores, we had to do this once a year but did it four times a year. After each season we counted everything and looked for things that took up valuable selling space but weren't worth stocking. When new merchandise came in, we would tag items with the date they arrived so it was easy to determine how old items were. We took things not selling and had our blowout sale and used the money to buy better merchandise. It sounds like a lot of work, but we broke our store down by section (swimsuits, surfboards, wet suits, skateboards, and so on) and my brothers and I divided and conquered—or did it a little at a time. You can do the same. Go through your home and tag items with dots. Red is things you love. Green dots for valuable, useful items. Blue for sentimental. Look for duplicate things you don't need or even like. As you go, ask yourself if you use this often. At all? Can you rent or borrow it if you need it? Can you make do without it? The best question of all is, does it support your goals?

Box It Up

Boxes are the best tool for cleaning out the clutter in a house. Andy Rooney did a routine about how much he loves boxes. He has hundreds of boxes of varying sizes and questionable condition. He keeps old letters in shoe boxes, office supplies in old check boxes, and loose change for parking meters is kept in empty Altoids containers. He claims to need a big box for all his little boxes. The one thing he doesn't like is to use boxes for what they were originally intended. (Sound familiar?) Boxes are best for sorting through clutter. Once you pick something up, put it where it goes or into one of these boxes. Have a pad of paper to write yourself notes as you go. Maybe you need batteries to make something work. Missing a cord? A trip to Radio Shack will remedy the problem.

Box 1. **To sell.** (Price as you go with a sticky dot, masking tape, or write on the item.)

Box 2. **To donate.** (Put it in a box for each charity or person you are giving it to.)

Box 3. **To return.** (Things you borrowed and photos to the people in them. You can have a pile or box by person or by store.)

Box 4. **To move.** (Things that need to go to their final resting place. Don't move them as you find them. It will be too distracting.)

Box 5. **To trash.** (Get a big trash can and extra bags.)

Box 6. **To recycle or reinvent.** (Many times you come across things and go, "Huh, I forgot I had this." Maybe you can put it to use or use it for something it wasn't intended for, but it will still work.)

Box 7. **To do.** (Things that need some additional action go here.)

Box 8. **To repair.** (It's nice to have a basket for stuff that needs repair or mending, along with needle and thread, bin with buttons.)

Box 9. **Not sure what to do with.** (Put a date on the outside of the box to decide.)

Box 10. **To file.** (It's pretty clear what needs to be done here.)

Other containers can include: A shoe box for photos. A big envelope for letters to reply to. Something to sort and containerize small stuff like rubber bands, paper clips, nuts and bolts. Keep baskets around for grouping small, loose things. A piggy bank for all the change you find. By the way, I read that it takes about an hour to wrap fifteen dollars in coins manually—typically pennies—compared with two minutes by a machine. Many supermarkets (an estimated nine thousand nationwide) have installed cash-counting machines that will take your loose change and print a voucher, redeemable for cash.

CREATIVE CLUTTER

You don't have to discard all your old clutter. Jeff Davis loved rummaging through thrift stores and record shops, where he discovered an abundance of neglected vinyl LPs. He decided to recycle these relics into bowls molded out of old albums from everyone from Billie Holliday to Bruce Springsteen. Davis says, "Products made from other products have an inherent history and can convey layered meaning through our associations with them." Laminate some of your photos and turn them into place mats. Hollow out an old book and make it a place to stash valuables. Turn trinkets into Christmas ornaments. Melt old jewelry down and have it turned into something new and original. You think those are weird? I know a guy who had a bunch of youths' football helmets lying around (that were deemed unsafe) so he sanded them down, painted them with the local team's colors, and converted them into mailboxes. He sold them at the local swap meet for fifty dollars! Another guy had tons of tools so he bought a bunch of closeout clocks, welded on various tools, and started selling his "Tool Time" clocks over the Internet. He also uses old billiard balls cut in half as the numbers for another series of his custom clocks.

TOP TEN

In the movie *High Fidelity*, John Cusack and Jack Black are always coming up with Top Ten lists. This is a great idea for organizing. If you could just keep your top ten of everything, you would have a lot less clutter. These are the items that get the prime location in your life, the rest is either stored out of the way or let loose. If you were on a deserted island and you could only have your top ten DVDs, CDs, and books, what would they be?

HOW TO CONQUER CLUTTER

Bill Gates is the richest man in the world—his dog is number five. He has over ten million dollars in change sitting on his nightstand.

—Jay Leno

Some of the things we hang on to, I'll tell you, are amazing. What's more incredible is that some of it survives through disasters, divorce, and is then shuttled from destination to destination during moves. Nothing seemed quite as unusual, though, as what renowned big-wave rider Greg Noll saved for his friend Rick James. Over two decades ago, James, while shaping a surfboard in Noll's shop, accidently cut off his thumb. After Noll rushed his buddy to the hospital, he returned to find the bloody thumb. So he cast it in clear resin for safekeeping. He kept the thumb on display in his surf shop showcase (where stunned shoppers would suddenly notice it alongside the sunglasses and stickers) until Rick came in one day and asked his friend not to put his thumb on display anymore. After that Noll used the thumb as a paperweight in his office until he eventually closed his shop. Now, years later, there is some debate about who owns the appendage. It seems that although the thumb originally belonged to James, Noll has had it in his possession longer. This is a true story!

Maybe you don't have a severed thumb amid your clutter, but it's likely that you do have all kinds of other strange things. Much of it is pretty worthless really. Do we really need everything that we keep? What about the stuff you never use? Is there another use for it? Could it be made to look better or work better? It's fun to find creative uses for stuff that is collecting dust. Here are some suggestions to rid yourself of some of it.

Pass It Forward

Comic strips, useful articles, photos—send them to family and friends. Don't save things for your kids or grandkids. Give it to them now, even though they may not want it. Go through your stuff and see who you could send some of it to and make their day. If one man's junk is another's treasure, share some of the wealth.

Rent or Borrow but Don't Buy Equipment You Only Need Once in a While

Maybe not having every single piece of equipment is a good thing. It gets you out of the house to talk to the nice lady at the copy center or the cute clerk at the equipment rental place. Not owning everything you use once in a blue moon frees up a lot of space.

When Cleaning Out Clutter, Decide As You Go

Go with your gut. How do I feel about this? Do I LOVE it or just like it? Does it give my energy a boost, or is it a bummer? Then use your logical side. Is it really useful? When was the last time I needed this? Save some sentimental things. Useful items are not clutter. Keep things that will help you reach your goals. Put them in places for easy access. Keeping your favorite dress for sentimental reasons is fine.

Make Counters and Desks Off-limits for Clutter

Put baskets, bins, or hooks where clutter collects to get it up and out of the way. Fine family members for violating the clear airspace rule.

Put Storage Where Things Are Used

Put a shed or storage container outside to contain toys or yard and gardening tools when done.

Get Rid of the Things That You No Longer Use and Trade for Something You Will

I went through the stuff on my boat that nobody ever uses, like water skis. Everyone wakeboards now. I traded the skis in for a new nonstretch wakeboard rope and vest.

Rearrange Things and Rotate Them in and out of Storage

Rearrange your space so you don't always feel that you need new stuff.

Create Things That Don't Collect Clutter

Painting the pavement with pigment dates back to sixteenth-century Italy when starving artists created chalk paintings in the hopes that appreciative passersby would throw them a coin. Artist James de la Vega is an artist in New York who writes on the streets and sidewalks of the Big Apple and makes people think. His favorite quote: "I just bought real estate in your mind." As an artist stuck in a crowded studio, this gets you outdoors, some good exposure, and when you are done your masterpiece can't come home and clutter up your studio. Take a picture for posterity.

Turn Your Clutter into Cash

If something is sitting around collecting dust, but it may be worth something to someone else, sell it. Jeff Hamilton and Robert Platts came across a forgotten stash of flat life-sized cardboard figures. Since one of the two was behind on the rent, they decided to recycle these discarded cardboard people and began renting them out to production companies as extras. Profit from peddling all kinds of stuff. There's a customer out there for just about anything. Start by selling duplicates. Hold a garage sale. Try selling online. John Freyer unloaded all of his possessions by putting them up for sale online. Then he used the six thousand dollars he made to visit his old stuff wherever it ended up. (He's engaged to the woman who bought his kitchen table.) He then went from clutter peddling to publishing with his book *All My Life for Sale* and on to a movie deal.

Have a Party and Invite People to Bring an Item They No Longer Need or Use and Do a Little Show-and-Tell About the Item

Then donate all the items to a charity.

Give Back Things That You Are Storing or Holding for Others

Swap Stuff with Friends and Coworkers

Rotate your CDs, DVDs, books, and clothes with friends. When you tire of them, trade. This keeps stuff moving, flowing.

Get Rid of Gifts

Send a thank-you note along with a picture of you (or your child) wearing that god-awful sweater and then get rid of it. If you feel funny throwing away holiday cards, save the best for next year and slip them in your picture frames to create a more festive atmosphere in your home. (You can also cut out the front of a greeting card you got, punch a hole in it, and create a hang tag for future gifts.)

Lend Your Stuff to the Library or Museum

Just don't forget to get it back. In the Center School in Old Lyme, Connecticut, hung an old Victorian painting that nobody paid much attention to during the sixty-five years it was on the wall in the school's library. Then one ten-year-old student took an interest in what turned out to be an 1878 oil by artist Walter Crane that sold at Christie's in London for $560,000 in 2002. Get your stuff out of the dark corners of your closet, attic, or garage and let others enjoy it while you lighten your load.

Establish Clutter-Free Zones

Places like your bedroom or the place people see the most (entryway, kitchen, and living room) are always kept clean.

Establish a Place That You Can Clutter All You Want

Have a junk chair to consolidate clothing mess in one central location. An armoire full of your favorite things. Maybe a shelf or closet to stuff your stuff is what you need. If that's not enough space, dedicate a room (with a door) to house your mess.

Use Off-Site Storage

This could be a friend's garage, a corner in the warehouse of a family business, or a self-storage unit. (This way you can take a trial run at living with less.) The father of a friend of mine retired from his business, which sold an assortment of fasteners. When he ran his company he relished finding and selling all kinds of strange fasteners—nuts, bolts, nails, and screws. His urge to find these fasteners didn't wane when he retired. So he bought a cabin and started a fastener museum. (I'm not making this up.) Now Mel has a place to store (and display) his stuff.

Take Inventory

Joanne Perez, the wife of vaudeville performer Pepito the Spanish Clown, cleaned out underneath her bed and discovered the only existing copy of the pilot for the TV series *I Love Lucy*. Desi Arnaz and Lucille Ball had given it to Pepito as a gift. He guest starred on that episode but put it under his bed, where it stayed for forty years. Take the time to sort through your stuff to see what you have and organize as you go.

What You Can't See Won't Hurt You?

Author Paula Jhung says to hide laundry in a hamper with a lid, put bills in an attractive shoe box, and clean them out when they overflow. Position a beautiful basket by the door to hold outgoing mail, library books, and other roving matter. Weed it regularly so nothing takes root. Hide stressful stuff until you make time to deal with it. If easily distracted, put pending clutter in containers and keep them out of sight and out of mind. I do this when I am in the middle of writing.

Closet Case

Julie Bowen, who played Carol Vessey on the NBC show *Ed,* values vintage clothing. When visiting her aunt's house she found a closetful of beautiful clothes in the attic that nobody else in the family could fit into. Keep out-of-season clothes in an out-of-the-way closet.

Simplify

When asked what she brings on tour with her, singer/songwriter Tracy Chapman said, "Mostly black stuff. It's easier to match—like adult Garanimals." Supersuccessful musician Moby admits to preferring a simple design in his home. He says he is a minimalist and has very little furniture and NO clutter. (Oddly, he has no mirror over the bathroom sink and no shower curtain.) I know I've mentioned this in other parts of the book, but it's appropriate that I mention it here. I simplified my life and it changed it—for the better. I liked to collect odd things. Let me rephrase that: I collected a lot of everything. As a result I was feeling weighted down by my mess. I had saved so much stuff I couldn't find anything. Having more than enough of everything should have brought me peace of mind but instead it took a piece of *my* mind. It was stressful to salvage, save, sort, store, and sift through items that had no real value any longer—to me. I looked around and made a decision to simplify my life. I started by selling off everything I had more than two of. To make a long story short (see, I really am living simply) I pared down to the bare essentials and organizing is so much easier and I feel more freedom than I have ever felt. Not once have I needed one thing I got rid of. I will admit that at first it feels funny, scary even to have less, but after a while you begin to wonder why you had all that stuff in the first place.

Display Your Stuff

Derryl DePriest keeps his immense collection of 450 G.I. Joes in glass cases. He has one of the largest collections in the country of the action figures. Martin Short keeps memorabilia and mementos in his studio, including photos of family, friends, and fellow actors. On his bookshelves are carefully preserved reels of audiotape from the pretend talk show he produced as a teenager in his bedroom. Clutter isn't bad if you have the room and it's stored in a way that lets you display the cool stuff and save the rest out of the way. Organize what you want to keep. Not everything has to go. Some clutter can stay, but keep it out of the way of your everyday living.

Clutter Is Okay If It Is Organized

My friend owns a design firm and keeps binders categorized to spark creative ideas in the beginning of the design process. This includes visual images, headlines, slogans, and samples of other successful campaigns. Leeza Gibbons loves candles and devoted an armoire to organizing and storing them. A guy I know is a fishing fanatic and has every type of rod and reel you can imagine. To say his gear is organized is an understatement. One lesson I learned from him is that he freely intends to add more gear (although his wife doesn't know this yet) and has planned ahead and has spaces set aside for his new equipment.

Ask for Gifts That Won't Clutter

Gifts like massages, a vacation, edible things, tickets to a show, or a housecleaning certificate reduce clutter. Also ask for gifts you need and will use. My good friends Donna and Glenn sold off everything they owned and for their honeymoon traveled around the world for almost two years. For wedding presents they asked for money or you could help pay for portions of their trip.

Trade Your Stuff That's Not Good for You Where It Can Do Some Good

Clothes can be donated to organizations that help men and women get dressed for interviews or help battered women. Books go to the library. Computer gear and sporting goods go to schools. You get a tax deduction, and others get a shot at a better life.

Tackle It As You See It

When you go from room to room, pick something up and drop something off. Keep a bin or box for things you want to scoop up and put away. Each time you pass a pile of clutter, toss one thing.

Get Rid of It

Drag some stuff to the curb, put a price tag on it, and wait for Winona Ryder to come and take it. (I'm joking.) If you didn't hook it up, turn it on, fix it, use it, then chances are it's not as important as you may think.

Remove the Temptation by Limiting Your Storage Space or Put an Expiration Date on Things for When They Will Be Fixed or Moved Out of Your Home

Right-brainers have a problem letting go of things, whether they are scraps of paper or rubber bands. The rule of throwing anything out that you haven't used in a year is harsh, so set your own expiration date.

If You Can't Part with Stuff, Clear Some of the Clutter with Off-Site Storage

It's a start. What's considered clutter? Too much of a good thing. Organize it or move it away to long-term storage. (Better yet, get rid of it. You will not miss most of it.) Store most used, most loved stuff in key areas and get the rest out of the way.

Unclutter Your Personal Life, Too

Get rid of the people, habits, and thoughts that drag you down and no longer serve your life.

Moving Experience

Moving was a major turning point, a testing ground for my own organizational skills. The thought of hauling all of my stuff, again, was too much of a burden to bear. I was ruthless. Not only did I not want to pack things up, but I didn't want to have to unpack them either. I looked at my new home as a chance to create the environment I'd always dreamed of: comfortable but uncluttered. Because I live by the beach, people come over to hang out all the time. I wanted to make it easier to keep clean and make a good impression. Last move I just stuffed a lot of my things in boxes and didn't open them for five years. I wanted to lighten the load this time, and it was terrifying to part with some of the items I knew had to go. It was also very revealing. What a waste of space! I had saved hundreds of tapes from old radio interviews. I had boxes and boxes of old business cards, rough sketches (thumbnails) from past projects. I took one box a day until I was done. That was my goal, and it worked.

Turn Clutter into Arts and Crafts

My nephew and I turned old socks into hand puppets, used LEGO and other long-since-forgotten toys as part of the set, painted old boxes for a backdrop, and put on a play for my family. It was fun and started me thinking of alternative uses for otherwise useless clutter.

Put Things That Need Action in a Bin or Basket and Leave It Where You Will See It

These could be sewing, crafts, photographs, and other projects. Make it easy to act. Keep tools and supplies with the project if possible. Put a visual reminder pad of where you left off and what you planned to do next when you quit. Add in any supplies you may need to buy or borrow.

Have a Ceremony

Have a burial if you are having a hard time parting with your clutter. Burn it, bury it, or send it out to sea. Learn to let go. Live in the moment. Don't buy or bring stuff into your life because you might need it some-day. Live for today. A friend of mine said to me as we looked at all the stuff in my garage, "Are you going to continue living in the past or do you want to move forward and clear some room to be in the present?" I had old art school projects—and many of these were bad. I looked through a lot of my stuff and asked myself, present or past? I celebrated successes but let go of the bulk of the items. I kept the award, for example, but ditched the banquet program, menu, and napkin. Get rid of items that stir up bad memories and keep the ones that produce a positive response.

Recycle

Old T-shirts make for great rags. Coffee mugs become pen holders. A cupcake pan or tray is the perfect place to mix paints. Artist Mark Dion would rummage around in the San Diego dumps culling materials for use in his art. "I wanted to make an entirely human-disrupted environ-ment," says the San Diego artist. His piece, called "Landfill," follows the style of dioramas in natural history museums.

Duplicates Can Always Go
Two's company, three's a crowd.

Who Are You?
Life changes so take a look at what to keep and what to toss based on who you are *now* and what you *want* to be.

80/20 Rule
Keep less stuff, but keep the best. Buy things that make you say WOW! Find things that fit, flatter, and make you feel good. Look at what you like and buy more of it—but get rid of things that just don't "do it" for you.

The Best Defense Is a Good Offense
The best way to control clutter is to stop it from happening in the first place. Find a way to curb your need for new stuff. I know, we all like shopping for something new. New is exciting. It's our tendency to hold onto the old well after it's usefulness has run out, adding it to our recent acquisitions, that makes any attempt at organizing a mess. Think before you buy. What would happen if I didn't buy it? Do you need it NOW? Is it worth the time and expense to store and clean it? Will it fit in your home and in your life?

AS IF?

When I am in my boat or scuba diving, I like to run "What if" scenarios. What if the engine breaks down in the open ocean or I run out of air sixty feet under water? This helps me to prepare. On the surface you would think this is an excuse to save every-thing so that you are prepared for every possibility. The truth is, if you run the "What if" scenario and you can buy, borrow, or rent something when you need it, then why have it hanging around? (When under water, this is not an option.)

GOT JUNK

There is a business called 1-800-Got-Junk that will come and haul away just about anything and have, including body bags, frozen animal carcasses, and boxes of breast-enlargement pills. Good to know these people are out there.

WHEN THESE ITEMS HAVE OUTLIVED THEIR USEFULNESS

Item	Shelf Life (Apprx.)
Rubber bands	2 yrs
Mascara	3 mos
Sunscreen	1 yr
Lipstick	1–2 yrs
Toothbrushes	3–5 mos
Canned food	1 yr
Nail polish	1 yr
Fragrances	2 yrs
Pens	2 yrs
Eyeliner	3–5 mos
Calendars	Get real!

(Check expiration dates on all medications)

SIMPLIFY

My experiences have shown me that life truly is a journey, and the less baggage we carry the easier the ride.

—Wally Amos

More than ever people are more important than possessions. Since 9/11 I have observed that people are living a simpler life, focusing less on purchases and more on people. What's more important, having ten different mobile phone covers to color-coordinate with your clothing or having important people call and say, "I love you"? Having a happy, healthy family that you love and loves you, friends who care, and clients that are a pleasure to work with is a priority for most people who first thrived and then barely survived that wild ride that was the nineties. A big home filled with the finest furniture is being replaced with a more responsible approach to life. A lot of us are simplifying and getting back to what's really important. Doctors will tell you that people facing death don't talk about the magazines they have amassed, the piles of paper on their desks, or the crap cluttering up their garage. They talk about the people in their lives, those they've loved and who've loved them. Don't let an overabundance of stuff get in the way of living your life. What do you really want out of life?

Less stuff can mean more life. To simplify is to make good use of your time because time is all you have. It is your life. Anything that doesn't move you toward your goals or make you happy is a waste of time. Simplifying means you can stay centered, calm, and in control despite all the chaos and craziness that swirl around you. Jamie Oliver, otherwise known as the Naked Chef, made millions from his books, cooking shows, and restaurants, which feature his "stripped down" recipes. Ironically he was quoted as saying, "I'm trying to be a bit more organized." His simplified recipes are liberating. I hate to admit this, but I will make semihome-cooked meals by adding a few fresh ingredients to prepackaged foods. Shhhhh, don't tell anyone because I take the credit for making the whole meal myself—from scratch.

Everyone is so busy living a grueling 24-7 marathon with too many things to do and not enough time to do them, there isn't time to stop and think—let alone organize. Simplify and streamline. Focus on what feels right. Rebel. If your Palm Pilot or planner is packed, slow down and get a handle on your time and your life. All of those devices that manage our lives—have they really helped or hurt? Don't buy gadgets that take a ton of time to set up and learn how to use. Before buying something, make sure it doesn't need special care. You want low maintenance.

When were you most happy? Was it when your life was simple? You can get back to that if you want. It's all about choices. If you only have a certain number of plates or coffee cups, eventually you will have to wash them. Think about what really makes you happy and get rid of gear that no longer serves you or your life. Birds, baking, watching boats drift by—not buying things we don't need, don't use, and can't really afford. Get back to nature. It's there for you when you need it. You don't have to hoard it. It is richly satisfying to lie in the cool grass in the park and look up at a clear, cloudless sky. Sunsets and sunrises. Walks. Thoreau and Walden Pond had it right. Less stuff equals less clutter, which means more time, which means more life. Sentimental items that don't produce a positive feeling should be banished. Say NO to things that will add to the clutter and chaos in your life. Stop piling it on— yoga, Pilates, soccer, cello, committees, languages, karate, and all the gear that goes with them. I'm not saying abandon everything or stop doing mundane maintenance tasks. Find a way to enjoy them. We are always looking for the big event, something for the highlight reel. What about enjoying the simple, mundane things in life? Make cleaning the kitchen a family affair. Find a friend to help with filing. A house unkempt cannot be so distressing as a life unlived.

eight

DON'T BE A "LOSER"

How to Find What You Need When You Need It

Not all that wander are lost.

—J. R. R. Tolkien

I f organizing is being able to find what you need when you need it, then disorganization is NOT being able to put your hands on something you are looking for. When it comes to organizing, this is a VERY important point. Life is a lot easier when you can find things when you need them—organizing will help. We have all misplaced things at one time or another. But if you are chronically losing things, this is usually the result of being disorganized. According to the *Harper's* Index, we waste a year of our lives looking for misplaced things. A year! Life is a lot less stressful when things are where you expect them to be. You know, where items almost fall into your hands when you want them.

It's no fun to be in a constant state of frustration. It's not helpful to our health, relationships, creativity, or career. Where have forgetfulness and flakiness gotten us? We can't be all we can be when we are absent-minded and keep losing things. Blanking on someone's name, missing an appointment, forgetting to follow through on crucial details, or falsely accusing others can leave people thinking we are unreliable, unintelligent, unfriendly, and, of course, very angry and upset. Not to mention disorganized, disinterested, and, sometimes, dishonest. That's the image we project and what others will think of us if we are disorganized. It's certainly not going to win us any promotions or new friends. It can be extremely embarrassing. Our reputation is on the line—organizing is the answer.

As if I haven't laid enough of a guilt trip on you already, let me also add this. Being forgetful and unable to find things can do more than tarnish your image—it can do a lot of damage and cause disasters in other areas of your life. It can be very dangerous to be disorganized. Forgetting to lock the door behind you, not turning off the iron and losing your wallet, keys, or important papers can all result in dire consequences. Let's see, you're sitting across from an IRS auditor who asks you to produce receipts you have long since lost. Uh-oh.

As you can see, there are serious consequences to being forgetful. Yet, strangely, there are some creative types who actually want to be seen as absentminded. They mistakenly think it's charming or eccentric. "Hey, I'm an artist, so it's expected of me." You may think it's charming, eccentric, and creative to be forgetful, but most people don't see it that way when you borrow an item and don't return it. When you miss appointments, deadlines, run late, or forget anniversaries. Not good. They see you as unthoughtful, ungrateful, and unreliable. "Every year, I would forget my family's birthdays. When they called me on it, I made up these dumb excuses like, 'Nobody reminded me!' Finally, they just stopped inviting me to the parties altogether. Now I write down everything I really need to do. I've become a giver, not just a taker," says Joan Rivers. Miss one anniversary and you'll *catch* it later. Careless is not carefree. Freedom of mind is not trying to keep everything in your head. It's also not trying to forget everything, either.

SEARCHING IN "EARNEST"

When you misplace something, eventually it turns up. Losing something for good is much more serious. Consider this story as a worst-case scenario. In the 1920s, Ernest Hemingway was to meet up with his wife, Hadley, in Europe. While en route, she left a suitcase containing virtually all his stories and poems (both originals and carbon copies) unattended and the suitcase was stolen. This left Hemingway no option but to rewrite everything that was lost. To say their marriage ended in divorce is stating the obvious.

GREAT MINDS THINK ALIKE

Right-brainers have the natural ability to be able to juggle several different things at once. Why not use this, as well as our natural curiosity and notoriously short attention span, to produce some profits? Leonardo da Vinci "dabbled" in science, math, philosophy, and music, in addition to art. Picasso tried his hand at writing plays. Ben Franklin was a bestselling author, media mogul, printer, editor, publisher, inventor, statesman, and a very rich man. Samuel B. Morse (the guy who invented Morse code) was, in addition to being an inventor, a painter, sculptor, and professor at the National Academy of Design, which he cofounded. With organizing, it is possible to spin several plates without dropping even one.

REMOTE, REMOTE

According to a study by Magnavox, about nine out of ten U.S. homes have TV remote controls and eight out of ten report losing them. Where is the remote usually found? In or under furniture, in the kitchen or bathroom, in the bed, and in the refrigerator.

QUIZ

How observant are you?

1. On a standard traffic light, is the green at the top or the bottom?
2. Whose face is on a dime?
3. On the American flag, is the top stripe white or red?
4. What is the lowest number on the FM dial?
5. What two letters don't appear on the telephone keypad?

Answers: (1) *Bottom,* (2) *Roosevelt,* (3) *Red,* (4) *88,* (5) *Q, Z*

"I KNOW IT'S HERE SOMEWHERE"

I do not seek to find.
—Pablo Picasso

Right-brainers have a unique kind of memory. We can remember the look or feel of something we came in contact with as a child, but are unable to recall where we put our keys five minutes ago. We're great with faces and feelings, but not so good at recalling names or numbers. It is a strange phenomenon that can make everyday living frustrating, but in other ways it's beneficial in our creative endeavors. It is the richness and vividness of past experiences that tend to surface while we are in the throes of work. Since we are very visual, seeing really is believing. Let's face it, as much as we would like to have everything out where we can see it, we just don't have the room. (Leave out the things that you use most often, but those items that we rarely use or won't need for a while need to be stored somewhere else.) Some of the traits that make us unique (and wonderful) are also behind the reasons why we lose a lot of things. We are usually going in a million different directions at once; we prefer to burn the candles at both ends, keep our heads in the clouds, and rarely write anything down. Mostly a lot of lost and forgotten things are a direct result of our chaos, clutter, and disorganization.

TRUE STORY

A friend and I were playing tennis when he received a frantic call on his cell phone. His wife had locked her keys in the car—again. My buddy and I rushed over to the mall to rescue her. On a whim I checked the passenger side door and it was unlocked. That's when my friend's wife whispered in my ear, "Quick, lock it before Scott notices!"

"IT'S NOT LOST, YOU ARE."

We're lost but we're making good time.

—Yogi Berra

Three third-graders from San Diego won a national science contest with their invention called Finders Keepers, which helps people find commonly lost items. This neat little project came from the question posed by their teacher: What bugs you? The answer: lost items. They attach a small battery and transponder to small items and it sends a signal to a laptop. It's like a Lojack for lost keys. Here are several suggestions that can save you the frustration and heartache of losing or misplacing things in the future. Since we can't put a LoJack on everything we own, we'll simply have to use a "mental" detector instead.

Let There Be Light

Could it be that there isn't adequate lighting to see things in your closets, trunk, or workspace? A keylight or miniflashlight is handy for finding things in the dark.

Home Base

Things that float around get lost—period. Having a designated, consistent place where you keep like things together is the best way to not lose something. There is a lot of truth to the saying, "A place for everything and everything in its place." Create a special place to keep items that you frequently lose (keys, cell phone, and glasses), using either a hook, bowl, or designated drawer.

Be a Lean, Mean, Cleaning Machine

To us, "I can't find it," really means what we were looking for didn't fall directly into our outstretched hands. We are lazy. We are much more likely to leave something lying around than put it back where it belongs. Could it be our disdain for cleaning up after ourselves (and the clutter that creates) that keeps us from finding things? Take a couple of minutes at the end of the day or after completing a project to clean up. This saves all kinds of time, considering how long it can take to hunt for lost things. Don't put something down temporarily until it is in its final, permanent resting place. The less stuff lying around, the less is lost.

Designer Labels

When you put anything in boxes and stick it in deep storage, mark what's inside the box on the outside. If you want to get creative, draw a picture of the contents. Any kind of label on a box you can't see into or that is stuffed to the brim saves time. Looking at a label is a lot easier than having to pull the box down and empty it just to see what's inside. (The same thing applies to labeling your computer disks.) For keys, label them with a tag so you know which key opens what. (By the way, you can affix a hang-tag to just about anything.)

Get Closer

Keeping things close to where you use them makes it easy to find them when you need them. For example, tape an instruction manual to the bottom of an item. If the thing stops working or you need to adjust it, just turn it over and the manual is right there. Use a chain so your glasses "hang around" when not in use. Have a pen tethered near the phone. Velcro the remote to the top of the TV.

It's a Group Thing

Things that are spread out are harder to find. Things you use together should be kept together. Grouping like things together in boxes means less gets lost. For instance, keep your sports equipment together rather than scattered in several places. Stored with or near your bikes would be your helmets, locks, and a pump. An all-in-one organizer wallet with calendar and address book means everything is always together. Small, but similar, things can be kept in cases so that you can move them from pack to pack, place to place.

Clones Are People, Too

Who likes to be sitting outside in the rain freaking out because we lost our keys (again) and are locked out? It gets worse. We have to spend money to have a locksmith (who happens to be preprogrammed into our cell phone) come out. Of course we never got around to stashing a key or can't remember where we put it. Instead, have an extra set of keys made and give them to a friend, relative, or neighbor. Stash a set in a safe place (that you can access in an emergency). Keep an extra set in a drawer by the door so you never spend more than a minute searching for your keys. (Grab your spare set and look for the lost ones later.) This thinking also applies to glasses (keep a spare pair handy), pens (buy in bulk and put several in places where they are needed), and tools (buy an extra screwdriver or two). I realize this contradicts what I mentioned in chapter 7 about ditching duplicates, but this is THE exception to the rule.

Living Color

Brand all your stuff. All my buddy's tools have a small spot of fluorescent paint on them. When working side by side we can quickly distinguish his tools from mine. Color code your keys with key caps to reduce fumbling. You can feel the raised bumps in the dark. I also have a distinctive key chain that makes it hard to lose. Mine includes my first name and phone number, which have saved me on several occasions.

Put It in Your Path

Get a holster you can wear around your waist for your TV remotes. Put two-sided tape on the sleeves of your shirt and stick stuff to it. Carry a Sharpie pen with you and allow others to write right on your tee. I know, that's crazy. What we need to do is put things in our path so we can find them when we need them. When I store my scuba gear, I stick stuff in the pockets of my buoyancy copensator (BC) vest. That way my knife, dive light, and logbook are almost impossible to miss.

Loaned Out Is Lost

Don't lend things. If you do, put a sticky note in the place where you would look for the item you lent out, indicating who has it and how to get hold of him. Or, keep a log of what went where.

I'm Floored

Keep things off the floor and you lose less of your stuff. Use bulletin boards, baskets, bowls, hooks, and hangers to get items up and off the floor.

Try, Try, Try Again

Make a lost-and-found box for loose items like single socks, game pieces, and other strange stuff that don't seem to have a home.

Cheap Trick

To find a small, valuable item that was lost on the floor (like an earring back or contact lens), put a nylon stocking over the nozzle of a vacuum cleaner. The tiny item then will stick to the stocking.

Déjà Vu

Have you ever had amnesia and déjà vu at the same time? It's when you think you've forgotten something before. When I lose something, I wait to look for it. The delay allows my left brain to get out of the way. If I relax, my right brain seems to work better. Nothing good comes from freaking out and running around the house cursing myself. Begin the search by using your memory and intuition. Where do you think this thing is or should be hiding? Where was the last place you remember seeing it? Retrace your steps. Look there first. If not there, it's probably nearby. Then use logic. Where *should* I look for this? If I were this item, where would I hide? If you still can't find it, look in the same places again. You say, "But I looked there!" Yes, but this time look closely, slowly, calmly, and confidently.

SCAVENGER HUNT

In ten minutes or less, could you locate any of the following items: dictionary, keys, Band-Aids, pen, business cards, glasses, an AA battery, birth certificate, instruction manual for the television, vacuum bag, medical records, umbrella, film, safety pin, sales receipt for your computer, spare lightbulb, recipes, car registration, past three years' tax returns?

"WHAT WAS THE QUESTION AGAIN?"

The journey of a thousand miles must begin with wondering if you turned off the iron.

—William Rotslert

We don't forget things; we just can't seem to access the information. Unless we did it with our eyes closed or in our sleep, there is a record of it somewhere buried in our brain. The problem is we have two minds, one for momentary awareness and another for everything else. It's like when a computer is spooling. It's printing something out and you can do something else while waiting. It's funny, I can sing the theme song to *Gilligan's Island* and dozens of commercials from when I was a kid, can tell you the address of the first girl I made out with, the make and model of every single car I've owned, but I forget where I put a piece of paper five minutes ago. This is partly because like a lot of right-brainers, I'm easily distracted. I don't pay attention to details like where I put something down or what someone's name is. We wouldn't have the World Wide Web if it's creator didn't have a problem making random connections. Tim Bernes-Lee admits he was terrible at recalling names and faces. In 1980 he wrote software to help keep track of links. The rest is history.

HOW TO REMEMBER WHAT WE FORGOT

First you forget names, then you forget faces, then you forget to zip up your fly, and then you forget to unzip your fly.

—Branch Rickey

The key to organizing is being able to remember where you put something so you can get your hands on it when you want it. Here's how organizing can improve your memory.

Reminders

My buddy wrote on his arm to pick up his wife from the airport. He noted the flight, time, and terminal. That cool fall day he wore long sleeves and didn't see the note until it was too late. Trouble! We need visual clues to improve our memory. Attach a string to a finger, staple a note to your purse strap, attach one to your keys, or tie a ribbon on your backpack as a trigger. You can even write a reminder right on the bathroom mirror. Some people will put their watch on the opposite wrist or a ring on the opposite finger as a way to remember.

Associate with Things You Already Know

I go to a place we call the Tiki Bar all the time for a burger and a beer. Next door is a marine supply store. I'll usually pick up a part for my boat and then eat. One day I went in to order my burger first and then headed over to the store. I said to the woman behind the counter at the Tiki when I ordered, "Do you want my name?" She said, "Oh no, I see you in here all the time." Then she wrote something on a piece of paper. I was flattered they remembered me. When I got back my burger was ready and there was the note she wrote taped to the bag: "Blonde guy in black tank top." If you associate something you want to remember to do, tie it to something you are unlikely to forget, like your birthday or daylight savings. Put a reminder on the back of a clock so when you go to change the time you also remember to make your semiannual physical, for example.

Everyone Has a Photographic Memory, Some Just Don't Have Film

Confucius said, "I hear and I forget. I see and I remember. I do and I understand." When dismantling something, take pictures with a digital camera or Polaroid of each step to make sure you remember how to put it back together. If it's something like furniture, put the screws in a bag with instructions and label the bag.

Concentrate

Stop for a second and look at where you are leaving something. Take a mental snapshot. Mel Ash, author of *Shaving the Inside of Your Skull*, suggests imagining you have a pad of Post-it notes in your head and you can label your thoughts, ideas, and reminders and paste them into your brain. Say it out loud when you put something down. Write a note to yourself with your nonwriting hand to shake things up.

Don't Trust Your Memory

You can diminish worry and anxiety by getting the clutter out of your head and onto paper, your PDA, or a safe place in your computer. (As a bonus, the act of making a list or mind mapping also triggers your memory.) Dates to remember go in your calendar. When you are handed a business card, write notes to yourself on the back. Keep a running list of things to remember when you go to see your doctor, take in your car, or have an upcoming meeting. Make a checklist (and laminate it) to trigger your memory as a reminder of the things you need to take with you and do when you travel and put it in your suitcase. Keep a dry erase marker in the bathroom and write notes to yourself—or your partner—on the mirror. It washes right off. Any surface will do. Rapper Missy Elliot writes lyrics on the wall, the floor, and even on herself. Jimmy Buffett gets his best song and story ideas while flying. He admits that many of his lyrics and much of his prose are jotted on navigational charts. Anyone who gets ideas should carry a pad of paper with her at all times even if it's just to transfer scraps of paper into it.

Make a Forget-Me-Not Spot for Your Stuff

Organizing helps you improve your memory, especially when you pick a place to put things that you need to take with you by the door. When it's time to leave, you can just grab and go.

Don't Try to Remember It All

If your brain is on overload, be more choosy about what you put in your brain. Read self-help books with a purpose in mind and an idea of how you will apply it. Pick out the main idea or a few key ideas rather than trying to remember the whole thing. When I am working on a book, I make a list of things to do when I am finished. These are things I have neglected, like medical appointments, chores, and projects I've put off. I also have a list of things I WANT to do. This way I stay on track with my writing and don't forget to do things when I'm done.

Put Things in Several Places

The Just-in-Case pillowcase is an actual product with a little pocket for a condom. The strange twist is that this pillow was invented by a mom who made the first one for her college-bound daughter. Keep extras of things you use often in different places around your home or garage near where they are used.

Have Others Remember For You

I've been married for ten years, and we've been together for fifteen years. My wife remembers mistakes I made YEARS ago. She'll bring up something I may have done or said when we first met. I just shrug and agree. My thinking is this: there's no use in two people remembering the same thing. I believe a partner is someone who knows that song in your heart and can sing it back to you when you have forgotten the words. Significant other unreliable? Single? Use a computer program that reminds you of deadlines, birthdays, and anniversaries. Take advantage of automated payment programs. This means less paper and less to remember.

Use Your Senses

To remember where you put something, involve as many of your senses as possible. When putting your keys down, listen to them hit the counter, run your hand over the surface, take a mental picture, and attach some meaning to the act. I bet you can recall where you were and what you were doing on September 11, 2001. That's because we were able to make a visual and emotional connection. We CAN remember when we want. When we are interested and focused, we remember.

Put Things Out Where You Can See Them

On HBO's *Project Greenlight,* one of the aspiring screenwriters commented that she had gotten a tattoo on her finger to remind herself to always be an artist and creative. That's a bit much. Instead, put things in your path. Attach directions for the next day's appointment to your key chain. Leave a drawer open to remember to put something back. Put a bulletin board or a chalkboard by the door for reminders. Leave luggage out a week before a trip and throw things in as you think of them.

Do It Now

Do something when you think of it—or at least write a reminder to yourself. Clean the cutting board with bleach before you put it away. Put things in your car the night before so you don't forget them in the rush of the morning. Take care of that task if it will only take a minute or two. Now you don't have to remember to do it later.

Label It

The first time I went parachuting I had to take a half-day class to learn the basics of the sport. One of the most important lessons I learned was what to do in case my primary chute did NOT open or the lines got tangled together. You cut away the malfunctioning main chute with one handle and open the secondary one with another. If you do this in the wrong order, you end up with what is known as a screamer—you screaming as you plunge to your death. Not good. The problem was I could not remember which handle was which. So I suggested labeling them. This was a lifesaver for me when my main chute was tangled, and I had to cut it away.

Visual Reminders

A guy I know showed me what his wife had inscribed on the inside of his wedding ring. It said, "Put it back on. I love you." There is nothing wrong with having visual reminders all around you. A friend of mine posted the word "yes" all over his home to improve his outlook on life. I keep copies of all ten of my books along with the awards I've won for my writing on a shelf above my computer. I've seen people post software shortcuts on a cheat sheet attached to their monitor. You can even make reminders you can carry with you at all times by turning an important phrase or goal into a bracelet or key chain.

Write It Down

Write the things you want to remember down on the calender (appointments), a pad of paper (things to do), sticky notes (reminders), Rolodex cards (contact information or key codes). Create a cheat sheet so that when your computer crashes or you just completed a complicated task, you have a written record of the steps you took to come to a solution.

Make a note and attach it to the bottom of that ugly vase you got as a gift so you don't accidentally send it back to the person on his birthday.

Anticipation

Buy birthday cards in bulk, address, stamp, and date them at the start of the year, and then drop them in a tickler file or mark your calendar. Have you ever taken a virtual tour of a place or event before it actually happened? If you run a "what if" scenario and put yourself in the picture, you can anticipate problems and see what you may need to tackle them. For instance, put a pen and paper in your car, by the bed, in your briefcase or backpack because chances are there will come a time when they will come in handy.

LOST AND FOUND

When you lose something, the right brain will try to remind you where it is with nonverbal clues. This is because the right side of the brain lacks verbal skills and needs to find other ways to communicate to you. If you can get back to the situation and the sensations that went with them, these will allow the picture to become clearer. When it comes to looking for lost things, picture yourself during the day and rewind the movie in your mind. Where were you going? What were you doing? Who were you with? If that doesn't work, try to recall where you found the item the last time you lost it.

FOR FUN

My buddy lost his job so he became "Mr. Mom" while his wife went to work. The first day he had to get the kids ready for school was a nightmare. His wife left for work and didn't have time to pull the kids' clothes out of the drawers so she left a message on the answering machine about what the kids should wear. My friend still struggled when it came to finding the kids' clothes. When his wife called him later in the day and asked if he found everything okay, he replied, "Oh, sure." "Really, where was it?" she asked. "Uh, Target," he replied.

ONE OF US: JENNIFER STULTS

"I write everything I need to remember in one place, my very small and portable planner. I also use Post-it notes and put them everywhere to remember important things—on the computer, my purse, and even on my planner. If I can't write something to remember down, I will call my voice mail and leave myself a message. I've also been known to e-mail myself reminders of appointments. For a little more peace of mind I set the alarm function on my computer to remind me of appointments. I love e-mail alerts about friend and family birthdays."

THE GOOD, THE BAD, AND THE UGLY OF A LOST ITEM

The Good: You and your husband agree, no more kids. The bad: You can't find your birth control pills. The ugly: Your daughter borrowed them.

TABLE SCRAPS

Arrange whatever pieces come your way.
—Virginia Woolf

Can't break the habit of writing things to remember on little scraps of paper or whatever's handy or within reach (matchbooks, napkins, envelopes, bills, any semipermeable surface)? There's nothing inherently wrong with this technique, except for the fact that you wrote a note on your palm and washed your hand before copying it down somewhere more permanent. If you prefer this type of system, here are ten tips.

1. Make notes on full-size sheets of paper and stick them into the file of the relevant protect. Don't worry about wasting a whole sheet for one small note. At least it won't get lost or crumpled, and there is room if you need to add more information to the page later.

2. Create a "Scraps" file in your computer and scan and save your most important scraps of paper for a more permanent record.

3. Try using a clear or translucent (string tie), plastic, letter-size envelope to keep scraps safe. You can organize and sort these scraps by using different-colored envelopes.

4. Post and sort small random pieces of paper on your bulletin board, which is divided into quadrants—"To Do," "To Call," "Waiting for a Follow-up," "Urgent," or "Personal."

5. There are clear check organizers that are perfect for saving and sorting scraps of papers because they are portable and have twelve separate sections that can be labeled.

6. Have a fishbowl for scraps. This acts as either an in-box or a dump site. To make it work, review the contents regularly and when it overflows take the time to thin out the current from the crap.

7. When you're making a note on a scrap of paper or envelope—use both sides. That way you have a 50 percent chance of finding the note when you need it and only a 50 percent chance you'll toss it by mistake.

8. Buy a notebook that has clear sleeves to keep your scraps of paper. A photo album with sticky pages also works well to secure loose notes.

9. Staple scraps to a large piece of paper or card stock, which can be folded in half and made into a tent. If it looks like a ransom note, so what?

10. If you write reminders on your palm, use a permanent marker!

POST-IT NOTES: THE ULTIMATE REMINDER

If you want something to happen, you have to make space for it.
                                                            —Unknown

The impact of innovations by creative individuals affects us every day. Thomas Edison's lightbulb, Alexander Graham Bell's telephone, and Art Fry's amazing Post-it note. Seriously, this little yellow sticky thing has become the right-brainers' best friend—a key weapon in our arsenal against the onslaught of little bits of information that continues to come at us. Plain and simple, these little sticky things work! There are more than 250 Post-it note products, from the original pastel yellow pads to bright neon colors to notes shaped like feet (foot notes?), to notes that smell like pizza, to big easel pads, to repositional wall decorations for a child's bedroom (it's never too early to start kids on Post-it notes). The uses are unlimited; that's one of the reasons they are so great for a creative person. There is no wrong way to use Post-it notes. They inspire creativity. The key advantage to the Post-it note is in its ability to stick cleanly—to files (or piles) of papers, planners, banners, memos, demos, phones, walls, stalls, doors, floors, chairs, or computer screens. I see nothing wrong with Post-it notes plastered all over your office, home, and car. Here are some creative ways to use Post-it notes to remember what you have forgotten.

Signs
Crease a Post-it note at the adhesive line so it stands up straight and becomes a better visual reminder.

Messages
The brightly colored Post-it note is perfect for leaving family members a phone message on a mirror, instructions for the delivery driver on the door, or a note to yourself on the doorknob.

Bookmarks
Use a Post-it note as a marker in your Yellow Page directory for frequently referred to information, marking the favorite passages of a book, affixing directions to a map as a reminder for future trips to that area.

Survival Tool
In the book *Longshot* by Dick Francis, the lead character is a survival expert who always carries Post-it notes for crucial activities, including marking a trail and helping to start a fire.

Daily Planner

The beauty of Post-it notes is that they are flexible. When it comes to planning your day, make a heading at the top of a piece of paper that says, "Things to Do" and "Places to Go" and "People to Call" and put your Post-it notes under the appropriate heading. Put them on a time line or in the order in which the tasks need to be done. Number them and move them around if you have to. Use a freestanding board, wall board, or card stock so you can organize tasks written in individual Post-it notes based on urgency, mood, category, and move them around as the day or week progresses. You could also divide them into categories like "Family," "Work," and "Me." On a calendar arrange appointments, meetings, or calls on the tentative day. You get the picture. It's easy when the day is done—just peel off undone tasks and move them to the next day. If things change, move the Post-it note to another day. If you turn a Post-it note on its side it becomes a perfect (sticky) things-to-do list.

Motivators

Motivate yourself with inspirational quotes and affirmations stuck all over the house. I came across a story of a single father raising his only daughter the best he could while working two jobs. Even though he left early in the morning for his construction job, he always made his daughter lunch and inserted a Post-it note with a nice message letting her know how much he loved and cared about her. Since it only took a minute or two, he doubted it mattered all that much. However, one day when he went into her room and closed the door, he found every single note he had ever given her arranged in nice neat rows stuck to the back of the door. (Sigh.)

Communication Tool

Country singer George Jones featured Post-it notes in a song and music video where the leading lady leaves messages on sticky notes scattered throughout the house to communicate to her no-good husband who never listens.

Training Tool

One woman put notes on things like the ice tray her husband left on the counter that said, "I'm not a magic ice tray. Don't expect me to refill myself," or for cereal boxes left out, "I can't fly. Can you put me back in the cupboard?" For dirty socks left around, "I don't have legs. Will you put me in the hamper?" After years of nagging, this finally did the trick.

MASTER LIST

There is no fun in having nothing to do. The fun is in having a lot to do and not doing it.

—John Roper

To give you an idea how a master list works, picture a large warehouse. This warehouse is stocked with your ideas, errands, reminders, people to call, unfinished business, and various tasks you have yet to tackle. They are stored there, awaiting shipment to your to-do list or calendar when (shelf) space opens up. This is the equivalent of a shipping and receiving department. Things that need to be done or remembered come in and eventually get shipped out. The master list acts as a holding area. An inventory of the things you have to do. When you ship them out, they are taken off the inventory. A list like this is a very efficient way of juggling several things at once without having to trust your memory.

nine

ORGANIZING TIPS
AND TRICKS

Quick Fixes for Any Mess
You Get Yourself Into

Worrying is less work than doing
something to fix the worry. . . . Every-
body wants to save the earth; nobody
wants to help Mom do the dishes.

—P. J. O'Rourke

The goal is to get a system in place so that getting and staying organized are a no-brainer. The tips and tricks in this chapter have helped others who were even more disorganized than you. Even though these ideas take into account the right-brainers' natural tendencies, each of us has our own unorthodox way of doing things. So as you read through this chapter, see which suggestions literally jump off the page and make the most sense to *you*. I have test-driven almost every single one of these ideas in my own life, and I know they work. Will they work for you? There is only way to find out—try some of these suggestions on for size.

Most times we achieve our dreams and goals through a series of small steps. So think big (everything flows in and out of your life effortlessly, and you can find what you need when you need it), but start small (organize a drawer in the kitchen or the contents of your wallet). The first step to an organized home or office may start with a clean kitchen or a purged purse. So included in this chapter are tons of tips to organize almost everything in small, simple steps. Look around and start to notice what really bugs you. These are areas about which you continuously tell yourself, "Someday I am going to organize this," but you don't because you don't have the time, tools, or the techniques to do it right—or right

now. Well, that excuse is now bogus because here are so many simple solutions that will work wonders on just about everything that ails you. You
can't fail. Make a list of one hundred things that annoy you. This should
take about ten minutes. (Or put sticky notes on the things that frustrate
you.) Think about it. You pick up your cell phone and realize you are
scrolling through hundreds of outdated names and numbers. You get in
your car and can't find your keys. You have more books and magazines
than your local library. Wait, some ARE from the local library, and the late
fees are piling up. Find at least one solution to each situation and then
DO IT. Try to get rid of a couple of annoyances a week. Maybe you hate
the lump of clothes in the corner. Simply put a wicker basket there, dress
or undress next to the hamper, or make nice, neat piles. It's really that
simple when you take it pile by pile, room by room, mess by mess.

BATHROOMS

My wife and I have separate showers because our styles of getting ready
are so different. I have a combo shampoo and conditioner, a bar of soap,
and a towel. That's it. Simple, easy. She has ten different treatments for
her hair, all kinds of washcloths, scrubbers, shavers, body washes, gels,
treatments, and things whose function eludes me. She also cleans the
shower after each use. I don't. My total time taking a shower is about five
minutes. Hers is like fifty. Then there is the battle over the toilet seat. I
like it up; she insists it should be down. I argue, why should I put it
down when I am going to simply have to lift it up again later? Well, the
night she practically sleepwalked into the bathroom and fell into the toilet was a turning point. The scream she let out literally scared me into
being better about "doing the right thing" and putting the seat down.
Picture this. Both of us standing over the toilet, label maker in hand as
we affix a little reminder to the underside of the toilet seat cover that
says, "PUT ME DOWN, DARN IT!" (This is a true story.)

We do a lot of things in the bathroom. I'll spare you the details, but I
think it's safe to say that for many people, what we call a "bath" room is
also used for reading, relaxing, reflecting, and "other" stuff. It's also the
room where many right-brainers get their best ideas. Yakov Smirnoff,
the Russian-born comedian/actor, and his wife invented Shower Notes

in the late 1980s. It's waterproof paper for jotting down notes in the shower. One artist I know writes notes to herself and doodles with a dry-wipe pen on her bathroom mirror. To make your bathroom into an idea center, put in a basket, bin, or container with the needed supplies so that when inspiration strikes—even if you are naked and dripping wet—you can capture it. Your bathroom can be a sanctuary or an insane asylum; it's your call. With a few clever adjustments we can make getting ready simple, easy, fast, and functional as well as quick to clean.

Privacy Please

According to a study I read, nearly half of all people who come to a party will take a peek at what's in your medicine cabinet, so be careful about what you leave "out in the open" (anywhere that's not locked).

Bathroom Groupies

This tip comes from Laura Love, a Feng Shui expert living on Kauai. "A mental trick that I use (and this works especially well with kids) is to create 'homes' for things, where they then 'live.' It often helps to subdivide storage spaces so that everything doesn't slide back into one big jumble of 'stuff.' For example, one single drawer in my bathroom has a basket with hair ties, several separate small boxes for different types of jewelry, and a couple of small, open bowls for hair pins and elastic hair bands. That way, when I take them off, I know right where they go, and when I'm getting ready in the morning, I can find things easily! It's especially nice when I'm only half-awake." Thank Laura, I "love" it. Along these same lines, a bowl with soaps, scents, and other bath paraphernalia works really well. Containers and baskets are great for grouping items such as curling irons, hair dryer, hair clips, and backup supplies. Keep cleaning supplies in the bathroom in a carry-caddy.

Hookers

Many bathrooms lack storage space, and that's the most common cause of clutter on and around the counters. The solution is to be creative with how you store things. Putting hooks on the back of the door, inside the shower, on the wall, or on the back of cabinet doors can double your space. My friend's home is done in early Hawaiiana, and he installed a bamboo pole with hooks to hold robes, toilet paper rolls, and towels. A shower caddy can be useful for all those loose little lotions and gels or a squeegee. A shoe bag hanging on the back of the door can hold a hair dryer, brushes, and other assorted items. Install a hook by the sink for the blow dryer. How about a hook to hang the next day's outfit or to "steam clean" a wrinkled suit while you take a hot shower?

Ministorage Units

Actually, you can use any kind of container for storage in the bathroom, even if it was designed for elsewhere. I bought small containers at the hardware store, which I believe were meant for nuts and bolts (a five-inch-tall tube with a removable top), and I put my nail clippers, eye drops, and other small stuff in them to make more space in my medicine cabinet. You can add more storage by putting in another medicine cabinet. The aftermarket over-the-toilet shelf systems are also helpful. Under-the-sink containers with drawers are one of my secrets to sorting my supplies. Skirt the area under a freestanding sink for more storage. Countertop acrylic containers are perfect for cotton balls and Q-tips. The idea for this next tip came from my boat. I installed mesh holders in various places (near the engine, on the back of the seat) to hold the things that are often used in that area. The beauty is that they drip-dry because the nylon mesh material allows it to breathe. You can put these on the back of the door, inside a cabinet drawer, or with suction cups in the shower. They are prefect for bath toys because they drip-dry.

The Reading Room

I have heard quite a few people say they do their best reading in the bathroom. If these people are willing to *admit* that, then there must be many more who feel the same way but keep it to themselves. A magazine holder fits nicely next to the commode or install a magazine rack on the wall. A basket in the bathroom where you throw articles or catalogs you want to catch up on also makes sense. Would a bookshelf be too much?

Something Stinks

One of the lessons I learned the hard way is that many of the things contained in the medicine cabinet go bad after only a matter of months. I was rushing to give a speech, and I grabbed an old bottle of cologne (Drakkar—the name alone lets you know how old it was), and it had taken on an entirely different scent after sitting around for a few years. Not good. When I got home I showered and then I went through my bathroom and got rid of a lot of old or expired items. Take inventory of your bathroom. I'll bet you have duplicates and outdated and disgusting items whose time has come and gone. Many cosmetics go bad pretty quickly. (Eye shadow and mascara should be replaced every few months because of contamination.) With a Sharpie pen, put the date you bought something on the bottom.

Move It Out

Keep frequently used items in the most convenient places and rarely used items out of the way or out of the bathroom altogether. Things you have in duplicate can go in your travel kit. Move your ratty old towels to the garage for use in washing the car.

FAST FACT

If you work for forty years you will have spent five thousand hours getting ready for work. (That's figuring only thirty minutes a day of grooming.)

BEDROOMS

Since your house is now divided into zones based on use, it's clear what goes where, right? The bedroom is probably the main exception. It can be used for reading, relaxing, sleeping, and, uh, "other stuff." Most of these are not messy (oh, stop), but eating in bed is one thing that may be a big turnoff. Leaving crumbs is one thing. Leaving dirty dishes or an empty Ben & Jerry's carton on the nightstand is gross. It's stuff like this that makes me believe there ARE monsters under the bed. (Monsters and all, under the bed is a good storage space for nonperishable, clean things.)

A bedroom should be the one place you can really rest and relax. This isn't the place for half-finished projects. It should also be a sanctuary where clutter is kept at bay. Anything that doesn't make you feel restful or relaxed should be kept elsewhere. If it has to stay, stash it out of sight. How about a trunk at the end of the bed for your blankies, jammies, and "other" goodies? If seeing clothes strewn all over the place isn't doing it for you, put a hamper in the place where you change and drop clothes. (If you have to pick them up and *carry* them to a hamper, chances are you won't.) If you read in bed or watch TV, make storage that matches that need. Have a basket or container with all the supplies—glasses, books, magazines, paper, or a cool box for your remotes.

GOING OVERBOARD

Everything I learned about organizing I learned on my boat. (These very same lessons can easily be applied elsewhere.) On a boat you learn lessons fast or you are in serious trouble. If my engine quits and I want to keep my boat from banging into the rocks, I need to get that oar out quickly. When approaching the dock, I need ropes at the ready. What if I drop my keys overboard in the middle of the ocean? It's a good thing I have an extra key stashed on board. If the Coast Guard decides to board my boat, it's helpful to have all my paperwork in order and accessible so they don't start digging around in the boat looking for contraband. When a line from a lobster trap wraps around the prop, it is a lifesaver to know that I have a mask and dive knife stored under the seat. It's never a good thing when someone trips on something left out and falls overboard. That's why everything that's nonessential is kept in a container and stored out of the way. When I run out of room for storage, I rotate the gear based on the activity that day or the season. I have also come up with creative ways to hold all my gear. All the above scenarios have happened—and then some. The solutions I mention have also saved me from some harrowing situations and would work on land, too.

FAST FACT

Of readers questioned 43 percent said they finish a book once they start reading it; 42 percent use a bookmark; 39 percent dog-ear it.

BOOKS

"I'm not intellectual, but I'm very curious. I love reading everything I can," says Nancy Bass, owner of the Strand, Manhattan's famous bookstore. Wow, if I could own my own bookstore I would be in heaven. Most people will say that reading is one of their favorite things to do. I agree! I LOVE books. L-O-V-E books. The problem was I had too many. (I really could have opened a bookstore.) I was keeping more books than I had room for. My books were crammed into every corner and two deep in my bookcases. Most of these were titles I would never look at again. Still, I knew that getting rid of *any* of my books would be too much of challenge to do alone, so I invited my mom to come and help.

With her help I set a limit (four bookcases) to how much space I'd dedicate to books and thus how many books I could keep. As we went through my extensive collection of books, my mom had to literally rip some of them from my hand, even though it was a title I had in triplicate. (I would buy the same book over and over again because I was never quite sure what was already on my bookshelf.) Since I was donating my excess books to the library, it wasn't as traumatic as it could have been. (I could go visit them if I needed to.) Some of my reference books were so old the information was obsolete. (I had an Atlas with countries that no longer exist.) Any old reference books with really old copyrights were thrown in a recycling bin. A lot of books I gave away to friends, which made me look like a great guy. One of the great things about this process was that I decided to reread some of my favorite books instead of going out to buy more.

When it came time to organize my remaining books, I used my favorite independent bookstore (Warwick's) as a model of how to do it. I put the new releases up front and the rest were divided by category. I now keep only my own personal bestsellers. I added extra shelves for my small books to take up wasted space.

Did you know that 36 percent of U.S adults haven't visited a library in the past year? Sad. So I also decided to create a lending library for some of the books I could live without for a while. I put a pad of paper on top of the bookcase with titles I have lent out and to whom. As Edward Robinson said, "Friends: People who borrow my books and set wet glasses on them."

Finally, I now keep reference books close to where they are needed. I put automobile repair books in the garage, my dictionary and thesaurus are in my office, and cookbooks are kept near the kitchen. I also moved my gardening books near my gardening tools. It makes no sense to run upstairs with muddy boots to check and see if a plant is meant to be in full sun or partial shade.

MUSIC

As Summer Brannin made her way to work, she would often pass a truck that was covered with British-pop bumper stickers. She didn't know who owned the truck, but based on the stickers she made a mixed tape of songs that she thought the owner would like. This was something Summer loved to do. She loved making tapes for anyone and every-one—especially her boyfriend. Summer died of cancer at the age of twenty-one, two months after she was diagnosed. At her funeral her boyfriend made a mixed tape of Summer's favorite songs and gave them away to her friends and family. *Music is meant to be shared.* That's why I started to better organize my music and gave away the CDs I no longer liked or needed. Other CDs I lent out (and I kept a list of who had what). Some I sold for cash. From what was left I made my Hot 100, and these most important CDs are in a tower that is truly a work of art and a part of the decor. (Of course this tower is next to the CD player.) For portable CDs I bought the carrying case that came with the most sleeves. (Having your loose CDs stacked is asking for scratches and makes it harder to find what you want when you want it—like when you are driving.) The rest I archived and put on shelves, organized simply by genre. It's not perfect, but it works. No matter where I pull a CD from, I always leave the case sticking out a little so it will be easier to put back.

My way is one of many ways you can organize your CDs. For exam-ple, on the HBO show *G-String Divas,* the DJ at the strip club (er, gentle-man's club) has a BIG binder with sleeves. This can be a good way to go if you don't want or need the case. (Many artists do not list the songs or even their own name on the actual CD, so sometimes the cases are worth saving.) With a big binder you can carry all your CDs with you and store a lot more. Using binders with loose-leaf sleeves allows you to have a binder that stays at home and one you can carry with you. I have seen these binders organized by style, artist, alphabetically, and even according to mood. Baskets are great for quick storage. I throw videos and DVDs into one that looks a lot like a grab bag at Blockbuster. Who says CDs have to be neatly arranged by title? Add more shelves and space them close together to hold your CD collection. Label the shelf based on how you sort them. (I know, all are sorted under "miscellaneous.") There is no right or wrong way to do this. There is only your way—as long as it works.

All this talk about CDs is mostly moot. Downloadable music is changing everything. However, give a right-brainer iTunes, a CD burner and allow our wandering minds to go wild, and you have a logistical nightmare. (Think: half-finished compilation CDs.) Keep blanks and a Sharpie handy and mark as you go. Organize songs by grouping them together (love songs, breakup songs, dance songs) so you can match your mood.

FAST FACT

In a recent survey of what motorists keep in their glove compartment, 50 percent said they keep a map, 33 percent said they have insurance information, and 23 percent said they stash their sunglasses there, according to a *USA Today* poll.

CAR

Whenever one of my friends says, "Let's take your car, Lee," this usually means that his is full of junk and out of gas. A disorganized car can be a killer when it comes to taking clients out to lunch or a date to dinner. However, some clutter is okay when it comes to a car. I often wonder what one of Tony Soprano's "associates" would keep in the trunk. Guns? A shovel? Duct tape? Plastic? Cement? I guess it depends on the "job." Believe it or not, there is a lesson to be learned here. If you have a shelf in the garage near your car, you can use clear plastic containers and pack what you need based on what you will be doing that day. Where are you going? Going to the beach? *Badda bing,* grab the container with the towel, sunscreen, and other beach supplies. Doing a workshop? Grab the container with your seminar supplies. A container that you use to carry stuff to and from your home to the car is also handy.

The thing to remember is that your vehicle has many uses. It can be used as a shuttle for the kids, a tour bus for trips, a school bus when you listen to books on tape, or a race car when you are running late. What it isn't is a trash truck. The reason I bring this up is that a guitarist I was jamming with offered to pick me and my drums up in his truck. Hey, I'm cool with a little clutter, but this was out of control. Remember when Burger King's logo was orange? Exactly, that was a long time ago. There were literally dozens of old wrappers with half-eaten Whoppers still in them. Yech. I also could have done an experiment on all the dirty coffee mugs strewn about to find if a caffeine-laced mold may make for a better form of penicillin. I asked him, as I gingerly put one butt cheek on the seat, "So do you date much?" He replied, "Nah, I'm going through a dry spell." Wonder why. On the other hand, a friend of mine who always "hooks up" keeps a blanket, cards, poetry, portable CD player, thermos, and other romantic items in his trunk for an impromptu picnic or some stargazing—and his car is clean.

So how much stuff is too much? That depends on the size of your vehicle and what you use it for. Here are some suggestions for items that will make all that time you spend in the car more efficient and enjoyable, whether or not you are taking multitasking to a new level with one knee holding the steering wheel, the other pedal to the metal, and one hand is holding a nonfat latte and the other cradling a cell phone.

Join AA
That's short for Astute Automobile owner. And an astute automobile owner is a member of the Automobile Association of America.

This Is the Key
Have an extra set of keys around the house or give them to a trusted neighbor. You can also get a credit card–sized plastic card with a cutout of your car key from AAA.

Home Away from Home

A car is more than a car, it's a home on wheels. Some of us will eat, sleep, drink (sodas only, please), and transport people and things. For others it serves as a mobile office. Keep toys in clear plastic containers, office supplies in a tackle box, and have trash bags handy.

"Can I See Your License and Registration, Please?"

There are quite a few papers that are kept in the car. Of course you carry registration, proof of insurance, and a blank accident report. No? Keep your papers organized, using a set of envelopes or a checkbook organizer. Both are good for the glove compartment. In these, put coupons, receipts, or a mileage log.

Roadside Safety

In addition to your cell phone, it's helpful and handy to carry flares or flashing triangle, a first-aid kit, Fix-A-Flat, flashlight, traction pads, a severe weather survival kit, Swiss Army knife, extra oil, jumper cables, and most important of all, water. I also stashed a fifty-dollar bill in an envelope in case of an emergency—of any kind.

I'm a Promotion Machine

One of the most important things I keep in my car is a promotional kit (in a plastic container), complete with business cards, press kits, postcards with my book cover on them, point-of-purchase displays, copies of my books, as well as pushpins and tape (to hang flyers), and a camera for photo opportunities.

Oh, Brother

It's such a pain to refold maps. That's why a Thomas Guide is such a godsend when lost. No, I still won't ask for directions, but I will look them up. A handheld global positioning system (GPS) is handy, too.

Think Tank

It's a fact we get good ideas while driving so have some way to capture them (without crashing).

Mobile University

Butch Trucks of the Allman Brothers is on a continuous program of self-improvement. When he motors around Florida he likes to listen to college lectures on audiotape. This makes perfect sense, since we spend more time in our cars commuting—so make it count.

You Never Know

That's why (if you have the room) keeping a couple of things in your trunk (containerized, of course) to counter any situation that comes up is a good idea. These can include books and magazines to read in case you are waiting for someone or have some found time. An errand box is also handy. In it you carry items to return to stores, cleaning supplies in case you pass a self-service car wash, or library books that need to be returned. Other items to carry are workout wear or yoga mat, an extra coat or sweatshirt, camera, and spare hosiery.

A Trunk in the Trunk

A box or bin for stuff that you have to schlep in and out of your home is helpful. Installing a shelf next to your car where you keep related supplies works well. Then, depending on where you are heading, you can grab the container with the gear you need and go.

Ten and Two

That's the position I learned in driver's education of where to put your hands on the wheel. Cup holders are not a novelty; they are a necessity. A hands-free cell phone car kit is also a must. So get a grip and keep from crashing.

FAST FACTS

The average wallet contains $104 and change. Seventy-five percent of people polled store their bills in numerical order—singles in front and larger bills behind. Also, one-third carry condoms.

CARRYING CASES (BACKPACK/PURSE/ WALLET/BRIEFCASE)

We carry around all kinds of things (mostly "emotional" baggage). There's more to carry than ever before. I saw a woman falling down the stairs while juggling a cell phone, planner, keys, and a book. Bestselling author Mattie Stepanick doesn't let muscular distrophy slow him down. Maybe you've seen the young poet on *Oprah* or *Larry King Live* promoting his *Heartsongs* collections. When he goes on a cross-country book tour, he has to tote a lot more than most. His wheelchair is loaded down with equipment and also his personal stuff.

WHAT'S IN YOUR BAG?

I did a little study asking friends (and even strangers) to dump out their backpacks, purses, and empty their pockets. In addition to finding some truly frightening things (moldy and hairy candy bars and an assortment of unmentionables), I found some fascinating things, too. Backpacks are not just for kids and campers anymore. What do you put in your pack? Circle anything you may want to add to your bag: aspirin, breath freshener, calculator, cappuccino mix, cell phone charger, coin holder, condoms, coupons, diary, deodorant, dog treats, extra car key, gloves, Handi Wipes, inspirational little minibooks, lighter, loose change, lotion, mending kit, miniportfolio, nail repair kit, notepad, panties, pantyhose, paper clips, pen, photo album, Polaroid camera, Post-it notes, promotional materials, scrunchies, sketch pad, snacks, Speedos, sunscreen, workout wear.

As a writer, my backpack is one of my most important pieces of equipment. Of course it contains my laptop, plus a lot of other supplies vital to my "survival." Angelina Jolie, the actress, is learning to play the drums and brings her drumsticks with her everywhere. I have been doing the same thing for years. Einstein got many of his insights and ideas while sailing. I'm no Einstein, but I've got a backpack with lots of little pockets so that loose items don't fall overboard when on my boat. I can't tell you how many times I said, "I wish I had my camera." Now I don't miss those Kodak moments by carrying a small, disposable camera. Did you ever notice that Clarence, the angel trying to get his wings in *It's a Wonderful Life*, carried around a Mark Twain book? He read it while George was busy "discovering" himself and the meaning of his life. Having a book "on board" is perfect for reading while waiting in line or when you want a break. In the book *The Stars*

continued on next page

on the Set: Stolen Moments, numerous photos appear of stars like Marlon Brando, John Wayne, and Marlene Dietrich playing chess, checkers, or cards between takes. Anyone can carry a deck of Uno cards. Or, if you know what you're doing, a deck of Tarot cards can make any party more fun. I carry a memo pad like reporters do and also use sticky notes for quick notes to myself and others. I love to doodle, and when I was single I would draw caricatures of people and use them as an icebreaker. I have made sketches while at the nursery looking at plants so that I would remember the care or watering instructions. For the artist within, I have to haul around all my supplies, including canvases, brushes, and paint. How do I carry all this stuff without getting a bad back? I use the bag-within-a-bag system. That way I can mix and match what I need for the day.

WALLET

In a man's wallet there is probably one photo. In a woman's wallet there is every person she ever met, and most of these photos are years old. In addition to more photos, a woman's wallets can be a clutter catcher. Although Sheryl Crow wears a leather wrist wallet designed by Tamera Lyndsay, herself a rocker who performed in girl bands and needed a place to hide money while playing late into the night. Even if you carry a "George Costanza" wallet (stuffed) it can be organized. A lot of lessons can be learned when it comes to organizing a wallet. It's a microcosm of organizing in general. Dump out everything in your wallet onto the counter. Make piles for credit cards, cash, business cards, other cards, photos, driver's license, and other "stuff" you carry around. Let's start with what you MUST have in your wallet. You need your license or picture ID, medical insurance card, and credit card. Then there are the things you WANT. These include cash and things that help you reach your goals (library card, business cards, or an association card) or make you feel safe, secure, and happy (AAA card, family photo, and condoms). Items that are handy and helpful include claim checks for a quick pickup of repairs, your kids' shoe and shirt sizes or model numbers for copiers and printers that need cartridges. Keep numbers instead of the actual cards (like frequent flyer). If your wallet is lost, it is easier if you only have to replace the essentials. (Photocopy everything in your wallet and store it in a safe place.) What you don't need is a wallet stuffed with irrelevant receipts and all kinds of papers and cards that take up room and do you no good. (You can keep some receipts but do a dump-out once a month.)

PURSE

Is it time to clean out your two-ton purse and lighten up? It's time to take out some of the items that no longer serve your life and organize the rest. How do you do this? Since I do not carry a purse, I turned to my wife and some of her friends for ideas. Here are some of the best. One suggested carrying items that do double duty. For example, Bazooka gum is a good thing to have since it gives you good breath, a sugar rush, and something to read. Another woman says she carries a product by Lola that is both a lipstick and a key chain. Many of the ladies I talked to keep their things in small, *clear* containers so there is not a bunch of loose stuff they have to sift through to find what they need. Have two bags in one—a big bag and a clutch. One for when you are lugging everything and the kitchen sink and a smaller bag for a lighter load. Organizing your small stuff makes it easier to find things. Most of the women have divided their purses into zones so they know in general where everything is. Have a portable manicure set or nail clipper for downtime, floss for a moment when you have spinach stuck between your teeth. One woman had a credit card–size set of tools that contained a knife, pen, scissors, and tweezers. One of the single girls carried cab fare for when she might want to bail out of a date gone bad, as well as a few items in case she got lucky. Make sure you have an extra pair of stockings, spare set of keys, and a bottle of quick stain remover. Stash some cash in case of emergencies. Have a place where you can hang packs and purses, like a coatrack or a shelf with hooks.

MAKEUP

Actress Anne Archer has two complete sets of makeup—one is set up at home and the other is organized into a portable bag she carries with her. She learned how and likes to do her own makeup on the set. A friend of ours is an actress, and she shared some of the stuff she uses to create the glitz and glamour that are Hollywood. Her makeup kit includes the usual: eyeliner, mascara, blush, lipstick, and lip liner. It also includes foundation, concealer, pencil concealer, finishing powder, lip balm, bronzing powder, a sponge, and Q-tips. She always takes her makeup kit to a shoot just in case the makeup artist doesn't show up. She thinks actresses should learn to do their own makeup anyway. Use a clear container for your makeup so you can see what's inside rather than rummaging around.

CHORES/CLEANING

According to a Time Project study, women spent fifteen hours a week on housework in 1995, which (surprisingly) is thirteen hours less than they did in 1965. According to a poll by Clinique Laboratories, only 43 percent of the women polled predict that men will share household duties equally. Most feel they will always be primarily responsible for those chores. My wife asked me, "What's on the TV?" I said, "Dust." Next thing I knew the remote was ricocheting off my skull. Now I help with housework, and I would like to offer these ten tips to help any of you out there who hate this stuff as much as I do.

1. **Not just health department clean, but Monica clean.** This is in reference to clean freak Monica Gellar on *Friends*. Lower your expectations of what clean is. When having people over, focus on key areas—toilets, for example. Go ahead and push things into the closet. Dim the lights and light some candles. Let some things go that people don't see (like under the bed) so you have more time to entertain. (I'd like to thank author Paula Jhung for writing the book *How to Avoid Housework*.)

2. **Multitask.** Clean the shower while in it. Catch up on your "reading" by listening to books on tape while cleaning. Talk on the phone while dusting.

3. **The faster, the better.** Cleaning your house vigorously can burn about 450 calories an hour. Time yourself and see how much you

can pick up and toss within ten minutes. Do a five-minute cleaning run before bed and pick up and put stuff away as fast as possible.

4. **Make it fun.** Make it fun for everyone to help. Put socks and
terry cloth outfits on your kids and allow them to slide across the
floor to get it clean. In Dave Barry's syndicated column, he
shared a letter one of his readers sent him. "Julia" told her husband that watching him do the laundry made her hot. (Not true,
but the effect was the same.) She insisted that watching him fold
the laundry got her even steamier. Her wiles finally got him to do
the housework. She has even made love to him right by the
washing machine to prove her point.

5. **Keep cleaning supplies near where the messes occur.** Keep
carpet cleaner close to where you eat. Dustbusters are cheap
enough to have in more than one place. Stash pop-up wipes in
every bathroom in the house and swipe the counters, mirrors,
and sinks regularly.

6. **Do a little each day and then you don't have to waste a weekend cleaning.** Clean things as you notice them and do what's in
front of you. Do a quick pickup every day. Take a second to clean
up before you leave. Wouldn't it be nice not to have to spend
your weekend cleaning up and doing chores? Just a few minutes
a day, and you won't waste a weekend. Break down cleaning up a
rather large area into thirty-minute increments. You can clean
out a fridge in half an hour or scrub a bathroom in that amount
of time.

7. **The more clutter you have the harder it is to clean.** Enough
said.

8. **Be a basket case.** Use a laundry basket and go around the house
picking up stuff and putting it back where it belongs. A friend of
mine always has a kid on one hip and a basket on the other. I forget what she looks like without either one.

9. **Keep dirt out of the house.** When I lived in Hawaii, it was a
constant battle with the red dirt that got tracked into everyone's
homes. It's a good thing it's "Hawaiian Style" to take your shoes

off before entering a home. On the mainland there are all kinds of pesticides, poop, and other foul things that would be tracked in if you didn't get into the habit of taking your shoes off outside and keep them organized with a shoe rack by the door.

10. **Got it maid.** Hire help.

A NEW WRINKLE

Whirlpool Corporation claims that 57 percent of all clothes taken to the cleaners were done to remove wrinkles. So how about this? Steam clean while you shower.

CLOSETS/CLOTHES

"I'm such a pack rat that when I lost over a hundred pounds, I couldn't throw away my fat clothes. I just bagged them up and put them in the garage, next to my dead husband's clothes—next to my dead husband," jokes Johnnye Jones Gibson. A well-organized closet is one in which it's easy to take things out. Closets are not a place to pile stuff in and leave in there. For the things that are piled high and stuffed in the back of a closet or on a high shelf, it's almost as if they are not there at all. To make matters worse, when it's difficult to put things away in a cluttered closet, guess what? You won't do it, which creates a mess in other areas of the home. Getting a handle on your clothes closet is the beginning of an organized home. The same rules apply here that apply to organizing anything. Make the items that are worn most the easiest to get to. For us writers, it's our best loose and baggy flannels, sweats, and comfy clothes that get prime position (easy to reach) with the suits and dress shirts in the back. Workout wear in front? Not! My fat clothes are in my closet (again) and my I-wish-I-was-this-thin-again clothes are in another closet—in the garage. If you live in North Dakota, do you really need your thongs out where people will see them? (Not those kind of thongs.) It's nice to have an overflow closet to keep your out-of-season or out-of-style clothes in and then "rotate your stock" based on seasons.

Are you afraid to open a closet door because an avalanche of loose items will topple on you? Are your closets so crammed full of random clutter that you can't find anything without a long and (usually fruitless) strenuous search? That's why I find it better to designate a closet for one type of clutter so that you know (generally) what's in that closet and it doesn't get too crowded. Perhaps the way to start in your clothes closet is to get rid of all that stuff that doesn't belong there—gift-wrapping supplies, books, boxes, and bags. Then weed out old and unwanted clothes and make room for a better wardrobe. I know, your closets are full, and you still have nothing to wear. Move out the things you never wear, don't fit, or are ripped or stained. The truth is, we all have our favorites—clothes that make us look good, feel good, or are from a good designer. Yet we keep a bunch of crap that we almost never wear. What if we just kept the best and stashed the rest? Well, I did just that. During a move and a change of seasons, I evaluated my entire wardrobe and ditched or donated the clothes that, "hello," didn't fit me anymore or didn't fit my current (casual) lifestyle. It became a lot easier to organize my clothes when I had fewer of them to deal with. To help me I held a marathon makeover with my wife and her fashion-forward friends. I tried on and "modeled" my clothes, and they gave me a thumbs-up or thumbs-down. The result was I ended up with a lot fewer clothes that did nothing for me—or those around me. (I also ended up with a slight fashion inferiority complex.)

Comedienne Rita Rudner's take on shopping is this: "A saleslady holds up an ugly dress and says, 'This looks much better on.' On what? On fire?" I can now see the wisdom of having a personal shopper. At Nordstrom they're free, and they show you the right look for you, help create outfits, and mix and match items together. This can save space and money. Maybe you don't need more clothes but just need to make better use of your existing clothes. It's a lot easier when black is the base "color" for the bulk of your clothes. (That's how I simplified my wardrobe and my life.) Inventor Kamen wears the same outfit no matter what the occasion—even the National Medal of Technology awards ceremony at the White House: blue jeans, a denim work shirt, and Timberland boots. Come up with your own simplified color palette.

The Clean Closet

Imagine a closet that is clean, uncluttered, and color coded. It can happen, and you don't have to become an obsessive-compulsive clean freak to do it. I recommend you hang a picture on or inside the door of what you want your closet to look like. (These photos come from catalogs or magazines showing you what's possible.) Step one is NOT to pull everything out all at once. This is way too scary. You clean out a closet a little at a time. (This is not our normal approach to *anything*, but it works for this project.) First, organize all the stuff lying around the outside of the closet and on the floor. Then do the racks one section at a time. To do this, you'll need some supplies. Boxes are best for sorting out the clothes by the category they fall into inside the closet (pants, shirts, skirts, and so on) or those that you need to mend or clean, donate to charity, give to friends or family, sell, store elsewhere, trash—or burn. You can also have a box for the "undecided" items. Leave them out for a designated time and then, if they don't fall into one of the above categories, tape up the box, put an expiration date on it, and store it out of the way. Now it's time to deal with what's left. If you can afford it, get good hangers. (Empty hangers go in the front so they're easy to find.) The next decision is how to hang your clothes. There is no right or wrong way to organize your clothes, but it is easier to get dressed if you do it by color, category, or group outfits together. You want it to be visual, easy to mix and match, and most of all, easy to maintain. Along those lines each time you take something out or put it back, do a little straightening up.

The Creative Closet

Closets do not have to be boring. Why not make your closet an expression of your personality and creativity? What if you painted it a pleasing color or did a mural on the doors? Would beautiful baskets or colorful containers make it more appealing? What if you made it smell nicer? How about a dry-wipe board or a pad of sticky notes on the door to leave yourself reminders and (positive) messages? You might also pin up pictures of possible outfits and ideas you've seen in fashion magazines and want to try on for size. You could also come up with creative solutions to organizing challenges. A friend of mine mentioned that she put a corkboard on the inside of her closet door and uses pushpins to hang necklaces and bracelets. My buddy's girlfriend assembled a week's worth of his outfits on a rolling rack kept in a corner. (Trust me, this is a BIG help for this "fashion emergency" friend.) Old-fashioned hat boxes can be decorative and hold a lot of loose items. My wife uses clear containers with different-colored lids on a shelf in her closet to sort accessories. Faced with purses piled high in her closet, a reader wrote me that after the pile collapsed on her (while she was already running late) she bought a hat rack and converted it into a purse tree.

The Custom Closet

Even the people who are picky about almost everything else in their life will usually leave a closet the way it came. The people who designed and installed your closet likely had no idea what your needs were and how it would better suit your clothes. That's why there is so much wasted space. With a quick trip to the home improvement store and a few tools, you can create a custom closet that is adjustable, flexible, and fits YOUR needs. Need more shelves? More rods? Both can be added by creating a wood divider to cut your closet in half while doubling the amount of bars and shelves (and with adjustable runners and hooks, there are a lot more options when you want to "raise the bar"). If you add a shelf also add a rod underneath it so it does double duty. If you have a high ceiling in your closet, add another shelf to take advantage of space at the top. Use the high space to store luggage, which can double as a container. For a wasted area underneath your clothes, you can put an old dresser into a closet for more drawer space. You can also add cubes or crates for additional storage. Hang all the short things together so that you can use the bottom space for other clutter. Create more closet space in an alcove or corner by adding a bar and covering it with a curtain. Use a bookshelf to store folded clothes like they do in retail stores. There is a product that is both a bookcase and a closet door. Hang stuff on the wall or the back of the door. Use a heavy hook to temporarily hang your dry cleaning, the next day's outfit, or clothes that aren't quite dirty enough for the hamper. Have you ever considered hanging a stain remover on a string? How about hooks for a flashlight, lint brush, or iron? You can also hang a minisewing kit in the closet so when you notice a loose button you can pull out a needle, some thread, and stitch it up.

The Shoe Closet

Shoes, shoes, and more shoes. I saw an interview with diva Mariah Carey. Her closet is a full-blown salon. I half expected José Eber to pop out. It looked like a clothing store. Of course she has a shoe room. A shoe ROOM. One thing I took away was the fact that she had amazing lighting. It's dark underneath your clothes (which is not the best place to put shoes) and it's hard to find anything in the dark. Add a light in your shoe closet if there isn't one now. (They make push lights that don't need to be plugged in.) Kimora Lee Simmons takes Polaroids of her shoes and puts the pictures on the outside of clear containers. You can do the same with original shoe boxes. Granted, she has three hundred pairs of shoes. She also calls the area she keeps her shoes in her meditation room. I read in a woman's magazine the following tip: don't let your man count your shoes. He'll never understand why you need so many. I poked around in my wife's shoe closet (yes, she has a whole closet for her shoes) and counted fifty black pairs, all varieties of white, including off-white, sand, salt, and powder white. Hmmmm. I never see the new shoes come into the house. How she does it is a mystery to me. Shoes were one area that my wife and I spent the most time trying to get a handle on when we moved—and we did it. In addition to allocating half the house to her shoes, we came up with a system. She shifts shoes by season and keeps the out-of-season shoes on the shelves or behind the more current and often-worn shoes. Shoes she wears the most were put in a prime position. We got an over-the-door shoe holder for sandals, and running shoes, slippers are stored by the door, and the rest are kept in plastic containers with a Polaroid photo on the front. The shelves we got are adjustable so we can adapt them to type and time of year. (Boots in winter, sandals in summer.) By the way, my three pairs of shoes and flip-flops are on a rack by the back door. Speaking of racks, women who use a shoe rack are seven times more likely to be on time to work, according to a survey by Ikea.

FAST FACT

Fifty-four percent of people polled hang their clothes up right away. Who are these people?

ASK A PRO: MARIE KINNEMAN, INTERIOR DESIGNER

"As an interior designer I like to be organized in a way that is creative and also looks good. I recommend baskets in all shapes and sizes for a multitude of organizing solutions. In the kitchen: a basket (wicker or wire) near the stove holds cooking oils and spices that are used often—they are always accessible and the bottles and jars these days are very decorative and look great when gathered together. In a bookcase: a way to keep little books, pamphlets, and maps together on a bookshelf is to gather them in a basket and then place the basket on the shelf among the larger books. In the bathroom: an oval basket without handles works wonders in a bathroom with little storage—the basket can sit on the countertop and hold lotions, powder, hair products, and the blow-dryer. Keeping everything together this way creates a sense of tidiness and looks pulled together."

DESK

Automobile designer Doug Halbert describes his desk as a gravel pit and bemoans the clean desks of would-be designers. "The richest things happen in the messes along the way." Unless you are a surgeon, a sterile desk doesn't do a darn thing for me. A little life left out and about shows that you are busy, able to juggle more than one thing at a time, and most of all, normal. A really messy desk sends a different signal. *You see* creative, cool, controlled chaos. *Others* see undisciplined, unreliable, and unfocused. Coworkers are afraid to leave a note on your desk for fear it will be swallowed up by the clutter monster. I have an idea that will please both parties. I am guessing you have lots and lots of toys and tchotchkes out and about. Encourage those uptight, clean-off-their-desk-every-day folks to use your "collectibles" to tape notes to and hang stuff on. Now your Godzilla figurine is both fun and functional. Fill your *Star Trek* coffee cup with pens and pencils. Maybe your desk is where you do your work and you need a clearing. Put things in bowls or on bookcases. Bind two stacks of old magazines and put a piece of wood across and voilà, you have another desk. Make a wall collage with your cool stuff to get it off the desk. Add a shelf around the rim of the office. Use the ceiling. It can look like a TGI Fridays. The goal is to make your cave work for you and not frighten others—much.

Actors

I have quite a few friends who work in the film industry so I have some insight into their lives. One actress I know has devoted a portion of her desk to promotion (she keeps her head shots, Rolodex, and résumé there). Another corner is where she works on her craft (she has a mirror, recorder, red pen, and script holder) for rehearsing. On her desk is a big calendar where she enters her acting gigs as she gets them. She also has a framed photo of her idol (Meryl Streep) on her desk and a binder filled with notes from her acting classes. Her portable makeup kit is next to the door. Since she is a master multitasker, she also has a small TV nearby. Finally, a big bulletin board hangs over her desk where she posts reviews and fan mail.

Artists

I can't tell you how many articles about artists start with "Despite the cluttered condition of her studio, the artist does great work." Wouldn't it be nice if they just mentioned the great work? A potter I know had a very crowded and cluttered work area. We used clear plastic containers and other tools to organize a lot of his loose stuff, and it looks so much better. He didn't have much money to spend on organizing so we used gallon milk containers cut in half, old bowls, and empty buckets for his various knives and tools. The lids of glass jars were screwed into the bottom of a shelf (and labeled with a Sharpie) to hold a lot of loose little items. We built cubbyholes for the rest of his supplies. We installed shelves so he can display his work around the room and get projects off the ground while they are drying. He also created a shipping and billing area with boxes, invoices, and a scale. Maybe the best thing we did to clear the clutter from his desk was to hang several clipboards with orders and photos/sketches attached to them.

Authors

Bestselling author Janet Evanovich has two desks in her New Hampshire home office. One is for writing and the other is for answering mail and taking care of business. Writer Joe Queenan says he has about twenty assignments lined up and decides which one to tackle depending on what mood he is in that morning. If he doesn't have the energy to work on a major article like a piece for *GQ* or the *New York Times,* he'll do a movie or book review for the *Guardian.* Since writers generate a lot of paper, anything to organize them is welcomed. Tents and three-way stands (like restaurants put on tables to advertise daily specials) are perfect for putting on top of piles. Binders are best for organizing a lot of loose papers. For frequently dialed numbers (agent/editor/shrink), you can use a nice font and frame them. I enlarged and framed a sheet with the meaning of all those wacky symbols editors use to mark up my manuscripts. (If this sentence survives the edit, I'll be surprised, and I'll know just the mark they'll use to do it.) I created zones on my desk. This way I can switch off and not have to put everything away. When I was working on this book, I was at the writing zone; and when I needed a break, I would make copies or answer mail at another portion of my desk. The supplies for these tasks are all near to where they are performed. If I have to get up to grab a file, the distraction could pull me out of my work mode.

Musicians

Maybe your desk is a music studio that includes a computer, mixing board, keyboard, and a host of other gear. Create zones based on what area of making music you are engaged in—writing, recording, or performing. Drummer John Robinson created a home studio with V-Drums, keyboard, mixing board, and a desk for writing and corresponding. Almost every recording studio I have ever been in is organized. It has to be. Keep a clock in plain view since time tends to get away from us.

DRAWERS

Professional organizer Evelyn Gray suggests making labels that list (in general terms) what is in each drawer in your desk and attaching them to the lip. This way you can clearly see what's in that drawer with a quick glance. Things need a home, and the label makes it a more permanent place. She adds that you can also color code the drawers with a sticky dot at the top. Then add dots to papers, files, or other items so you remember where they go when you are finished with them. Good advice.

When I was growing up, every drawer in our house was a junk drawer. That doesn't mean they weren't organized. Using a combination of odd containers and drawer dividers, all those loose little things (paper clips, rubber bands, pens, glue, scissors, and screws) were sorted and stored separately. It made it easier to find things by not allowing them to commingle. This way, when you opened the drawer, you could see everything in one quick glance. In my own home I believe it's best if drawers only serve one purpose.

ENTRYWAY

First impressions are sooooo important. Your entryway is the first and last thing others see. People pick up on all kinds of visual clues and their subconscious mind makes instant judgments based on this input, and it is almost impossible to counter them. If these are negative signs—they have to step over a pile of papers or push aside a box to get into your office or home—this is not good. Impress them with your organization. It doesn't have to be perfect—a little quirky is okay.

Try the three bowl system. This consists of one bowl for keys, your cell phone, wallet, and other items you use and need every day. The second bowl is for impulse items (things you don't want to forget to take with you), including notes to yourself, library books, and outgoing mail. The third bowl is for junk, like loose change, coupons, and oddball items you don't know what to do with. I personally have a shelf next to the front door with baskets on it and hooks underneath to hang anything and everything.

GARAGE

Garages are mostly meant to store automobiles but are so much more. Almost every single musical group began as a "garage band." Quite a few companies were launched out of a garage (Apple Computers, the Walt

Disney Company, and Hewlett-Packard), and a lot of small business still operate there. Of course the garage is also the place a lot of things go to die, thus causing a lot of clutter. If you saw my garage, it would scare you and not in the way you are thinking. It is so well organized wives have brought their husbands over and, while admiring the cleanliness, say, "See! This is what I want." What I tell the wives is this: if I can do it, he can do it, too. What's the secret? It's the same as it is with organizing anything. Group like things together and store the most often used items in the easiest-to-reach places (and label the boxes). To do this, divide the garage into zones based on the activity that takes place there. You may have a car-care center, laundry room, workshop, sporting goods center, and a long-term storage area with the related items stored either in containers, hung on the wall, or in boxes. At your local home improvement store there are all kinds of cool hooks, shelves, cabinets, racks, and bins to make organizing easier so you can make the most of your garage. This isn't including the lumber department, where you can build custom storage solutions.

GEAR

I was watching Mick Fleetwood being interviewed (the drummer of Fleetwood Mac) on *Dateline NBC* and in the background was a case/rack that held all his snare drums. The shelves were labeled and they adjusted for the different-sized snares. There were also drawers for small parts. Being in bands since I was a teenager, I recognize the importance of organizing. We tag and tidy up our cords. We bought cases and containers to organize and store a lot of our gear. (We also use Ziploc baggies for the little loose stuff.) When it comes to playing live (and late at night), it makes sense to keep a backup for everything and anything and to be able to find things before the audience notices anything is wrong. This takes organization.

Create Zones

Big wave surfer Mike Parsons has every type of gear for every type of surfing situation. The unusual thing is how organized his San Clemente garage is kept. In his "surf zone," there is a rack for his wet suits, stacks of large plastic crates filled with surf accessories, each clearly marked. This is in addition to his watercraft and over thirty surfboards hanging on the walls according to size.

Keep Things Where They Are Used

The key is to put things that are used often within easy reach and store other stuff out of the way. Keep your gardening gear in a caddy you can carry or set up a station where you dig in the dirt. In-line skaters may consider buying the Rubbermaid storage bin/bench to sit on while removing their Rollerblades and storing them inside, along with the safety gear.

Less Stuff Is Easier to Organize

Instead of buying a bunch of items you'll only use once or twice a year, rent them when you need to. Keep a box for stuff you no longer need, and when it's full, donate or sell it.

Label Everything

Always label boxes! Always. Right brain, left brain, it doesn't matter. This is a no-brainer. Like they do in a repair shop, put broken items on a shelf and attach a note saying what's wrong with them or what parts are needed. Some people mark off what goes where with painted lines on the floor so that there is no doubt where the designated spot is for bikes. Same with pegboards and your tools.

Keep It Simple

Have a "What the heck is this?" box for odds and ends. Limit it to one box, and when it's full go through it and throw out anything that isn't useful or valuable and find homes for the rest (or let it stay in the box a little longer). Maybe that's its home.

Make the Most of Your Space

There's lots of hidden space if you look for it. Bikes can hang from the ceiling, coolers go inside coolers, add more shelves, put car-cleaning supplies in a bucket, store luggage within luggage, hang stuff on the wall. Drill a hole in the handle of almost any tool, put a cord through it, put a nail in the wall, and hang it.

ACTION ITEM

Take a piece of paper and fold it in half (horizontally). On the left side draw your ideal environment. This is your dream space. In your picture make cartoon balloons with words and statements that describe it. On the right side describe how it feels to be in this space.

IDEAS

Businesses have been launched off napkins, envelopes, and maybe even matchbooks. But what if the original concept had been lost? Many people have great ideas, few write them down, and even fewer ever act on them. Keeping hold of your creative inspirations for later use is simply a smart thing to do. How you capture your genius is up to you. Leonardo da Vinci was constantly doodling and scribbling on any paper he could find. He didn't want to loose all the ideas that filled his head. What's interesting is that next to his plans for projects and finished drawings were notes to himself like "I feel like making miracles!" and lists of things to buy. Stephen Bishop wrote a book called *Songs in the Rough,* which features original drafts of seventy-five pop songs. Some songs were written on toilet seat covers, scraps of paper, envelopes, restaurant bills, wedding invitations, and airline tickets. "Life forms illogical patterns. It is haphazard and full of beauty which I try to catch as they fly by, for who knows whether any of them will ever return." There were legions of secretaries who recorded every word Gandhi uttered (including the previous quote), eventually filling over ninety volumes.

You can actually increase your creativity by using it more often. Honor it. Flex it like a muscle. If you are an artist, you should practice your craft and carry a small pad. Writers should look for dialogue or interesting ideas. An actor friend of mine would keep an acting notebook filled with emotions and inspirations, depending on what he was asked to play. Always carry a notebook with you and write down your thoughts, ideas, and insights. Even if you never look at these again, the act of writing them down may make you remember better. After a while you will start paying more attention to everything while jotting down your thoughts. Throughout the day jot down anything that surprises you or captures your attention. Sift through these entries later for ideas you can use.

Ideas can come to you at the most inopportune times. You may be driving, walking, or sleeping. You need some way to capture these brain droppings. Keep a notepad near you when you watch TV, in the bathroom, nightstand, at work, in the car, purse, or pack—remember, ideas can happen anywhere. Believe it or not, you are most creative first thing in the morning. For the first fifteen minutes after you awaken, your brain is in a dreamlike state and this allows for increased creativity. The only catch is you have to capture these ideas right away or they are gone forever. As a writer I find that my subconscious mind is still writing the novel and trying to figure out what happens next while I snooze. I keep a notepad next to the bed so I can write it down and then go back to sleep.

I sometimes forget my idea journal, but there is usually something to jot down some of my crazy ideas onto. Then I transfer them into the journal when I get the chance. (I've never lost my idea book, but I still put my name and phone number in it, just in case.) Have you ever left a message on your voice mail of a great idea or important thought? Brian Sweeney, a passenger on one of the hijacked planes of 9/11, left this message for his wife: "Know that I love you and no matter what, I'll see you again." A friend of mine aptly named Sunshine has lived a VERY interesting life and wants to write a memoir, but she was having a hard time getting it down on paper. I told her to start carrying a microcassette recorder, and it's working.

What your idea catcher looks like is up to you. It might just be an old trunk where you can throw scraps of papers, napkins, and matchbooks with your thoughts or sketches on them. You could use a legal pad, spiral-bound notebook (so it lies flat), or a stack of index cards. This way you can make a kind of table of contents on the cover. Otherwise, it's hard to find some of your brilliant brain droppings. You can write with sixty-four colors of crayons or one color of pen. Feel free to paste pictures, articles, samples, and draw in it. I am always tearing articles from magazines, and I am not very discreet about it either. These are things that give me ideas or inspiration.

Award-winning author Jonathan Franzen (*The Corrections*) keeps a thick binder with a year's worth of notes. He says, "It's a record of the struggle to figure out what the book was supposed to look like and how it was supposed to be built." Grammy Award–winner Beck will work on a song and if it's not happening, he'll shelve it and come back to it later. What you keep in your journal is up to you. It could be a success journal, which helps you sell yourself and build your confidence. What if you wrote down everything you adore about your loved one? Then you will have something to say when you have a fight and want to make up. Take it one step further and make notes about your lover's favorite things and other important information. This will come in handy when you need an idea for a gift. Add in his or her shirt, shoe, and ring size. Believe me, you don't want to buy any clothing for your spouse that is too big. (Been there, done that, have the scar.)

KIDS

"Cleaning the house before your kids are done growing is like shoveling the walk before it stops snowing," advises Phyliss Diller. She's got a point. Some parents have found creative ways to keep kid clutter under control. With kids (and adults) a place for everything and everything in its place are the best method for making sure stuff gets put away. (Bins with a picture of what goes in them are a good idea.) Toys can also hang on the wall. Hang stuffed animals, backpacks, toys. Get it off the floor and you lose a lot less stuff. It's nice to have a cubbyhole for each kid by the door, like in kindergarten. Actress Lauren Holly keeps her two children's room safe, clean, and fun. Their toys are kept in easy-to-reach wicker baskets on shelves. There are maps on the walls, toys on the floor, and a chalkboard/magnet board at kiddie level. Pamela Anderson's kid's room has big wicker baskets filled with toys. There are an easel for painting and a whole wall devoted to artwork, report cards, and pictures.

KITCHENS

If we are what we eat, I'm cheap, fast, and easy. I do not spend a great deal of time in the kitchen. My wife does the bulk of the cooking—we both prefer to eat out, however. She also handles the cleaning of the kitchen. About all I do is wipe the chocolate stain off the milk container in case we have company. I know, I'm a bad, bad man. I am also not normal. For many people the kitchen is the most used room in the house. The command center of their home. In addition to being a place to cook, the kitchen is a place a lot of people eat, socialize, store stuff, post messages and artwork on the fridge, and do "other" things on occasion. Where do people hang out at a party? Usually the kitchen—whether it's a kegger or canasta night. You want a cozy, comfortable, clear, and CLEAN space. Cooking can be a joy when the kitchen is well organized and clean. If a restaurant looked like your kitchen, would you want to eat there? We need room to spread out and work and do what we do best—multitask, space to have appliances out like a toaster, and tools so it is task efficient. The key to the kitchen is to divide it into zones and store related supplies in each zone. Don't put things away where they fit, put them where they are used. Cluster things used together in the same place. The most often used stuff is up front and within reach. Kids' cups and plates should be low enough so they can get them out and put them away themselves. We want to make it as easy as possible to put things away. Ask yourself when you put something away, is this the best place for it?

Take Out to Dine In

Are you more of a take-out, order-in type of person? It's okay. Just admit it and maybe you won't spend so much on buying gourmet cooking utensils that take up valuable space and collect dust. Put your take-out menus in a holder in a prominent place in the kitchen. Aw, it's okay.

Chillin' in the Fridge

Combine and conquer. Condense the four ketchup bottles into one, assuming they haven't all gone bad. Repackage some bulky stuff in smaller bags. If your refrigerator doesn't have a lot of built-in containers, create some. Tupperware or Rubbermaid works well. To have an organized fridge, begin by getting rid of all those unidentified items. Rotate the stock like they do in the grocery store. Pull older stuff to the front. How do know what's been around the longest? Some items will quickly show their age and grow hair. With others you may want to write the date on the container (use tape) or mark the box (Chinese takeout).

Cook the Books
Cookbooks and recipes can quickly become a disorganized mess. You may have recipes scribbled on all kinds of loose little pieces of paper. Instead of rewriting them, staple, glue, or tape them to a letter-size piece of paper and put them in a binder or attach them to an index card and stick them in an (attractive) recipe box you leave on the counter. Organize recipes by category: drinks, desserts, healthy dishes, dinner, and so on. Keep cookbooks in the kitchen. Build a bookcase or use bookends if you have to. You would think this is obvious, but I have seen them everywhere but the kitchen. Create your own cookbook system with recipes clipped from magazines, using a binder and sheet protectors or a photo album with clear pages—put all the scraps in there and seal it.

Tools of the Trade
Under-the-counter appliances save a lot of counter space as do combo appliances. Store appliances you rarely use out of the way.

Coffee Talk
Make a coffee station like they have at coffee shops. Hang the mugs on a mug tree and keep the coffee and condiments near the coffeemaker.

Bag Lady
Save shopping bags. Have an area or container and when it's full, that's it, you have enough.

Spice It Up
Most-used spices should be in front and within easy reach. Put spices in a handy little carrying case so you can pull it out and put it where you're cooking. I made a BBQ kit out of a wicker basket to hold the spices I use

while cooking on the grill. Use the step, stadium-seating method for your spices, says organizer Stephanie Denton. Old Spice? Get rid of duplicates. I love cajun spices, but I had four of the same Chef Paul ones, two of which had solidified.

When Your Cups Runneth Over
It's a sad day when the last clean cup in the house is the one from your Yahtzee game. Use cool coasters you can leave out when not in use.

Labels Out
Organize your pantry like a grocery store. Divide your pantry into zones—baking, quick meals, breakfast, soups, and sauces.

While You Were Out
Hang an information center or bulletin board for notes, pictures, art, a calendar, important phone numbers, reminders, phone messages. Hmmmm, maybe we need two bulletin boards. You can divide one up into sections or by person.

You Are What You Eat
Decide on your favorite dishes and just rotate the menu from week to week. Less ingredients needed and easier to shop.

Tupperware Party
Small plastic containers are great for loose stuff—corn holders, bag clips, corks, openers. Use cute ones and store them on the counter. Transfer cereals and pastas (all your carbs) into clear containers. Put the date on the bottom on a strip of tape. Have an organizer or plastic container for all those loose packets of spices and mixes.

Let's Shelve It for Now
I saw a kitchen where shelves were assigned by meal—breakfast, lunch, and dinner. The cabinet was labeled so everyone knew what was where. Cabinets usually have adjustable shelves so move them around to fit your stuff. Add a shelf if needed. Put shelves under cabinets or on counters for spices or other small stuff.

Less Stacks, More Racks

When someone says, "Nice rack," don't slap them, thank them. Smaller compartments and dividers are handy so that it is clear where things go. It's hard to pull out plates when they are piled high so you don't have to lift ten plates to put one away. Use a shelf within a shelf for plates. Racks to hold and divide pans and lids are awesome. Wire dish racks let plates drip-dry and don't clog the drain. Vertical dividers or spacers underneath keep stuff sorted better. A strip of wood can become a knife holder. Make grooves so knives are out of the way. (Make one space a sharpener.)

Leftovers

A lot of the stuff in your kitchen has gone bad. Flour has a shelf life of only one year. Tea bags a year-and-a-half. Pasta keeps for two years. (Twinkies *do* last forever, I hear.) Pull all old cans and cake mixes and pile on counter. If you can't bring yourself to throw older items away, try creating a dish using as many as possible until all are gone. Yuk!

An "Apple" a Day

You would think a mouse in the kitchen would be a bad thing. Maybe not. Put a computer in your kitchen so that all your recipes are there along with contact info. Go online for coupons, restaurant ideas, and shop while you cook.

Neat Trick

A butler tray is a great idea because it makes it easier to carry things back to the kitchen after you have eaten. A wheeled tray with a butcher block top is even better. Put a measuring cup in the containers for flour, sugar, coffee (less mess).

A Quickie in the Kitchen

Have some grab-and-go munchies. For quick snacks use paper plates and plastic cups to eliminate sink clutter. When cooking, make more than you need and freeze it for future dinners.

Kitchen Clutter

Designate one junk drawer. Use baggies to get a handle on the small items. Use a Sharpie to mark the bag.

Everything Out

I saw a kitchen with no cabinet doors. Everything was out. There were small shelves for wines and spices and oils, all utensils were hanging, a basket was on the floor with mats and napkins, dishes and bowls were on shelves. It looked like a Crate and Barrel showroom. There was a ledge with little drawers for small items like recipes and another for fasteners. Both fruit in a bowl and flowers were out. Hang utensils. Keep the table set. It's one less thing to do, and you're less likely to pile stuff on the table. A pegboard in the kitchen is kinda cool to hang all those strange utensils they sell at William Sonoma. Use the underneath of cabinets to hang stuff. Cook caddies are a catchall for all those kitchen utensils that we want out and visible.

Lazy Susan

Slide shelves, spinners, or lazy Susans are great for hard-to-reach places. There are also organizers for tall, narrow spaces like next to the fridge. These can be a roll-out spice center, pantry, or overflow area for seldom-used items.

Birds of a Feather

Put baking stuff into a basket so that you can grab all the items at once. Stack stuff inside each other, like Tupperware, for example.

Less Is More

Get rid of duplicate items. I had tons of coffee cups that were gifts from talks I had given. I lined them all up, took a picture, and then gave most of them away. We had wedding gifts that we never used, never would use, and had no real use for. We made a note of who gave what and "regifted" them.

Unlisted

Put a blank pad of paper or bulletin board in the kitchen for your grocery list or a magnet clip on the fridge to hold a large envelope on which you can write things you need and put coupons inside.

LITTLE STUFF

Put a drop zone by the door so you can scoop the things you need to take with you on your way out. A list on the front door with all the things you need to remember to take with you for the day is another way to go. Have a pad with a pencil on a string so you can add items to it as you think of them. How about a bowl in each room for loose change, keys, earrings, pens, coupons, batteries, paper clips, rubber bands, stamps, and other small clutter? Velcro small stuff and stick it where it's often used.

FUN FACTS

Valuable toys include a 1959 Barbie, nineteen sixty-seven G.I. Joe, and battery-operated Robbie, the Robot—all worth more than three thousand dollars each.

MEMORABILIA

"There is a very fine line between 'hobby' and 'mental illness,'" says Dave Barry. "I collect a lot of things. I'm one of those swap-meet whores," boasts Pamela Anderson. Actress Selma Hayek collects art. "I have a small house. I lease my car. All of my clothes are borrowed. I spend my money on art." Actress Jamie Pressley collects buddahs, books, and boats. To house it all she created a knickknack room. "All the stuff that doesn't fit anywhere else I put in the knickknack room." Demi Moore had to buy a home for her doll collection. That's right! She purchased a Victorian home just for her collection. Jerry Seinfeld has a warehouse for his Porsche collection. Rocker Sebastian Bach is a big fan of other bands, especially KISS. His memorabilia include comics, concert tickets, stickers, and his prized KISS Vomitizer that spits blood. He uses these items to fuel his own creativity. Many right-brainers are avid collectors of this and that, and we switch interests as fast as we change socks. Collecting things that bring you pleasure is a plus—even if others laugh at your Hulk Hogan dolls. It's a problem when these things are so disorganized that *you* don't enjoy them.

THIN IT OUT

Actress Holly Marie Combs leads a "charmed" life. She collects horse-riding memorabilia, including trophies she won when she rode, but she keeps a piece of an item (with a photo) rather than the whole thing. (I'm NOT talking about the actual horse here.) Think about what you collect. Maybe bulky isn't better. What if you collected money from around the world rather than buying things to bring home? (It's more valuable, too.) Rotate what you display and get rid of anything that doesn't produce a positive memory.

USEFUL

Functional memorabilia are the best. Souvenirs that do double duty are the kind you can hang on the Christmas tree. A buddy of mine keeps all of his old surfboards, but they become a table, shelf, or a bench. One woman collects hats, and many came in cool hat boxes. She stacked the boxes and they became a table, plant stand, and decorations. I also know a guy who collects vintage guitars—Gibson's and Fender's. These are works of art, and he hangs them on the wall. He also plays them.

STORE IT

A man I know pasted and then varnished many of his baseball cards (his "common cards") on the wall. This is extreme, but he liked his stuff where he could see it. If you like to store things away, create a memory box. Put programs, photos, and other items in an old travel trunk, hat box, armoire, or even an old lunchbox. Just as long as it's safe, dry, and protected. One woman has a shoe box under her bed filled with notes, clippings, photos, and mementos for a book she hopes to write. Ask your local pizza place for a few empty (clean) boxes. These are good for keeping each child's creations and clippings. Mark the outside with their name and year.

DISPLAY IT

You might want to come up with a gallery or museum look for your best stuff. Beautifully displayed is better than a bunch of things thrown around the room. Build or buy a bookcase to hold your collectibles. Put them on a bookcase and use them as bookends. It doesn't have to be perfect. Hodgepodge and eclectic is cool. It's always in motion and reflects who you are, who you love, where you've been. It's a record of your life, family, travels, hobbies, interests. It is a little like an antique store with your stuff on display. Put your best stuff up front and rotate it around to keep it interesting. You can add steps to allow items behind to be seen. Make blocks out of wood to give depth and varied levels. Build a wall unit for knickknacks. That way they are out, but if you keep them behind glass they are both safe and dust free. Do a retrospective of your career, year by year. Seeing your body of work as a whole is inspiring. Have a binder for each decade of your life (toddler, teen, twenties, and beyond) or each area of your life (career, mother, friend). Make a collage/sculpture of things you've collected. Make it creative, artistic, functional. Glue it all together and it's a centerpiece, a conversation starter, a work of art. You can frame just about anything, not just art. Put the clutter on the wall and out of harm's way where you can see it—magazine covers, photos, postcards, stamps, your first (good) review, awards, sheet music, a degree, certificates, wedding or honeymoon mementos, or baby stuff.

FAST FACT

A mint condition copy of Simon and Garfunkel's *Sounds of Silence* would fetch about twenty dollars. A copy of Bob Dylan's *The Freewheelin' Bob Dylan* should go for about fifteen thousand dollars.

MOVING

After her divorce was final a woman went to the DMV and asked to have her maiden name put back on her driver's license. "Will there be any change of address?" the clerk asked. "No," the woman replied. "I see," the clerk said, "*you* got the house." Moving is a great time to declutter and get organized. For each item decide if you really want to pack, move, and unpack it. It has to pass this test before it's boxed. Anything not worth moving goes in a garage sale box. Have the garage sale before you move so you can lighten the load and use the cash to pay the movers. I thought I was organized until we moved—twice in six months. I found all kinds of hidden clutter. Since we moved to a smaller place, I had to decide what was most important. I got rid of a lot of things that weren't functional and wouldn't fit.

OFFICES

According to a study done by Logitech, half of the respondents who have a home office say it is a disorganized mess. Your office or studio should reflect your inner self. Cluttered and confused? Stuff everywhere and struggling? Peaceful and pleasant? Personal and professional? Crafty and creative? The office is an organizing nightmare. There's a lot of stuff in a small space, which is one of the biggest problems. I've seen home offices carved out of kitchen corners, closets, and other nooks and crannies. "I'm building my home office into the closet so that I can shut the door when people come over—and because we want to turn the room into a playroom for the kids, so there will be more room without the desk. I'm also hoping that having the office in the closet would force me to be neater, and thus, more organized," says freelance writer Scott Kramer. Make the most of the space through organizing. Arrange and rearrange until you find the right fit.

Clean off your desk by starting with those things you don't need or use. Keep the frequently used stuff out and move or remove the rest. Place equipment strategically for ease of use and to minimize distractions. In a nutshell, fix what's not working. The way your office is organized (or disorganized) could be the reason you procrastinate or hate to go to work. Revitalize by rearranging and reorganizing. Twenty-seven percent of those surveyed claim that the thing they need most to help them through the day is more storage, according to a Steelcase Workplace Index survey. Most offices are too small, with not enough storage. Maybe you could rent or borrow some of the bigger equipment you rarely use.

Maybe you can use a roll-up desk to hide the clutter. Put a table in the middle of the room so you have more work space. Use bookshelves as room dividers. Make the room multifunctional. A chair for reading also doubles as a place for clients to sit for consultations. Have a box for each project and put them on a shelf. Label or mark the containers so it's easy to throw stuff in them as you think of it. (It's also great when you want to switch from task to task.) Use a cart with supplies that wheels around the room. Get glass cabinets so you can see that what's in them is functional and nice looking.

KINKOS

There is a place in southeast San Diego called Kink-o's. The outside says, "We have NOTHING to do with office supplies."

ONE OF US: NICOLE PUGH, WRITER

"I am most definitely a 'right-brainer' and am constantly trying to 'trick' myself into being more organized! It seems as if I have more success when I can make organizing myself fun and creative at the same time. That is why, first and foremost, no matter where I am living, I always create a special space for my writing 'work.' This might sound simplistic, but I am always amazed at how many writers and artists I meet who do their thing from the kitchen table in between setting plates for dinner and helping their kids with their homework. I think that creating a special space for creative work is a major step in turning an 'interest' into something that brings in abundance and eventually could turn into a career!"

OTHER ROOMS

The true power in any household is determined by one thing and one thing only—who gets to control the remote control for the TV. (In case you were wondering, I am second in command of the remote behind my wife.) Here are some suggestions for dealing with this very "important" part of your life. Make a basket or bowl for all the remotes. Better yet, program one remote to operate all of your equipment and Velcro it to the TV.

PHONE

"The telephone is a good way to talk to people without having to offer them a drink," says Fran Leibowitz. I do find that the phone can be a time-saver, especially a cellular phone. The phone can also be a great organizer. Used correctly, it can cut the clutter. For example, instead of having to buy, address, stamp, and send a card, just reach out and touch someone. It can also be a burden. Take rapper Nelly, who has three cell phones. "One's for the family, one's for business, and a third I just like to keep natural. If you are lucky you get all three numbers," he says. That's two too many for me. You are probably pretty proficient with the phone, so I'll just include a couple of suggestions here.

If the Phone Doesn't Ring, It's Me

One way the phone can create clutter is when it comes to messages. One graphic artist I know put a dry-erase board by the phone for messages. A red pen (urgent) and a green one are attached by Velcro to the board. Carbonless message books are good for taking notes on calls. The spiral-bound ones work best because there is a backup record of who called and you can look up phone numbers from previously missed calls. Put pens (please put more than one) and paper all over the house, since most of us use cordless phones. However, make a message center where you post most messages. This can be on the fridge, by the door, or on a corkboard on the wall. You can create your own URGENT message pads, which are bright enough to get anyone's attention.

Two-Timer

When I was doing a book signing in Florida, someone raised his hand and asked if peeing in the shower was multitasking. I scratched my chin before saying, "Yes, it is. It's also kinda gross." My point is (and I do have one), having a hands-free setup is perfect for the multitasking right-brainer. Think about the possibilities. Keep a stack of easy-to-tackle tasks by the phone so you can talk and take care of business at the same time. If you are lacking room on your desk, consider hanging the phone on the wall or getting a phone stand to make better use of the space.

Let Your Fingers Do the Walking

Networking only works if you work it. Always have something to write down someone's phone number on. One woman I know carries a pen and 3 × 5-inch index cards with her wherever she goes. When she gets home she files them in a file box. The box is divided three ways. In the front it has one through thirty-one (daily tabs and) monthly tabs, which act as a tickler file. The third section is for long-term storage and is divided alphabetically. She will put business cards and phone messages in there, too.

Rolodex

The Rolodex is still a great tool. Tom Morey, the inventor of the original Boogie Board, kept a Rolodex filled with his thoughts on everything from shipping to sales. For example, some of the little cards included thoughts on advertising. "Promise benefits rather than features." Good advice! When you collect cards, staple them into a Rolodex. Easy. Mark the date and check it off when you enter it into your database. Note birthdays, names of people's kids, their alma mater, and any other pertinent information. Put a symbol next to the name: if it's a lead (money sign), a potential date (a heart), or a potential friend (a smiley face). Some people use colored Rolodex cards—yellow for business and white for personal, or colors for different types of contacts like the media, editors, customers.

Lazy Lee

What can I say? I try to cut corners when I can. For example, I encourage callers to leave their number on my outgoing message. That's one less thing I have to look up. Caller ID saves numbers and saves time. I just entered my speed dial numbers. I was always too busy or too lazy to do it until now. Wow! I put my voice mail number on speed dial and the code to retrieve messages on another. Better late than never.

PHOTOS

When Kodak advertises film they don't sell the actual pictures, they sell memories. Ask anyone what three things they would grab if their house is on fire, and I'll bet one of them would be their photographs. Preserve these permanent reminders of precious moments in your past. Photos can provide comfort, joy, and, in some cases, proof for insurance. Although you want to save photos in a safe place, you also need to sort, send, and save them in a way that allows you and others to look at them whenever and wherever you want.

The thought of going through and organizing old photos is daunting. Ask the people in the pictures to come over and help. It's always easier to put photos in an album when you return from having them developed. Have new photo albums ready to go. Weed out anything that doesn't touch your heart. Throw away all bad photos such as blurry, boring, "I look fat," and so on. Keep photos of people and places that inspire you. Organizing photos requires making some tough decisions, which can lead to a pile of photos and a project that never gets done. Make some space so you don't have to finish this major project all in one session.

The people in the pictures you shot would likely love to have their own copy, and you can get rid of unneeded duplicates. When you sort through photos, grab some envelopes, label them with the name of the recipient, and start putting the extra pictures in there and then send them out. Photos can also become instant postcards. Just draw a line down the middle of the back and address and stamp them. You can also scan photos and either post them to your Web site or send others an electronic version. When you save photos on your hard drive or to a disk, there's a lot less clutter in your life.

Scrapbooking (keeping photos in a creative, attractive way) is a craze that is catching on even with noncreative people. It's a way to preserve memories and an outlet for your creativity. There are retail stores where you can meet with other scrapbookers for a crop session. There is even an organization called Scrapbooking in America. Some serious scrapbookers have a dedicated room for their hobby. You don't have to become a scrapbooker to combine photos with other memories. Along with the photos, glue in related items—stickers, ticket stubs, matchbooks. Turn your photos into a coffee table book. Make a cover by laminating or spray-mounting a photo and title. Make an introduction and include photos of various sizes. Add captions to create a part photo album, journal, and book. Leave it out where people can see it. Since your memory doesn't get better with age, write on the back anything that will jog your memory about the date and the person or place in the photo.

Other ways to save and display photos include buying binder-style photo albums and creating several based on person, place, year, or occasion. These small binders can be stored on a bookshelf with a label on the spine for easy reference. You can create a "Best Of" or "Photos I Love" album, which you can grab in case of an emergency, or put it in a safety deposit box or safe. Some albums should be stored out of sight. Photos of ex-boyfriends you want to save but don't want to flaunt in the face of your current love should be kept out of the way. For fun you could create an "I Should Have Married" wedding album and slip in your photo next to Brad Pitt or George Clooney. Of course, framing photos and getting them up on the wall are a great way to display them. The future is here—digital frames with high-resolution displays. You can see something like fifty photos directly from your digital camera or computer. For the extra photos a shoe box is a good place to keep them safe and sorted. There should be a system to your shoe boxes. Mark the outside based on the years of the photos or the people in them. Inside the box, use dividers. You can stack these on a shelf or get custom boxes with drawers that make them easier to open.

TECHNOLOGY

"People in the computer industry use the term *user,* which to them means 'idiot'," says Dave Barry. Technology is a great thing, but when it comes to getting organized it's a double-edged sword. For example, the great thing about a notebook computer is that no matter how much you stuff into it, it doesn't get any heavier. That's the good news. The bad news is that the more stuff you store, without some sense of organization, it becomes just as lost as if it were buried under a pile of papers on your desk. It should also be noted that if you are unable to get organized with a notepad and pen, you're not likely to get organized with computer technology. E-mail, for example, is a true test for your organizational skills. The computer does simplify many tasks and can help you stay organized, but it won't *make* you organized. Some technology actually complicates your life. Bill Gates said it best: "Some people waste time in front of computers, but that doesn't mean that technology in general—or even computer technology specifically—is holding us back. A computer is a tool. You can use the tool appropriately, in which case it's a blessing, or inappropriately, in which case it can be a waste of time." My advice is keep it simple. More equipment means more manuals, warranties, wires, and chargers; and then there is the learning curve. What's important is what we can do with computers and not the device itself. Have a goal and use technology to help you reach that goal. Rivers Cuomo is the frontman for the band Weezer and one computer savvy guy. On his laptop he has an elaborate color-coded spreadsheet to keep track of every song he's ever written. These are all numbered and organized.

If you have too much paper but plenty of hard drive, maybe the best place for storage is in files—inside your computer. This can be your main filing system. Think of your computer as if it were a tree. Your hard drive is the trunk, the branches are the folders, and the leaves are the documents. Add in color coding and you have a system that should work well. Keep it simple by dividing folders into categories such as client or project. Keep frequently used documents and active files on the hard drive but archive the old stuff onto disks.

Electronic organizers come in two varieties—the prototype and the obsolete. These handheld electronic organizers are also called PDAs. I just like the sound of that, "personal digital assistant." Most people use PDAs as a datebook. Graphic artist Karen Larson wanted something extra from her Palm Pilot. She wanted to make "PalmArt" and turned her handheld into a mobile canvas, using drawing software and a stylus. We all know creativity can strike at any time and anywhere. Felicia Borges says to get a Palm Pilot! "A Palm is a great tool for right-brainers, they are 'fluid' and can easily keep up with your racing thoughts. You can make notes to yourself, update your address book or calendar, all within a few seconds. But the best part is how much paper it has cut out of my life. No more looking for the phone bill in the bottom of my purse to write someone's phone number down and then mailing off the payment before taking the time to rewrite the number into my address book."

WORKSHOPS/STUDIOS

Right-brainers are more creative than most and that means we need a space in which to indulge our artistic side, whether that is a workshop, studio, or just a corner of the den. Even though we believe what comes out of a workshop is more important than what goes in, organizing is still important. Some people will have patrons or clients come over, and it matters what your space looks like. Plus, if someone trips and falls because you left a mess, you could be held liable.

A good workshop grows with you and adapts to the various projects you will inevitably take on. You want to be able to leave things out or stash them away quickly so you don't miss dinner. It's a sanctuary you can come home to and dig in or relax. Maybe the reason a lot of your projects remain unfinished is because your workshop is a mess and disorganized. The more organized and clean it is, the more time you'll want to spend there. You probably need a clear area to work in, a place to put your tools and storage for the parts and pieces you need to keep handy. Put things where they are used, and the most often used tools get the best space.

Apply your creativity and craftiness to fitting all your tools and paraphernalia into a space that will likely be too small. Walk through your current work area and ask yourself what works and what bugs you off.

Start sketching some possible solutions. Visualize a project in progress and what steps and tools you might use. How could it be better? For example, what if you were sitting instead of standing for four hours? What if you could wheel your bigger tools around instead of having to drag them or push them with your butt? How could you better store your projects in progress? There is an old (and wise) saying that goes something like this: "Measure three times and cut once." Plan by mapping out the area on graph paper (to scale) and cut pieces of paper to represent your big tools. Then arrange and rearrange on paper until it makes sense. It's a lot better for your back to move around little scraps of paper than the heavy gear.

A workshop is a work in progress, and your needs change based on what you are working on. Pegboard is perfect for this reason. Make things adjustable when possible. Movable tool racks are good because you can put tools needed for a project near a workbench. Essential hand tools should be within reach above your work area. Store like supplies together. Keep tools and parts together. For example, put various blades near the saw and bits with drill press; use racks and hooks to hang tools, making them organized and easily accessible. Mount a magnetic strip on the wall and stick metal tools to it. Dual purpose Craftsman rolling toolbox is a good thing. It serves as a table and toolbox. A bucket with tool belt attached is very cool. So is the step stool with tools inside. A bench that opens up is good. It's like a lockbox. With a tool rack you know where things go at a glance; and the easier things are to put away, the more likely you'll do it. The most important tools are probably just two items—duct tape and WD-40. (Ha, ha, ha.) Another thing to consider when organizing a work space is lighting. A place to pin up plans, keep track of ongoing projects and their deadline, along with swatches and examples, places to toss scraps of materials, shelves for strange cans of stuff like paints, stains, and goops are important. Drawers are your friend. You can't have enough. Hardware and fasteners can be stored in smaller containers within a drawer. Baggies are also good for loose items. Mark them with a Sharpie pen. Plastic containers with dividers (or coffee cans) are great for keeping little loose items organized.

Part Four

HOW TO
STAY ORGANIZED

ten

I CAN SEE CLEARLY NOW

How to Maintain Your New
and Improved Way of Life

It's by acts and not by ideas
that people live.

—Anatole France

I meet some of the smartest people who have read all the right books, have a good education, and bought all the best organizing tools but can't seem to pull it all together. The trick is to turn what you know into what you will DO. This book is loaded with proven organizing ideas that work—if you work them. You have to take this knowledge and apply it to the problem of getting organized. I like to say that reading my books can change your life, but I want to amend that statement. Taking the concepts contained on these pages and *applying them* bring about true change.

I know this works because it works for me, and I am just like you. I'm a creative, right-brain pack rat (my wife would also like to add perfectionist, procrastinator, and easily distracted) who has managed to get and stay organized without losing my creativity, personality, or spontaneity. If you dropped by my house unannounced on any given day you would find what you would expect from someone who wrote a book about organizing—a showplace where everything shared in this book is put into practice. Everyone that comes to visit me says the same thing: "You are soooooooooo organized."

It wasn't always this way. Years ago my place was a cluttered, chaotic, disorganized mess. That's right, I was not always so together. Now I am the poster boy for organizing. How did this transition take place? By applying the same principles I share in this book along with a little self-control and a lot of creativity. I started small and eventually every single area of my home and office was organized. There is no way I could have written this book or any of the ten others if I couldn't stay organized. It would be impossible to live in my beach house with its limited storage if I didn't try and apply everything I set forth in these pages. I doubt I would be able to entertain as often as I do if things were as messy as they once were. I certainly couldn't have reached any of the financial and personal goals I have while living in complete chaos. I have lived a disorganized life and an organized one and there is no comparison—being able to find things, not being embarrassed when others come to visit, and having a home and office that run smoothly are best. I get more done in half the time and I am able to spend my time and energy on more important things, because getting and STAYING organized are better than being disorganized. If I can do it, so can you. If you set up an organizing strategy and structure that make sense and work for you, there is no reason you can't continue to be an organized person for the rest of your life. It will be one less thing to worry about and many more good things will happen to you as a result. It's also habit-forming. (Something right-brainers know a little about.)

My disorganized friend joined the navy and was stationed elsewhere. After serving his time, he came back with a whole new set of skills, including being more organized. I'm still not exactly sure what he did while he was away but it involved a lot of weaponry and equipment where keeping it clean and in working order was very important. This has become a way of life for him. Replace old habits and thought patterns with new ones . . . that work. The whole idea here is to eliminate anything that gets in the way of your goals. If clutter and disorganization have held you back in any way, then you have good reason to get it together and make some changes. What you don't want to do is look back and dwell on what you've done. The past is the past and does not determine your future unless you let it. Focus on your new life where everything flows and helps you reach your goals. You can change and improve so that the future is brighter, cleaner, and working well.

An idea that worked well for me was to walk through my home and office and take inventory to see what was working and what wasn't and to help get a handle on what I needed to happen to be happy. Fear of the unknown can be paralyzing. The truth is, things aren't always as bad as they seem. Pinpoint the problem and then solve it with creativity. Focus on the task and not on yourself for a minute. Don't judge yourself (that will be distracting and divert your attention away from a creative solution) and just do it. That's why, as frightening as it sounds, to see what you have and what has to be done is worth the effort. The key is not to judge and not allow yourself to feel overwhelmed by what has to be done. It's hard to not want to clean, repair, and organize everything, but the exercise is to just observe and take notes, mental or otherwise.

Why you want to get organized is more important than how when it comes to staying that way. All the tips and techniques won't work if you don't stick with it. It takes a powerful purpose to push you to continue to do the things it takes to control the chaos that your life can quickly become. It doesn't matter what your reason for wanting to be more organized is, as long as your goal gets you going and gives you the energy and determination to see it through and stay on course. When you want to give up and go back to your old ways, look for a deeper meaning. When you do get down and discouraged, figure out your feelings by asking, "Why?" and then see what your decision about what you are doing right now will do for your future. "If you really want something, you can figure out how to make it happen," says Cher. Find the reason why you want to get organized and how you'll benefit from staying that way. Focus on the how and the why and don't dwell on the why not. List or mind map the reasons why you want to be organized and what the benefits will be to getting and staying that way. That should make you motivated. Put a picture of your perfect environment up where you will see it: photos or clippings of places you admire. Keep your eye on the goal. Finally, you need a plan of action. Just put up a checklist of things you must do to get where you want to be organizationally and deadlines to do them. Ask yourself, "If I could get this stuff cleaned up and organized (in a way YOU want it to be), what could I do with this space? With my life? How much easier or better would my life or work be?"

So why are so many people disorganized? A lack of motivation is a reason why so many smart and talented people fail to organize. They know what to do, but they have a hundred reasons why they don't do it. When you're motivated you can overcome these excuses and realize your full potential. Getting organized isn't about making sure everything is in its place per se. It's about making your life work so that, well, your life works. So that clutter, and the frustration it causes, don't hold you back from being all you can be. Once you climb out from behind the clutter and let the light in, you can shine and do anything you want to do. "If we did all the things we are capable of doing, we would literally astound ourselves," said Thomas Edison. If you are unhappy with your current circumstances, then you have to decide to make changes and act on them. Anthony Robbins talks about people's motivations and says that people act to either gain pleasure or avoid pain. The catchphrase "No pain, no gain" is true. Nothing in life is free. The thing is, is the goal worth the price of the pain? My wife and I wanted children. Unfortunately, there were some complications that made the process more challenging. When the doctor told us she would require a nightly injection, her fear of needles was almost a deal breaker. But her desire to have children allowed her to overcome her fears, and she was able to give herself the injections. She kept the goal in mind, and it does become mind over matter. If you're wondering why I didn't give her the shots, the answer is I am even more afraid of needles than she is. (We are now proud parents.)

If you want to solve the problem, it's imperative to figure out what caused it and then fix THAT. This begins by getting your head on straight and your mind around the problem. Stop blaming your circumstances, your upbringing, or your personality type for being disorganized. Being a right-brainer is a reason why you are disorganized, not an excuse. Growth is choosing to act in a different way in the face of the same feeling. You can overcome. It's about the choices you make and making the right ones. Go around with large index cards, a pad of paper, sticky notes, tape recorder, digital camera, and start mind mapping, sketching, or taking notes about what you want to do. It's part plan and part brainstorming session. Look for areas that need the most help and for clues as to why things got this way. Notice the feelings and nonverbal sensations you get while you wander around your home, office, studio, garage, or storage area. Try to capture what you are seeing and feeling and what you would like to have happen. I think it's important to get it down on paper (I know, more paper, yikes) so you can see what means the most to you. It may surprise you about the things that both matter and bother you most. Then tape your notes with your thoughts and ideas to the problem areas.

If you haven't achieved all you believe you can, maybe you should ask yourself if it has anything to do with your lack of organization. You may think that being less than organized hasn't hurt you. Maybe that's true, but I'll bet it has had a hand in who you are and how much you have been able to do. Granted, the blame game doesn't do a lot of good, but if it finally makes you realize that there IS something to getting and staying organized, it is more helpful than hurtful. Your space is a reflection of you and sends a message, whether you want it to or not. What does yours say about you? What would you like it to say? Focus on the goal and not the work it will take to get your space looking the way you want and keep it that way.

Make a contract with yourself and write down not only your ultimate organizing goal but the smaller actions and steps you'll take to get there. Celebrate as you complete each step. This can be a turning point for you, a defining moment in your life. I know that getting organized doesn't seem like such a big deal, but it may be the thing that gets you to tackle and turn around other problem areas in your life. The effort of getting your act together can have a profound effect on how others see you and more importantly, how you see yourself. If you can, get rid of the excess baggage that is getting in the way of what you want. Couples fight over inconsequential things like who left the toilet seat up, all the unfinished projects lying around, the lost keys buried under a pile of papers, and so on. If your goal is to have a harmonious and more romantic relationship, then cleaning up your home could make a big difference. What's more important, a pile of unread and obsolete magazines that cause tension with your loved one or a little less clutter and a lot more love?

When you are beginning your new life as an organized person (yes, I am talking about YOU), there is nothing more important than getting off to a good start. Begin with a task you can tackle without much effort to show yourself (and others) that this isn't so hard. You can do it. Maybe you started and stopped several times before but that doesn't matter.

Don't focus on what you haven't been able to do. That's the old you. This is the new and improved you that does what she says and follows through. Start by choosing an area you truly want to see organized. Maybe this is your makeup, music CDs, or that miscellaneous drawer. Weed out the unneeded, unwanted, and unnecessary stuff so that the process of organizing what's left is a lot easier. The thrill of seeing a clutter problem to completion is highly motivating. Stand back and admire your success. You may even want to start an organizing journal and reflect on and record your feelings. Begin by breaking down the zones you need to tackle. What bugs you most? Organize the area that will give you the biggest boost and benefit. Then schedule the first step and each succeeding step on a calendar.

Take it one room at at time. Everything is done before leaving that room and moving on to the next. Take a break before going on to the next area. Walk in the door and literally do the first thing you see. Then you are off and running.

Look at the big picture and then use the solutions in this book. You design your own custom system for your style and special circumstances.

FACT

According to a study by the *Journal of Clinical Psychology,* 36 percent of us break our New Year's resolutions by the end of January.

MAKE IT LAST

I don't love you because you're organized. I love you in spite of that.
    —Chandler Bing to Monica Gellar on *Friends*

It's really not "Get organized", it's "Stay organized." One way to stay organized is to put Post-it notes wherever you leave a mess and to remind yourself what your goals are or scold yourself for going back to your old ways. Put notes in your calendar as reminders to stay organized. You have to have a new mind-set. You know what being disorganized is like. We both know there is a problem or you wouldn't have bought this book. This isn't for my good, this is for yours. You already have the book. The solution is for you to make some lasting changes. Keeping a place organized is a thankless task but worth the effort. If you value yourself, you will want to do it and keep things that way. Just because you are organized doesn't mean you can rest on your laurels. You have got to keep it up. Reaching a goal can be a real letdown, but you have to set new goals. Here are some suggestions to keep you on track.

Think Before You Buy

Start today by promising to not allow any new clutter into your life until you get a handle on what you have. The new you thinks about everything that comes into your life and wonders whether it is working for you or against you and doesn't allow things in that don't belong or help you reach your goals. Will this purchase make my life easier? Better? For example, when you buy bedding, is this complicated comforter and the ten pillows that go with it worth the time it will take to make the bed every morning? Pause and reflect before buying something or agreeing to do something that could clog up your life with clutter. You have a system in place so that you know what goes and what stays and where it goes. You have divided your home and office into zones with most-often-used items easy to get to and stored near where they are needed. You have a junk drawer, but before you fill it up you take the time to sort through and thin it from time to time.

Believe and Achieve

Say, "I am organized." This can't just be a phase. Write it down over and over again. Put it on your key chain. Turn it into a screen saver. Act as if you ARE an organized person even if you have to pretend and cast yourself in that role. Your home is the set. You can have a cast of characters to help out. You write the script complete with a happy ending. Schedule an opening night to show off the new organized you. That's commitment.

Set Aside Some Time for Organizing Tasks

According to a University of Maryland study, 85 percent of us feel rushed some or all of the time. Duh. You will always be too busy to get organized and find the time to stay that way. It doesn't take that much time to keep up your organized ways. You can sift through your wallet in a minute or two. It takes five minutes at most to go through a pile of publications and get rid of your oldest ones. You'd be surprised at how many pesky little projects you can clear off your to-do list in a few minutes a day. You can probably do a desk drawer in fifteen to thirty minutes. In one hour (with no distractions) you can conquer all kinds of clutter. Make the time to tackle organizing tasks like paying bills, putting photos in albums, repairs. Many of us go through seasons or cycles where we are extremely busy, and then there are the downtimes. Granted, some never get a break. It is during the off-season that you can conquer clutter and finally catch up on organizing projects, so do a little every day. Set a timer for ten minutes and see how many tasks you can accomplish and how many things you can put away.

Persistence Pays Off

"Persistence trumps talent and looks every time," says Aaron Brown. It will seem impossible that you will ever have everything in its proper place but by breaking down areas that need attention, you will find it is possible. Chip away and take on one area at a time. Getting one drawer of your desk in order does make a difference. Making a dent is a confidence builder. Take it one pile at a time. There will be peaks and valleys on your way to becoming organized. Don't give up if you get discouraged and start sliding down the hill. Pull yourself up and stay with it even if you suffer a setback. When you feel overwhelmed, take a day off and leave the endless chores alone and go have some fun.

Do Something, Anything

Build some momentum. Once one area is organized, you will feel so empowered you'll want to continue. Take out the big stuff first (binders, catalogs, books) so your piles get smaller sooner. Do the task you find the most appealing first. By beginning with the easiest or most exciting thing, you should see some success and start to get in the swing of things. Believe it or not, once you start you may not want to stop.

Find the Deeper Meaning

"All motivation is self-motivation. Your family, your boss, or your coworkers can try to get your engine going; but until you decide what to accomplish, nothing will happen," says Seth Godin. Post the reasons why you want to stay organized so that when you are tempted to quit you'll stick with it. Jim Carrey used affirmations before his big breakthrough. He was broke and struggling, but he still told himself, "I am one of the top five actors in Hollywood. Every director wants to work with me." Then he wrote himself a check inscribed, "For acting services rendered, $10 million." He credits much of his success to affirmations and the mind-set they can create. Make up your own that includes the words, "I am an organized person."

Rome Wasn't Built in a Day

Getting organized will take time. Don't give up if you don't get everything the way you want it right away. It's a lot like a diet. It's a lifestyle that you have to maintain for a lifetime. You make changes with the times and what's going on in your life. You find a system that works for you and stick with it. You may fall off the wagon but don't throw in the towel. You may feel like you are losing control; and in order to get a handle on things, you may need to get some help to get things back in order and flowing. Murphy's Law will always rear its ugly head and throw a wrench into your organizing wheel, so set realistic goals.

Take It One Day at a Time

Many of us will do what I call Olympic organizing. Once every few years we decide to get organized and we give it our best shot, but in between things tend to slide. My personal preference is to do a little organizing every day. I use found time to straighten up, put things away, shuffle my papers, and take care of pesky little tasks. I find that I work better in short bursts anyway, and I prefer to slip in organizing between more enjoyable things. When I am writing and need a break, instead of plopping down in front of the TV, I will make copies, put papers away, and take care of a multitude of mundane left-brain tasks. If you don't have a minute to spare, then you have to set aside some time to get to your organizing tasks. You can't function at full speed if you are being slowed down by clutter and disorganization. A little organizing a day actually saves time later and prevents tiny tasks from turning into monsters. Actress Lucy Lawless says, "I can be 'on' for about two hours, then I have to do something real—like cleaning the grouting."

Look for Ways to Mix It Up

Create new ways to do those same old tasks like paying bills, answering e-mail, updating your mailing list, cleaning the house, or doing the dishes. Walk around your house with duct tape on your feet, sticky side out, and pick up all those little loose items. Then you can sort them and throw away what's not worth saving.

It's a New Mind-set

When you are faced with new challenges to staying organized, look for solutions instead of giving up or giving in. Keep your eye on the goal, and what seems like a setback may not be a cause for concern or time to cave in. A state of effortless action is when you and the task become one. Find the tasks that give you that state of absorption that creates flow. One woman made her computer password at work "Organized" to make sure she thought about it throughout the day.

Celebrate Your Organizing Successes

For one week make a list of all the small successes you've had each day. Realizing this will motivate you to do more and keep you motivated. Put a jar on your desk, and every time you choose organizing and maintenance over chaos and clutter, put in a few bucks as an "atta boy" or "good girl" reward. When you get to a hundred dollars blow it on something fun and frivolous for yourself. Get rid of ten worn, unflattering tops and replace them with one nice new one.

Anything Is More Interesting than What You Are Doing Now

Use organizing as a break from boring work or when you have a mind block. When I am blocked or bored, I will switch from writer to landscaper, janitor, secretary, or whatever hat needs to be worn as long as it doesn't involve working on a book—this book. The truth is, we can't create all day long or we'll burn out. It's also true that you can't create in a vacuum, and you need outside experience to trigger ideas. I also believe that to get unstuck you can't force. The best thing to do is to get away from the problem and do something that allows your subconscious mind to work on coming up with a solution while you occupy your critical left brain. It may be while I am going through a pile of papers or catching up on my reading that I'll get the breakthrough I've been waiting for. What am I getting at? When you need a break, take it; but instead of watching another rerun of *Murder She Wrote,* clean out a drawer or catch up on some tedious tasks.

Make It a Habit

Believe it or not, organizing can become habit-forming. Start the day off right by beginning with a simple but important task that you can complete in a few minutes. It will give you a positive push by accomplishing something of importance that will propel you through the day. What if you were to begin or end each day by getting rid of one piece of clutter? Wow, in a week you would have lightened your load by seven items. If you did one more thing a day to get and stay organized you'd be a lot better off by the end of the week, month, and year. Get up early or arrive at work when nobody is there to bother you. Then organize. Do it at the end of the day to end on a high note. Ever notice how your local evening news ends the broadcast with a nice animal story so that it ends with something positive? It's always better to come in the next day to a somewhat organized space. Some people may prefer to stay up late and do it. Frank Zappa worked nights while his wife, Gail, did the day shift since Zappa didn't feel he could get anything done during the day. Some people get their second wind at night. A chore a day (or night) keeps the weekend work away.

Redecorate as Part of the Organizing Process

One couple featured on an episode of *Trading Spaces* was so enthralled with the transformation of their bedroom that they didn't even sleep in it for fear of messing it up. Of course they returned to their room, but now they say they will not leave clothes lying around because the room has to remain spotless. I think this is true of a lot of us.

Do It As You See It

Some of the rules that apply to staying on top of your organizing tasks include the rule that if you pass something on the ground, pick it up and put it away. In fact, don't put something down unless you put it away. Finish what you start so that a lot of loose ends don't clog up every surface and finished things can be stored.

Make Organizing Easier

When my wife wraps gifts, she has a system that includes all the needed supplies and a trash bag so that she can clean up as she goes.

Routines Are Not as Stifling as You May Think

In fact they can free up your creativity. It's important for people who tend to take each day as it comes and easily get distracted to have some structure. The key is to set up a routine that is realistic, and then stick to it. Put it on your calendar until you memorize it—a routine that will allow you to know what has to be done in order to stay on top of ongoing organizing. Pick a desk day to deal with paperwork, answer fan mail, put together proposals, and pay bills. Otherwise, things that must get done tend to pile up. Before you celebrate the weekend, transfer all those scraps and sticky notes onto one master list. Catch up on calls. Process the mail.

Break Big Tasks Down

Organizing the entire garage in one try is too much, but if you work on it for twenty minutes a day you can make a difference. Our attention span is probably about thirty minutes, but if we really focus we can work wonders in one hour. For big jobs break them down into "sitcom" segments (thirty-minute increments) so that it's not too long but long enough for you to make a difference. You can clean out the fridge in half an hour and have time left over to make a sandwich. Maybe you can use the thirty minutes just to assess what needs to be done and take one tiny step to getting started. You can always sneak in thirty minutes of maintenance between the bigger tasks.

Schedule Big Organizing Projects

Make a date with yourself to get rid of clutter. Until you have a deadline it's unlikely you'll do it. Tie it in with a move, holiday, tax time, your birthday, the rainy season, or when you paint your home. Whatever works. Sometimes it's a life-changing time of your life that gets you to organize. A child goes off to college, you get married or divorced, have a baby, move, or start a business. Schedule tough tasks when you know you'll have the energy.

Do More than One Thing at a Time

Multitasking helps you handle all the day-to-day organizing tasks that have to be done daily. In today's fast world it won't work to just do one thing at a time anymore or you'll fall behind. If you clean the shower while showering or iron a week's worth of clothes while watching your favorite show or wash the dishes while waiting for the water to boil, you'll stay a step ahead of the clutter waiting to collect. Keep simple projects by the phone or near the TV to do a little at a time.

ACTION ITEM

One woman slips cards into sheet protectors with her chores listed by room and then puts them in a binder. This way she can check off chores with a dry-erase marker when completed. Another way to do this is an index card box with dividers for chores broken down by room. This same system can be adapted with reminders of chores divided by month, week, day, or simply alphabetized.

FAMILY AFFAIR

Remember, no matter how bad a child is, they're still good for an exemption on your income tax return.

—Unknown

Now that you are more organized it becomes painfully obvious that not everyone is as motivated when it comes to clutter control. So let chaos reign with some restrictions. There are people (teenagers, roommates, husbands, bosses) whom you will have very little control or influence over. You can't just move their stuff or, heaven forbid, throw it away. The solution is simple. Agree to some mutual boundaries. Give them a room, closet, or corner and let them junk it up to their heart's content. It's their space. It's best when you can close the door or cover this mess in some way so that it won't feel as if you've failed.

- Make it easy for your family to stay organized. Give each family member a hook to hang his or her backpack or keys on. Make an in-box for each. Actress Jane Seymour was blessed with twins. That's a lot of stuffed animals. Since there were pairs of stuffed animals, Seymour went with a Noah's ark theme for the nursery. To keep things neat, she had a jungle mural painted on the wall, then had hooks added so the animals look like they are hanging from the vines on the wall. Fun and functional. Each person in your family has a unique strength when it comes to organizing. Find it and exploit it. Maybe one child enjoys vacuuming and another would prefer to mow the lawn. Let them do what they like or have a natural affinity for.

- My good friend has two children that, well, take after their dad when it comes to doing the dirty work—they don't. So I suggested he make a chart with all the chores that had to be done and then divide them up. Well, that didn't go over so well. So we wrote the chores on paper, cut them up, added in a few fun ones, and put them in a bowl. On Monday each kid (and my friend) draw chores. They could trade with each other, and a lot of bargaining went on. They then pinned the chores to the fridge with a magnet with each person's name on it. Kids can pick up and put away their own toys. Schedule a time (before dinner or bed) for them to run around and put everything away. Make it into a game and make it seem like fun. When kids get home from school, get them in the habit of putting things away rather than dropping them anywhere and everywhere. Each kid picks a room or project and tackles it. First one done gets to go outside.

- Finish errands without your children slowing you down. Ask a

family member or friend to baby-sit for a few hours while you zip
through stores and get more done in less time.

- Teach kids how to stay organized and allow them to teach you a
few things, too. Encourage them to come up with creative and innovative solutions to keeping your home organized. To help them
learn how to do basic household chores, make index cards and put
them in a small index card file box with tabs with step-by-step instructions about how to handle various chores. This teaches inde-
pendence, innovative thinking, and responsibility. Most kids at a
certain age want to be treated like adults. It happens at different
ages, but it almost always happens before you want it to. Why not
make it work for you? Give them adult responsibilities that help
you stay organized. Train them in simple life skills and boost their
confidence. Make a master list of things kids can do to earn extra
allowance and post them on the fridge with a price list. (Load the
dishwasher = one dollar or clean up room = two dollars.)

- You are the CEO of your corporation, HOME, Inc., and you
should delegate and reward success. Promote from within. Share
in the profits. Have a kid-of-the-month award, vary their assignments, give bonuses and raises for work well-done. Is there anything on your to-do list that can be done by someone else or that
doesn't really have to be done at all?

GET HELP

*Men fantasize about having a harem, a group of women that fulfills all their wishes.
Women don't fantasize about having a male harem. That's just more men to pick up
after.*

—Rita Rudner

Nothing is impossible if you don't have to do it yourself. If you have
read this book and still feel that getting and staying organized are too
much to handle, hire a professional. We do it when we need to travel (a
pilot), when we aren't feeling well (a doctor), and when our car is broken (a mechanic). There are personal chefs, personal shoppers, dry
cleaners who pick up and deliver, and gardeners. To me my computer is

a tool, and I don't want to take the time to learn how it works, I just want it to work. My time is better spent using my laptop to write books than reading the manual on *how* it works. So I have a computer doctor come over to diagnose and cure what ails my Mac. There is no shame in hiring help with something like organizing your home, office, or computer. When people offer to help you—accept. If someone volunteers to store some of your belongings, let him. If you don't need something in a couple of years, allow him to toss it.

Do what you do best and have other people do the rest. Allow your overbearing, know-it-all spouse, kid, roommate, friend, or some other left-brainer deal with the details of getting and staying organized. You have skills that you could trade for cleaning and organizing services. Find someone who finds filing fascinating and stimulating.

Hook up with someone who would actually enjoy organizing your hard drive. Make friends with a neat freak and invite him over for a cleaning session. Why deprive him? The most popular labor-saving device is a spouse with money. Pay for people to do the work (professional organizer, housekeeper, assistant). Be the big picture, idea gal, and let others make it happen by dealing with all the dirty little details.

My assistant is also a right-brainer so this hasn't quite panned out, but we share the burden of all the detail work that comes with my (so-called) career. If you can partner with your polar opposite, this is a win/win. What I find interesting is that when two totally disorganized people get together, one of them usually becomes slightly more organized. I think it's their survival instinct kicking in.

Can't we all just get along? The last time I went to the movies in Kauai, Hawaii, people picked up after themselves on their way out of the theater. It was surreal. (I had to go back and get my empty Junior mint box.) But if everyone picked up as they went along and put things back where they belong, maintaining an organized home or office would be a whole lot easier. "Roommates are tough. Even if you shared an apartment with the pope, I guarantee you that three weeks into it you'd be going, 'Hey, do you mind picking up that cape, man? And quit leaving the papal miter on the kitchen counter,'" muses comedian Jeff Foxworthy. You can make it a man-versus-woman debate if you like, but it seems as though the lines are getting blurred between women and men. Women now have as much equipment as men as they become more involved in sports and outdoor activities. Many like to work with tools, too. I doubt that women will ever leave the toilet seat up, but now you have his and hers golf clubs, surfboards, and guitars. "Anything you can do I can do better," seems to be the mind-set and that's great. But staying organized is less about gender and more about style and responsibility. It's not that *one sex is better than the other* at cleaning, filing, or fixing things anymore. You go with your strength—whether that means lifting your feet while the other vacuums or when it's time to pay the bills you affix the stamps to the envelopes.

It's so much better when everyone is with the program. If everyone is involved and knows his role, it is called teamwork. Teamwork. You can set up a rewards-based system to make it more fun by dangling a day at the beach or a night at the movies for helping to stay organized for one week. Or you can penalize someone for not doing her part—also fun. Put a sticky note or sticky dot on an item left out along with the person's name, date, and a fine (one dollar for each day it stays where it is) and post the total fines on the fridge. Collect the money and give it to the person with the least amount of infractions.

Here's an idea. Have a cleaning day and invite some friends over and pay them with some wine and cheese and first dibs on some of the clutter you are going to be parting with because it doesn't fit into your life anymore. Or it just plain doesn't fit. They can help organize, clean, fix, discard, and deal with the details. It's a lot faster and more fun than doing it by yourself—as most things tend to be.

If you need accountability, you can make an announcement to your friends, family, coworkers, or clients that you are going to get and stay organized and make them hold your feet to the fire. You can also get an organizing partner that shares your desire for an orderly, clean space and you agree to encourage, support, and help each other stay on track with monthly meetings where you announce your intentions for the month, and then check up on each other with surprise inspections, regular calls, and e-mails, where each coaches and counsels the other. If you can't think of anyone you'd want to partner with, take out an ad or post flyers around town looking for a teammate. Ask at church, the office, or even online.

PROFESSIONAL HEP

The place to find a professional organizer is the National Association of Professional Organizers, otherwise known as NAPO. To contact them go to: 35 Technology Parkway South, Suite 150, Norcross, GA 30092 or 770-325-3440, hg@hapo.net.www.napo.net.

ASK A PRO, JILL BALDWIN BADONSKY, CREATIVITY COACH

"Here is something that works for me and some of my clients. Because the task of organizing can be so daunting and overwhelming, to help break it down in doable chunks I put my favorite song on the stereo and make the goal of organizing the length of the song. Of course, once I start I continue because starting can be the hardest part—especially when something feels overwhelming. Another way to make it fun is to have a special organizing hat to wear or buy an entire organizing outfit. Somehow endowing clothing articles with the power of fueling energy to organize works for the creative person with the vivid imagination."

ABOUT THE AUTHOR

In addition to being the award-winning author of eleven books, Lee is an accomplished graphic artist, drummer, workshop leader, radio talk-show host, and the founder of five companies. Lee and his wife reside in their highly organized home in Mission Beach, California. For more about Lee Silber and his books visit www.creativelee.com.

CONTACT INFORMATION

HOW TO CONTACT THE AUTHOR

I would love to hear from you and continue to offer solutions and suggestions for your organizing challenges. Please feel free to contact me through my Web site or the mail.

> Lee Silber
> 822 Redondo Court
> San Diego, CA 92109
> leesilber@earthlink.net
> www.creativelee.com

HOW TO GET A FREE "RESOURCES FOR RIGHT-BRAINERS" PACKET

If you would like a free "Resources for Right-Brainers" packet filled with all kinds of cool stuff, send me a self-addressed stamped envelope (with one dollar in postage).

HOW TO JOIN THE FREE ONLINE BRAINSTORMING CLUB

How would you like to connect with other creative people from around the world? I found a way to link up like-minded people for support, encouragement, and idea exchange through online brainstorming. To participate and join the club, go to: www.creativelee.com.

HOW TO ATTEND A RETREAT OR WORKSHOP
FOR RIGHT-BRAINERS

Each year I hold free retreats for right-brainers in my hometown in San Diego. This is a chance to meet and mingle with other creative people. Attendees learn from one another and have an opportunity to show off and share their talents and skills. I also conduct dozens of free workshops around the country, many offered in a bookstore near you. For a complete and updated schedule of retreats and seminars, bookmark www.creativelee.com, or better yet, invite me to speak to your group by calling 858-488-4249.

HOW TO LEARN MORE ABOUT "RIGHT-BRAINERS RULE MONTH" (OCTOBER)

Right-brainers are often ridiculed and reprimanded for their unorthodox and creative way of doing things. Listed as an official annual event, Right-Brainers Rule Month is a chance to show how the right-brain person can survive and thrive in a left-brain world. To participate, contact me.

HOW TO HAVE "THE ULTIMATE REMINDER" SENT TO YOU

The Ultimate Reminder works wonders when it comes to improving your memory, making positive changes to your personality, and breaking bad habits. To get yours, send me a SASE and three dollars.

THE NATIONAL ASSOCIATION OF
PROFESSIONAL ORGANIZERS

This is THE place to find a professional organizer:

> NAPO
> 35 Technology Parkway South, Suite 150
> Norcross, GA 30092
> 770-325-3440
> hq@napo.net
> www.napo.net